# James Baldwin's
# Later Fiction

# James Baldwin's Later Fiction

# WITNESS TO THE JOURNEY

Lynn Orilla Scott

Michigan State University Press

*East Lansing*

∞ The paper used in this publication meets the minimum requirements
of ANSI/NISO Z39.48-1992 (R 1997) (Permanence of Paper).

Michigan State University Press
East Lansing, Michigan 48823-5202

Printed and bound in the United States of America.

08 07 06 05 04 03 02    1 2 3 4 5 6 7 8 9 10

*Library of Congress Cataloging-in-Publication Data*
Scott, Lynn Orilla, 1950–
James Baldwin's later fiction : witness to the journey / Lynn Orilla Scott.
p. cm.
Includes bibliographical references and index.
ISBN 0-87013-613-5 (cloth : alk. paper) — ISBN 0-87013-625-9 (pbk. :alk. paper)
1. Baldwin, James, 1924—Criticism and interpretation. 2. African Americans in literature. I. Title.
PS3552.A45 Z885 2002
813'.54—dc21
2001007861

Book and cover design by Sharp Des!gns, Lansing, MI

*www.msupress.msu.edu*

# Contents

# Preface

n 1963 my aunt, Orilla Winfield, sent me a copy of *The Fire Next Time* for my thirteenth birthday. I read it in the library of Headington School for Girls in Oxford, England, where I had been "exiled" for a year from my life as a teenage American girl who liked rock and roll and mini skirts, who ratted her hair and secretly smoked cigarettes. I was just beginning to learn that there were worlds very different from the one I had inhabited for the first thirteen years of my life. Headington—with its gray-blue uniforms, its daily prayers, its kidney pie, and its extremely studious young women— seemed like another planet from the American junior high school I had attended just a few months previously. The day I read *The Fire Next Time*, however, I got my first glimpse of yet another world, one that was also American, but a long way from the America I knew, as one of those white "innocents" at home that Baldwin so adeptly describes and addresses.

I have never been able to boast a photographic memory or even a particularly good memory, but I vividly remember reading James Baldwin for the first time—I remember where I was sitting in the Headington Library, what the room looked like, and how the book made me feel. I remember being unable to put it down, drawn in by Baldwin's tone of moral seriousness (rather than moralism) and by the intimacy of his voice—a voice that made me feel he was letting me in on his life, as he was, somehow, letting me in on my life as well.

My aunt, Orilla, was a strong advocate for racial justice and an avid reader, so it was not surprising that she had sent me *The Fire Next Time*. But I didn't know, then, of her friendship with Jimmy Baldwin. I soon learned that she was the white school teacher whom Baldwin first mentioned in "Notes of a Native Son," and that, periodically, they still kept in touch. However, it was not until Baldwin published *The Devil Finds Work* in 1976 that I really started to appreciate the significance of that relationship, not only for James Baldwin and my aunt, but for the legacy it left me and my family, a legacy of hope that we can cross barriers of race, class, and culture, that we can share a vision of the way things should be, that we can be friends, comrades, and lovers. In the *Devil Finds Work*, Jimmy writes:

> It is certainly partly because of her, who arrived in my terrifying life so soon, that I never really managed to hate white people—though, God knows, I have often wished to murder more than one or two. But Bill Miller—her name was Orilla, we called her Bill—was not white for me in the way, for example, that Joan Crawford was white, in the way that the landlords and the storekeepers and the cops and most of my teachers were white. She didn't baffle me that way and she never frightened me and she never lied to me. I never felt her pity, either, in spite of the fact that she sometimes brought us old clothes (because she worried about our winters) and cod-liver oil, especially for me, because I seemed destined, then, to be carried away by whooping cough.[1]

Yet it is another description from the *Devil Finds Work* that has stood out for me, even more than the one above, when I think about my aunt as a political activist and young school teacher: "Bill took us on a picnic downtown once, and there was supposed to be ice cream waiting for us at a police station. The cops didn't like Bill, didn't like the fact that we were colored kids, and didn't want to give up the ice cream. I don't remember anything Bill said. I just remember her face as she stared at the cop, clearly intending to stand there until the ice cream all over the world melted or until the earth's surface froze, and she got us our ice cream saying, *Thank you*, I remember as we left."[2] I can well imagine that scene and my aunt's expression (she could be quite undaunted), and it makes me smile. She was a woman whose values and principles always came through in her actions.

Standoffs with the police were not something Aunt Orilla talked about with me, although having been a member of the American Communist Party in the 1930s, like many idealistic people of the time, I imagine there was more than one. What she did talk about, when I asked her about the young James Baldwin, was his brilliance, the dignity of his family, and their extreme poverty. My aunt was only twelve years older than Jimmy Baldwin, making her about twenty-four when they first met. She grew up in a small farming community in Illinois, then had gone to Antioch College (until her family lost their home and land in the Great Depression), and finally to Teacher's College in New York City. She had been hired by the WPA Theater Project's Educational Division to put on plays in the schools and was assigned to Harlem on her request, because it was in walking distance from her apartment. The school she worked at was not only racially seg-regated (99 percent black, except for a couple of very blond Finns), but after the fourth or fifth grade, the classes were segregated by gender as well. The children she worked with were all boys, virtually all black, and all hun-gry. The children were fed at school. Orilla said, "It was the worst poverty I ever saw. I don't think people today have any idea of the poverty of that time in the cities."[3]

James Baldwin's classroom teacher welcomed help, was very support-ive of special programs, and allowed Orilla to take Jimmy out of the class as much as she wanted because he already knew everything the class was doing. Jimmy became my aunt's "assistant director," and they spent a lot of time together. She said, "it was a real break for me. He was a remark-able child." She recalled how they were both enthusiastically reading *A Tale of Two Cities,* and they would have these "long conversations up in the attic of the school about Dickens," which she "enjoyed more than the conversations about Dickens [she] had with adults." She felt that Jimmy should be seeing more theater and more of the world and asked permission to interview his parents. Thus began the relationship between my aunt and the Baldwin family. The relationship also included my aunt's husband, Evan Winfield, and her sister, Henrietta Miller, both of whom lived with her. They lived very close to the Baldwin apartment, within walking distance, and my two aunts and my uncle began to include Jimmy on their outings, "like a little brother." Orilla described him as a "very sweet child . . . always a pleasure to have around." The friendship continued for about two years. After James joined the church, Orilla and Evan saw less of him and then my uncle, a Merchant Marine, was stationed in Puerto Rico during the war, and they left New York.

Years later they would have a few reunions. One was in the mid-sixties when Baldwin was traveling with CORE in southern California. It was the first time Orilla heard him speak in public, and she was "utterly surprised." She described him as "an absolutely stunning and dramatic speaker. He had the whole audience in the palm of his hand." After the speech, and before he was hustled off to a Hollywood fundraising party, they only had time for a brief exchange. She described him, then, as "the most exhausted looking person I've ever seen." But to Orilla he was still that "sweet boy," now a "sweet man." Orilla heard from James Baldwin at occasional intervals. He was not an easy person to keep in contact with, but both Orilla and her sister, Henrietta, corresponded more regularly with Berdis Baldwin, James's mother.

My aunt has been gone for ten years now; she died four years after Jimmy, but the last time I saw her, about a month before her death from cancer, she asked me to read a letter to her from Berdis that had just arrived in the mail. This study of James Baldwin's later fiction is dedicated to my aunt, Henrietta Miller Tschannen, who is still with us, to the memory of my aunt, Orilla Miller Winfield, and to their children, my cousins: Steve, Ken, Tom, Mary, and Peggy. It is also dedicated to the memory of my mother, Margaret Miller Wasserman, to my father, Robert Wasserman, to my husband, Randall W. Scott, and to my children, Sara, Ziba, and Margaret.

Baldwin left a huge legacy in part because he filled so many roles as a writer, moralist, political activist, public speaker, and celebrity, but most of all because of his undisputed eloquence. Like all important legacies it has not been without its controversies, and I believe there is much to be done before we see a true assessment of Baldwin's contribution to American life and letters. This book is my effort to pass on a part of Baldwin's legacy, which I believe has been sorely neglected. It would not have been possible without the guidance of teachers, mentors, and friends. I want to thank Professor Barry Gross, who recently retired from Michigan State University. Over a quarter of a century ago, before there were any black literature classes at M.S.U., I took a master's-level seminar on Richard Wright and James Baldwin from Dr. Gross. It was my first encounter with Baldwin's work in the classroom, and it was a rigorous experience; we read everything Baldwin had written to date by 1974. Twenty years later I would pursue a doctorate in English from M.S.U., and Barry would chair my committee. I thank him for his many years of encouragement and patience. I also want to thank Professor Linda Susan Beard, now at Bryn Mawr. Dr. Beard guided my graduate studies of African American literature while she was at Michigan State University. She is an original, wonderful teacher with a very sly wit, who, like all good teachers, has a vision of teaching and mentoring that goes beyond the confines of academia.

I doubt this project would have come to fruition without the encouragement of two important Baldwin scholars, Professor Trudier Harris at the University of North Carolina at Chapel Hill and Professor Craig Werner at the University of Wisconsin at Madison. Professor Harris was kind enough to read my doctoral dissertation on James Baldwin. Her early feedback encouraged me to pursue the project. Professor Werner gave the manuscript a close reading and made a number of concrete and very helpful suggestions for revision. I delivered sections of this book at two recent conferences, which afforded me the opportunity to discuss Baldwin's work with other scholars currently studying his contributions to American literature and culture: the first was Challenging American Sociopolitical Hierarchy: James Baldwin at the Millennium at Howard University in February 2000; and the second was Looking Back with Pleasure II: A

Celebration, sponsored by the African American Literature and Culture Society at the University of Utah in October 2000.

I also want to thank my good friend Lovalerie King at the University of Massachusetts at Boston. In spring 2001 Dr. King taught a seminar on Toni Morrison and James Baldwin and included me as an electronic participant. I wish to acknowledge Val, her students in English 697A, and their fine work on Baldwin and Morrison!

Finally, I want to thank Professor Douglass Noverr, chairman of the Department of American Thought and Language at Michigan State University for a supportive working environment, and Randall W. Scott for his index to this book.

# Introduction

## I.

James Baldwin (1924–1987) is one of the great twentieth-century American writers. His career was long and prolific, spanning forty years and resulting in twenty-three books published in his lifetime, along with numerous articles and interviews, many of which have not yet been collected. His books include six novels, seven collections of essays, two plays, two collections of poetry, a collection of short stories, a phototext (a collaboration with Richard Avedon), two dialogues (one with Margaret Mead, the other with Nikki Giovanni), a screenplay, and a children's story. In 1989 Fred L. Standley and Louis H. Pratt edited a collection of Baldwin interviews (*Conversations with James Baldwin*), and in 1998 Toni Morrison edited two Library of America editions of Baldwin's work, one of his early fiction and the other of his essays.

When Baldwin appeared on the cover of *Time* magazine 17 May 1963, he was at the height of his public renown. Most Americans had at least heard his name and his books were widely read among college students.

Nowadays, the majority of undergraduates, at least the ones with whom I come in contact at a large state university, have neither read nor heard of James Baldwin, although many will have read something by Richard Wright or Toni Morrison. Even more surprising to me are the number of graduate students in literary studies that are completely unfamiliar with Baldwin's work. While the critical response to Baldwin's work was never unequivocally positive, even at its best, the decline in his reputation after the mid-sixties is only beginning to be reversed. The reasons for the decline, which I attempt to map in the first chapter of this book, are complicated. In short, however, those reasons involve the disavowal of Baldwin by the liberal establishment, the dramatically shifting style of political resistance to racial and sexual oppressions, specifically the rise of "identity politics," and the corresponding developments in academic discourses that began to newly theorize the cultural production of racial and sexual minorities. Baldwin, who consistently defied categorical thinking and practice, challenging the binaries of black/white, male/female, gay/straight, as well as the divisions of literary genres, particularly that between autobiography and fiction, seemed to fall outside the view of the scholars of the 1970s and 1980s, who were busy discovering and canonizing "other" traditions in American literature.

Two recent collections of essays promise a renewed interest in Baldwin's work.[1] A number of these essays argue that his work preceded important developments in cultural studies, as well as work in gender theory and queer theory. It is the central purpose of this study to build on this renewed interest and to expand Baldwin studies by giving serious consideration to his neglected last three novels, *Tell Me How Long the Train's Been Gone* (1968), *If Beale Street Could Talk* (1974), and *Just Above My Head* (1979). These works, along with his later essays, have been dismissed as less interesting, less complex, and less aesthetically viable than his early works. The supposed failure of these novels is typically blamed on Baldwin's political activism, anger, and his supposed ideological investment in black power. What is missing from most analyses is an understanding of the extent to which his later work is consistent with his earlier work, building upon, revising, and refocusing it, but never abandoning the critique of American

racial and sexual identity. I argue that Baldwin's later writing is of particular interest because of the way it traverses the cultural divide between the
fifties and late sixties. Baldwin's writing is a much more sophisticated negotiation of the rapidly changing politics of "difference" than has previously
been acknowledged. Just as Baldwin understood the way the universal
"white" liberal subject made racial and sexual minorities invisible, he also
understood both the power and the limits of strategies of resistance based
on difference, and, most important, he explored the way a resistant black
identity contained difference within it. His last three novels continue to
interrogate the way racial and sexual categories not only divide the
American landscape but divide and terrorize the "self." The focus, however, of the later novels does change: they are less concerned with mapping
the experience of internalized racism and homophobia, and, as Baldwin put
it, "the white problem" (now, in academic discourse, the "cultural construction of whiteness"). While these problems remain givens in the world
his characters inhabit, the last three novels shift focus by exploring the
sources of personal and cultural resistance to the pressures of a deforming
context. Beginning with *Tell Me How Long the Train's Been Gone,* Baldwin
revisits and revisions the subject of his first novel, the black family and
community. Self, family, and community become contested sites in the
struggle for freedom. Open-ended fictions that balance hope and sorrow,
these novels portray characters who are complexly situated as both subjects
and agents of their stories. Sources of black resistance are explored not only
thematically, but in the discursive strategies that Baldwin employs, strategies which signify on the tradition of black male autobiography and on the
structures of feeling in black music, especially blues and gospel.[2]

Baldwin's life was the subject of much of his own writing and has been
the subject of several biographies as well, the most recent by Professor
David Leeming, who was Baldwin's secretary and assistant in the mid-sixties and whom Baldwin designated to be his biographer.[3] Born out of wedlock to Berdis Jones, James Baldwin became the eldest of nine children. The
eight who followed were born to his mother and his stepfather, Rev. David
Baldwin. James Baldwin never knew his biological father, and his identity
has not been part of the public record. Raised in Harlem in extreme

poverty, Baldwin's early life was difficult. Nonetheless, there were a number of saving features, not the least of which was the close relationship he had with his mother and his love and sense of responsibility for his siblings. Baldwin's turbulent relationship with his stepfather is fictionalized in his first novel, *Go Tell It on the Mountain,* and is the subject of his early essays, including "Notes of a Native Son" and *The Fire Next Time.* David Baldwin was a puritanically religious man, devoted to his family, but very difficult to get along with and prone to angry rages. Baldwin frequently said his father "terrified" him. As an adult Baldwin came to understand his father's bitter pride and his distrust and hatred of whites to be a result of American racial history, which had humiliated, disempowered, and emasculated black men. Much of the trouble between the elder Baldwin and his stepson was caused by James's "worldliness," in particular his interest in books other than the Bible (Baldwin was an avid reader from the time he was a young child), his love of movies, and his friendships with white teachers and classmates. The emotional landscape of Baldwin's adolescence is best described in the character of John Grimes in *Go Tell It on the Mountain.* The novel culminates with the protagonist's fourteen-year-old religious conversion in his father's Pentecostal church, the Temple of the Fire Baptized. The novel also suggests the protagonist's yet-to-be acknowledged homosexual orientation by the coded homoerotic desire that marks John's attachment to Elisha, the older boy who brings him up from the "threshing floor" and welcomes him into the community of the saved. Like his protagonist, Baldwin experienced an adolescent religious conversion. Between the ages of fourteen and sixteen, the young Jimmy Baldwin was a successful boy preacher, and while he later described his ministry as a "gimmick," a way to temporarily save himself from self-knowledge and from his father's rage, Baldwin's early religious vocation continued to inform both the language and the sensibility of his adult writing.[4]

In addition to his family and the church, Baldwin's relationships with a number of teachers and mentors were very important to his development as a writer. He was recognized as an unusually gifted child from the time he was in elementary school by his principal, Gertrude Ayer, and by a young, white schoolteacher, Orilla ("Bill") Miller, about whom Baldwin wrote in "Notes of a Native Son" and later in *The Devil Finds Work*. Miller developed a personal relationship with James and his family, producing Jimmy's first play, taking him to plays and movies, unaware of the resentment she evoked in David Baldwin, who felt unable to deny the white teacher.[5] Of Miller, Baldwin wrote, "I loved her, of course, and absolutely, with a child's love; didn't understand half of what she said, but remembered it; and it stood me in good stead later."[6] Later Baldwin attended Frederick Douglass Junior High School, where his ability was recognized by two African American male teachers, Herman W. Porter and the poet Countee Cullen, who encouraged Baldwin to apply to the prestigious De Witt Clinton High School in the Bronx, where he was accepted and was "exposed to exceptional teachers."[7] Clinton was an all-male school populated by the sons of Jewish immigrants who tended to be left wing, politically active, and who "were bent on academic and social achievement."[8] At Clinton, Baldwin was much admired for his writing ability. There he became a regular contributor to the school's literary magazine, "The Magpie," and became close friends with classmates Richard Avedon, who was to become a famous photographer, and Emile Capouya and Sol Stein, who were to become publishers.[9]

The years following his graduation from high school were a time of intense conflict as Baldwin struggled to reconcile familial duty with his calling as a writer. In "Notes of a Native Son" he describes a miserable year in New Jersey, where he worked at a defense plant. While the money was good, the atmosphere was mindless and oppressive. During this period Baldwin's encounters with segregation and racial prejudice caused him to discover the depth of his own rage, which he described as "some dread, chronic disease, the unfailing symptom of which is a kind of blind fever, a pounding in the skull and fire in the bowels" that once contracted "can recur at any moment."[10] Following his father's death in 1943 and the birth of his youngest sibling, Baldwin moved back home to Harlem, briefly, but the menial jobs and the crowded living conditions were soon intolerable to the young man whose ambition was to become a famous writer: "'I had to jump then,' Baldwin always said, 'or I would quite simply have died.'"[11] Baldwin then moved to Greenwich Village, a gathering point for artists and radicals and the locale of a homosexual community that in the postwar years was just beginning to be open. Although the Village promised an environment more supportive of Baldwin's creative ambitions, it was a white environment, where blacks might visit, but few actually lived. The early years were particularly difficult, and Baldwin later described them as his "season in hell."[12] Targeted as a "queer" by "straight" white men who wanted to have sex with him, or as a "black stud" by white women who wanted to have a "Negro experience," or who wanted to "save" him from his homosexuality, Baldwin felt himself menaced by American racial and sexual myths. *Another Country* and *Tell Me How Long the Train's Been Gone* include fictionalized representations of this period of his life. While Baldwin wrote freely about bisexuality and homosexuality in his fiction, his essays (with three exceptions) did not treat the subjects.[13] In 1985, however, he broke his silence about aspects of his private experience that he had not previously written about in his autobiographical nonfiction. Looking back forty years, he described the loneliness and fear of the first years in the Village:

The American idea of masculinity: There are few things under heaven more difficult to understand, or, when I was younger, to forgive.

During the Second World War (the first one having failed to make the world safe for democracy) and some time after the Civil War (which had failed, unaccountably, to liberate the slave), life for niggers was fairly rough in Greenwich Village. There were only about three of us, if I remember correctly, when I first hit those streets, and I was the youngest, the most visible, and the most vulnerable.

On every street corner, I was called a faggot. This meant that I was despised, and, however horrible this is, it is clear. What was *not* clear at that time of my life was what motivated the men and boys who mocked and chased me; for, if they found me when they were alone, they spoke to me very differently—frightening me, I must say, into a stunned and speechless paralysis. For when they were alone, they spoke very gently and wanted me to take them home and make love. (They could not take *me* home; they lived with their families.) The bafflement and the pain this caused in me remain beyond description.[14]

As Baldwin often claimed, it was precisely because he was menaced by the myth of American masculinity from a young age that he understood its contradictions; he saw that machismo and queer baiting by "heterosexual" men concealed both a fear of and a longing for male touch and intimacy, both of which were paradoxically projected onto the black male body by the white male. Throughout his work, Baldwin exposed what contemporary theorists have understood to be a cultural construction of masculinity that depends upon a "racial dialectic of projection and internalisation."[15]

The relationship which most helped to sustain Baldwin during these difficult years was his friendship with Beauford Delaney, an African American artist who lived in the Village whom he had met while still in high school. In the introduction to *The Price of the Ticket* Baldwin says that Beauford became for him "an example of courage and integrity, humility and passion" and that "his example operated as an enormous protection" in the Village, which was racially "vicious, partly because of the natives, largely because of the tourists, and absolutely because of the cops."[16] Because of Beauford Delaney and Connie Williams, a restaurant owner from Trinidad, Baldwin felt he was "never entirely at the mercy of an environment at once hostile and seductive."[17] David Leeming credits Delaney with being the most important influence in Baldwin's life: "Here was a black man, an artist, an outsider, somehow a later version of himself. It was as if Jimmy had found his long-lost father."[18] Delaney taught Baldwin the skill of careful observation, the play of light on city streets, and the unexpected beauty to be found in the ordinary and the ugly. It was also through Delaney that Baldwin learned his love of blues and jazz, gaining an appreciation of black secular culture: "Delaney was to reconcile for his protege the music of the Harlem streets with the music of the Harlem churches, and this helped Baldwin to reconcile his sexual awakening."[19]

Baldwin's first break as a writer came when a friend introduced him to Richard Wright, who was then living in Brooklyn. Wright read an early manuscript of Baldwin's first novel, responded positively, and recommended the younger writer for a Eugene F. Saxton Foundation Fellowship, which he was awarded in 1945.[20] Baldwin lived in New York for another three years, gaining his first professional writing experiences: publishing book reviews, an important early essay, "The Harlem Ghetto," and the short story, "Previous Condition." The novel Baldwin had been working on, however, was stalled, and his personal life in disarray. In November 1948 Baldwin left for Paris with 40 dollars in his pocket. In 1959 he would write: "I left America because I doubted my ability to survive the fury of the color problem here."[21] As Emmanuel S. Nelson has argued, while Baldwin spoke of his exile in primarily racial and artistic terms, it is important

> to insist on the sexual dimensions of his exile as well. . . . Indeed, his flight to France was a flight away from American as well as African-American sexual codes. . . . France, then became a symbolic space of imaginative liberation—a space where American scripts of masculinity can be discarded, a place where sexuality can be explored in greater anonymity and freedom.[22]

Within a year of Baldwin's arrival in France, he published two key essays, "Everybody's Protest Novel" and "Preservation of Innocence." The first became one of Baldwin's most famous essays. Its rejection of the protest novel and the comparison of Richard Wright's *Native Son* with Harriet Beecher Stowe's *Uncle Tom's Cabin* caused a rift between Baldwin and the older writer he admired. "Everybody's Protest Novel" was to be a subject of controversy in literary circles for years to come. The second essay, published obscurely in *Zero* magazine, remains relatively unknown and has never been included in any collections of Baldwin's work.[23] It is, however, an insightful statement of the relationship between homophobia, misogyny, and American myths of masculinity. "Preservation of Innocence" is of direct significance to the ideas underlying Baldwin's second novel, *Giovanni's Room,* and is a forerunner to "Here Be Dragons," Baldwin's most explicit statement about his sexuality, published in the last decade of his life. As more critics become interested in Baldwin's contribution to studies of gender and sexuality, this essay will undoubtedly gain importance. Within less than ten years after arriving in Paris, Baldwin had written much of the work for which he became famous, including *Go Tell It on the Mountain, Notes of a Native Son,* and *Giovanni's Room.*

Baldwin lived and worked in France throughout most of the fifties, but returned to the United States in 1957 to report on the Civil Rights movement. At this time, he toured the South and met Martin Luther King and other leaders.[24] By the early sixties his writing, and his appearances on television and radio, had made Baldwin a well-known public figure. He would continue to take an active role in the black freedom movement in the years to come, supporting both the struggle for integration in the South and, later, the struggle for black power in the North. Baldwin again toured the South in 1963 for the Congress of Racial Equality (CORE), at which time he met James Meredith, the chief NAACP officer in Mississippi, a man who impressed him greatly according to David Leeming.[25] In 1961 Baldwin was interviewed on a radio program with Malcolm X.[26] Shortly afterward, he was invited to meet the leader of the Black Muslims, Elijah Muhammad, an encounter he was to write about at length in his 1963 book, *The Fire Next Time.* Although Baldwin had been critical of the Black Muslim movement and did not support an ideology of racial separatism, his relationship with Malcolm X evolved over the years and Baldwin grew not only to respect and admire Malcolm, but to identify with him. As David Leeming says, "Malcolm's message grew, like Baldwin's, out of real anger and resentment, out of a real experience of poverty and personal deprivation."[27] Dr. Kenneth Clark had arranged a meeting between King, Baldwin, and Malcolm X in February 1965, but two days before it was to take place, Malcolm was assassinated. In 1967 Baldwin met with Alex Haley and Elia Kazan to discuss writing a play about Malcolm X; the project received the support of Malcolm's widow, Betty Shabazz. Then in 1968 Marvin Worth bought the rights to Haley's *The Autobiography of Malcolm X* for Columbia Pictures and offered Baldwin the position of scriptwriter for the film. After some wariness, Baldwin accepted, but ultimately Baldwin and Columbia pictures were not able to agree on the portrayal of the Black Muslim leader or on who would play Malcolm. Finally, unwilling to script the Malcolm that Hollywood wanted, Baldwin gave up the Hollywood venture in early 1969. Three years later he published his original scenario as *One Day When I Was*

*Lost.* Much later the version that Baldwin had collaborated on with Arnold Perl became the basis for Spike Lee's film on Malcolm X.[28]

While Baldwin was working in Hollywood in the late sixties, he continued to be politically active by giving talks in high schools and churches in Watts. He appeared with Betty Shabazz before a House of Representatives subcommittee in support of a bill for the establishment of a commission on "Negro History and Culture"; he discussed President Johnson's Civil Disorders Bill on television with representatives of the World Council of Churches. Baldwin was in Palm Springs with his friend Billy Dee Williams on 4 April 1968 when he heard of King's assassination. It was a devastating blow, one that would mark a turning point in Baldwin's thinking. Two days after King's murder the Black Panther house in Oakland was raided and several Panthers were killed. On 12 April, Baldwin wrote his friend Engin Cezzar, one of the people to whom he had dedicated *Tell Me How Long the Train's Been Gone,* that he would struggle against despair even in the face of the murders of Medgar Evers, Malcolm X, and now Martin Luther King. He wrote, "At this point it was impossible to do anything but pray to those gods who are not Western . . . not Christian."[29] Baldwin's struggle with Columbia studios, King's assassination, the raid on the Panther house in Oakland, and the imprisonment and trial of Baldwin's former bodyguard, Tony Maynard, all took an emotional toll on Baldwin.[30]

Less than a month before Martin Luther King's death, Baldwin had introduced King at a Los Angeles fundraiser for the Southern Christian Leadership Conference, and later appeared with him in New York at Carnegie Hall for a celebration of W. E. B. Du Bois's life. Although Baldwin continued to appear in public with King and certainly admired him, his emotional affinities were with the younger, militant generation. In the mid-sixties Baldwin supported the new, more radical leadership of Stokely Carmichael and Floyd McKissick in SNCC (Student Non-violent Coordinating Committee) and CORE (Congress of Racial Equality), respectively. Baldwin spoke out in support of the idea of black power in 1966,[31] but he was also cautious of its potential misuse, writing his brother David that "he would resist getting caught up in 'some mystical black bullshit.'"[32] When

Carmichael's passport was confiscated because of his pro-Cuban and anti–Vietnam War sympathies, Baldwin wrote an impassioned plea in his defense and a strong indictment of the United States, which the *New York Times* refused to print.[33]

Baldwin first made contact with the Black Panthers in 1967, a few days before their leader, Huey Newton, was arrested. He later visited Newton in prison and helped to get him released. Baldwin met Bobby Seale (a Panther leader who had been arrested for demonstrations at the 1968 Chicago Democratic National Convention) through his friend Marlon Brando. Baldwin contributed to Seale's defense and later wrote a foreword to Seale's autobiography. During Baldwin's stays in California, he visited the Huey Newton School in Oakland on several occasions and worked with Newton, Angela Davis, and other activists on local projects. According to David Leeming, "the two men developed a real friendship and enjoyed spending time together."[34] Baldwin made several public appearances with the Panthers between 1967 and 1969, including hosting a birthday party-fundraising event for Newton in 1968. In the early seventies Baldwin also made several appearances on behalf of prisoners Angela Davis and George Jackson, in England and Germany as well as in the United States, which caused a great deal of trouble with the French authorities, who almost refused Baldwin residence papers. Baldwin expressed interest in doing a film on *Soledad Brother,* Jackson's letters from prison. When Angela Davis appeared on the cover of *Newsweek* in prison garb, Baldwin wrote an impassioned response to the *New York Review of Books* (January 1971), "An Open Letter to My Sister, Miss Angela Davis," which compared her to a Jewish housewife being taken to Dachau.

By the early sixties Baldwin had become famous not for his literary skill alone but for his role as a moral spokesperson and social critic of the rapidly changing political landscape of the American Cold War and Civil Rights era. By the later sixties his support of the more militant voices in the movement brought increased criticism from a number of his former liberal admirers. The pressure of public life in the United States was difficult to sustain. Baldwin lived in Istanbul for a while in the middle sixties and was to settle permanently in southern France by the early seventies. Doing most of his writing in Europe and frequently traveling to the United States, Baldwin came to refer to himself as a "transatlantic commuter." Throughout his career Baldwin also described himself as a "witness," a term which effectively portrays both his relationship to American and African American experiences and to the discursive strategies he employs in his texts of many genres. As a witness Baldwin saw himself as a participant in and a critic of American culture and the mythology which sustains it. As a witness Baldwin both gave evidence to his experience as a racial and sexual minority as well as testified to a moral vision of things to come.[35]

# II.

In exploring the new directions of Baldwin's later novels, I will focus on three interconnected themes that link these works to his early essays and fiction. They are the role of the family in sustaining the artist; the price of success in American society; and the struggle of the black artist to change the ways race and sex are represented in American culture. One cannot overemphasize the importance of family in Baldwin's writing. First, the relationship between parents and children and between siblings are important subjects of representation in just about all of Baldwin's fiction. Second, family relationships become metaphors for a spiritual intimacy among lovers, who are often described as being like brothers or like brothers and sisters. Third, the family in Baldwin's fiction is the site of desire and of self-knowledge, where characters struggle with questions of identity.

As a subject of representation, the black family is central to Baldwin's first novel, his plays, several stories and essays, and his last two novels. In fact, depictions of complex family relationships distinguish Baldwin's work from that of other mid-century black writers, particularly from that of Richard Wright and Ralph Ellison. The autobiographical father-son relationship depicted in "Notes of a Native Son" and *Go Tell It on the Mountain* has been the subject of several critical analyses.[36] However, it has been less noted that *Mountain* also tells the stories of mothers and daughters (the story of Florence), fathers and daughters (the story of Elizabeth), mothers and sons (the story of Gabriel as well as the story of Elizabeth and John), and siblings (Gabriel and Florence, John and Roy). Baldwin moves away from the subject of the black family in his second and third novels but returns to it in his plays. The relationship between a black parent and child is central to both *Amen Corner* and *Blues for Mister Charlie*. Sister Margaret in *Amen Corner* and Meridian Henry in *Blues for Mister Charlie* are ministers who seek safety through religion, respectability, and pacifism but must come to terms with the knowledge that in trying to "save" their children they have failed them. Baldwin, then, returns to the subject of the black family in his last three novels, with a new emphasis on the bond between siblings. The concerns of his story "Sonny's Blues," which depicts the reconciliation of brothers who represent the divide between black respectability and the creative artist, are picked up with variations in *Tell Me How Long the Train's Been Gone* and *Just Above My Head*. By the last two novels Baldwin's focus is a full revisioning of the black family. *If Beale Street Could Talk* and *Just Above My Head* each juxtaposes the values of two Harlem families in order to explore the black family as a potential site of resistance to the racism and economic exploitation in the larger community.

While the family, and the black family in particular, seems to all but disappear as a subject of representation in Baldwin's second and third novels, families continue to be an important theme even in their absence. The characters in *Giovanni's Room* and *Another Country* are driven by the failure of early familial relationships to create alternate models of intimacy or new families. The characters are limited in their ability to create "another country" or another family in Paris or in Greenwich Village by the extent to which they are bound to models of heterosexual and racial inequality and to a model of masculinity, which denies the possibility of intimacy between men. David, of *Giovanni's Room*, is afraid to make a commitment to Giovanni because he can only imagine himself as a "woman" in such a relationship. *Another Country* centers on three heterosexual relationships made dysfunctional by the characters' inability to transcend racial and gender inequalities. However, the stories of these couples (Rufus and Leona, Vivaldo and Ida, and Cass and Richard) have a counterpoint in the story of Eric, a white, bisexual actor who, unlike David of *Giovanni's Room,* gains self-acceptance and returns from France able to love and heal others. Trudier Harris has pointed out that Vivaldo, Eric, Rufus, and Cass form a "symbolic familial group" which anticipates similar arrangements in Baldwin's later fiction.[37] Eric prefigures Leo Proudhammer, the bisexual black actor and first-person narrator of Baldwin's fourth novel.

In *Tell Me How Long the Train's Been Gone* Baldwin returns to a representation of the black family through the memory of thirty-nine-year-old Leo Proudhammer. Leo's crisscrossing memories of his Harlem childhood, his life in the East Village as a struggling actor, and his current experience as an international celebrity bring together elements of all of Baldwin's previous novels. *Train* is Baldwin's bridge between the disparate worlds of *Go Tell It on the Mountain* and *Another Country.* Rufus and Ida, the black brother and sister of *Another Country,* pursue careers as a blues musician and a singer and in the process sever their ties to their family and to the black community. However, unlike Rufus, Leo Proudhammer survives and at the peak of his acting career returns home. Most significantly, *Train* is Baldwin's first portrayal of sexual love between black men, and he situates this love within the family, between brothers.

In Baldwin's fiction the family is a site of strong emotional and sexual desire. It is a place of longing and fulfillment where characters experience both abandonment and abiding intimacy. Families are the intersubjective ground where characters achieve, and fail to achieve, a sense of self-recognition. For Baldwin, the question of identity is always a question of intimacy with another; one cannot see oneself or experience oneself except through the eyes or the body of another. When families are absent emotionally or literally, characters in Baldwin's fiction form love attachments with others who become symbolic siblings or parents or both. For example, in *Go Tell,* when Elisha leads John through his religious experience on the threshing floor, he takes on the role that John's father has refused. Elisha, who is the repressed subject of John's sexual desire, becomes the surrogate father-brother who initiates the adolescent John into the community of the saved. Similarly, and much more explicitly, the middle-aged Leo Proudhammer's young lover, Black Christopher, in *Tell Me How Long the Train's Been Gone* is Leo's link to a lost brother and father. Heterosexual love, as well, is often described in filial metaphors. For example, Tish and Fonny of *If Beale Street Could Talk* grow up together like brother and sister and Leo and Barbara in *Train* are described as "the incestuous brother and sister." Both relationships are Baldwinian models of intimacy where lovers nurture each other in a hostile environment.[38]

Family, especially the dream of domestic harmony, and the artist's pursuit of worldly success are linked in Baldwin's work and imagination. The former provides the motivation for the later, but the later ironically makes the former an ever-distant dream. As a child Baldwin fantasized that worldly success would bring him approval and establish his place in the family. Furthermore, he would rescue his family from poverty. Baldwin's first biographer, Fern Marja Eckman, writes:

> As a child, he had tried to insulate himself against rebuff by spinning a cocoon of reverie about the future, about the time when he would be grown-up and successful. The dream had been recurrent:
>
> Clad in a gray suit, he would drive his big Buick uptown—uptown, from somewhere in the shining, white citadel—to the block in Harlem where his family lived. And they would all be there waiting for him, proud of him now, his father as well as his mother, proud of their son, James Arthur Baldwin, so wealthy and so famous. Then they would all pile into his car and he would drive them to his country house. And they would dine there together or in a restaurant, all of them close and loving.[39]

This fantasy finds its way into Baldwin's fiction in the imagination of John Grimes, who dreams of becoming "a poet, or a college president, or a movie star" to compensate for his father's rejection and to challenge his father's authority.[40] Running up a hill in Central Park, John next imagines himself a "tyrant," conquering the city for the multitudes who will welcome him with open arms, but fantasies of social prestige and political power are soon replaced by a vision of domestic bliss that will presumably result from such success. As John descends to Fifth Avenue his dreams culminate in a romantic vision of the American family: "Behind him stood his house, great and rambling and very new, and in the kitchen his wife, a beautiful woman, made breakfast and the smoke rose out of the chimney, melting into the morning air. They had children, who called him Papa and for whom at Christmas he bought electric trains."[41]

In Baldwin's last novel, *Just Above My Head*, written twenty five years later, the image of a country house again appears, bringing closure to the almost 600-page novel. Hall's reconciliation with the loss of his brother, Arthur, is figured in a dream where all the family members and friends, some no longer living, are walking in the driving rain toward the safety of a country house where Hall and his brother await their arrival.[42]

In a variation on the childhood dream that success would allow him to rescue his family from poverty, Baldwin told an interviewer in 1970 that his family had saved him and that they were the key to his success.

So when I say that they saved me I mean that they kept me so busy caring for them, keeping them from the rats, roaches, falling plaster, and all the banality of poverty that I had no time to go jumping off the roof, or to become a junkie or an alcoholic. It's either/or in the ghetto. And I was one of the lucky ones. The welfare of my family has always driven me, always controlled me. I wanted to become rich and famous simply so no one could evict my family again. . . . That's really the key to my will to succeed.[43]

This statement is both revealing and concealing. It reveals the extent to which Baldwin's overwhelming sense of familial responsibility came to shape the directions of his later work, but it conceals the extent to which his drive to succeed came into conflict with his family's expectations and caused a great deal of guilt. Becoming a successful writer required that Baldwin enter and embrace enemy territory. To conquer the city he had to learn the ways of, and live in, the white world that his father so distrusted and detested. To realize his dream of becoming a writer, Baldwin had to "abandon" his family, first moving to Greenwich Village and then moving to Paris, leaving behind his widowed mother and eight younger siblings, whose means of support were meager. Baldwin's most recent biographer, David Leeming, describes the day of his departure "as the most 'dreadful' he had experienced . . . his family's tears and expressions of incomprehension clouding his conscience."[44] Regardless of Baldwin's mature view that his family had "saved" him and that his desire to succeed was motivated by his sense of family responsibility, initially the process of pursuing a career as a writer drove him away physically, intellectually, and emotionally from the circumscribed black world in which he had been raised and from the black church which was at the center of his family life. In Baldwin's fiction, as in his life, the wages of success mostly conflict with, rather than facilitate, the dream of domestic harmony. However, the dream of the artist's return home remains a powerful image, shaping the direction of his later work.

By foregrounding the lives of black performers and artists in his last three novels and their relationship to "home," Baldwin focuses on questions of race representation. Baldwin's concern with race representation dates back to his early essays, "Everybody's Protest Novel" and "Many Thousands Gone." The later novels, in many respects, fulfill the call expressed in these early essays for a new type of representation of black life in American literature. Baldwin's critique of Harriet Beecher Stowe's *Uncle Tom's Cabin* and Richard Wright's *Native Son* comprise Baldwin's literary manifesto and assert his independence from Wright and the representation of the black male as a victim of racism who is only able to act out the roles that have been socially assigned to him. The "protest novel," argues Baldwin, "so far from being disturbing, is an accepted and comforting aspect of the American scene, ramifying that framework we believe to be so necessary."[45] In Baldwin's reading, Bigger Thomas becomes a mirror image of Uncle Tom, "a continuation, a complement of that monstrous legend it was written to destroy."[46] By arguing that the "protest novel" unintentionally reifies oppressive racial stereotypes prevalent throughout the culture, Baldwin puts himself in a position of double resistance to previous representations of race. For Baldwin the way out of the trap of race representation is through a commitment to representing the complexity of individual subjectivity as it evolves within the black family and community.

Arguing for the importance of complexity and paradox in art appeared to ally Baldwin with the literary culture of the fifties where he got his start, writing reviews for publications such as *Partisan Review, New Leader,* and *Commentary.* Critics from the left such as Irving Howe were unsympathetic with Baldwin's critique of *Native Son* and the "protest novel" and associated Baldwin with a conservative postwar outlook. Howe claimed that Baldwin's "formula evade[d], through rhetorical sweep, the genuinely difficult issue of the relationship between social experience and literature."[47] In order to canonize Richard Wright's work as central to an African American literary tradition, Houston A. Baker Jr. continued this line of criticism, thus helping to marginalize Baldwin's importance to the study of African American literature. Baker described Baldwin as promoting a "theology of art" and advocating a "poetic, analytical, asocial" kind of writing.[48] He claimed that Baldwin's early essays are paradigms of bourgeois aesthetics, arguing that it is not until the mid-sixties with the publication of *The Fire Next Time* that Baldwin's work becomes socially engaged.[49] Horace Porter contests this judgment by minimizing the differences between Wright and Baldwin, stressing the importance of Wright's legacy on Baldwin's early essays and novels. About "Many Thousands Gone" Porter says, "Baldwin in effect, becomes a spokesman for the collective rage of black Americans in a way Bigger Thomas cannot. . . . Baldwin speaks as Bigger Thomas would if Bigger's hatred for whites had not been, according to Wright's narrator, 'dumb, cold, and inarticulate.'"[50] Porter's argument is useful in countering Baker's idea that Baldwin's early work lacked social engagement. Certainly, Baldwin's work from the late forties to the late seventies demonstrates a much greater continuity of method and subject than Baker's criticism implies. Baldwin's argument with Wright was not over whether the artist should be concerned with the individual as opposed to social realities, but how the relationship of the individual to the social should be represented. There are, however, limits to Porter's intertextual approach. By emphasizing the influences of Richard Wright, Harriet Beecher Stowe, and Henry James, Porter tends to minimize the significant differences that result in Baldwin's unique vision. Regardless of whether one agrees with Baldwin's assessment of *Native Son,* his criticism of the novel reveals the direction of his own work. Baldwin would restore the family and community relationships that are missing from *Native Son*:

> Bigger has no discernible relationship to himself, to his own life, to his own people, nor to any other people—in this respect, perhaps, he is most American— and his force comes, not from his significance as a social (or anti-social) unit, but from his significance as the incarnation of a myth. It is remarkable that, though we follow him step by step from the tenement room to the death cell, we know as little about him when this journey is ended, as we did when it began; and, what is even more remarkable, we know almost as little about the social dynamic which we are to believe created him. Despite the details of slum life which we are given, I doubt that anyone who has thought about it, disengaging himself from sentimentality, can accept this most essential premise of the novel for a moment. Those Negroes who surround him, on the other hand, his hard-working mother, his ambitious sister, his poolroom cronies, Bessie, might be considered as far richer and far more subtle and accurate illustrations of the ways in which Negroes are controlled in our society and the complex techniques they have evolved for their survival. We are limited, however, to Bigger's view of them, part of a deliberate plan which might not have been disastrous if we were not also limited to Bigger's perceptions. What this means for the novel is that a necessary dimension has been cut away; this dimension being the relationship that Negroes bear to one another, that depth of involvement and unspoken recognition of shared experience which creates a way of life.[51]

Baldwin's analysis of what's missing from *Native Son* is a blueprint for *Go Tell It on the Mountain*. By decentering the protagonist, John Grimes, and embedding John's story in the stories of his father, mother, and aunt, Baldwin restores the "dimension" of black life, "the relationship that Negroes bear to one another," that he found absent from *Native Son*. The story of John Grimes's conversion to his father's church also suggests "the complex techniques [Negroes] have evolved for their survival." Baldwin's interest in representing a complex subjectivity does not reflect an ideology of individualism, as Howe and Baker suggest. It does reflect Baldwin's strategy for deconstructing racial myths, interrogating the psychosexual dynamics of racism, redefining identity as an intersubjective process, and exploring the possibilities and limits of love as liberation.[52] Baldwin completes his project of restoring the missing dimension of black life in his last three novels.

# James Baldwin's
# Later Fiction

# 1 Baldwin's Reception and the Challenge of His Legacy

## I.

When James Baldwin died in 1987, five thousand people attended his funeral at the Cathedral of St. John the Divine in Harlem. The people came to celebrate his life and to mourn his passing because he had changed their lives; he was "quite possibly for his times their most essential interpreter."[1] Literary agent Marie Brown described Baldwin's passing as "the end of an era." He was "the last survivor . . . of those few most powerful moral articulators who could effectively lecture the society, among the very few whom we could quote almost daily as scripture of social consciousness."[2] A substantial number of leading American writers, intellectuals, and musicians came to pay tribute to Baldwin. Maya Angelou, Toni Morrison, and Amiri Baraka each gave eulogies, and many more wrote tributes to Baldwin's life and work that were published in newspapers around the world, some later in Quincy Troupe's *James Baldwin: The Legacy* and other venues. In her funeral address Toni Morrison said that Baldwin, like the Magi, had given her three gifts: a language to dwell in, the courage to transform the distances between people into intimacy, and the tenderness of vulnerability:

> No one possessed or inhabited language for me the way you did. You made American English honest—genuinely international. You exposed its secrets and reshaped it until it was truly modern dialogic, representative, humane. You stripped it of ease and false comfort and fake innocence and evasion and hypocrisy. And in place of deviousness was clarity. In place of soft plump lies was a lean, targeted power. In place of intellectual disingenuousness and what you called "exasperating egocentricity," you gave us undecorated truth. You replaced lumbering platitudes with an upright elegance. You went into that forbidden territory and decolonized it, "robbed it of the jewel of its naivete," and un-gated it for black people so that in your wake we could enter it, occupy it, restructure it in order to accommodate our complicated passion—not our vanities but our intricate, difficult, demanding beauty, our tragic, insistent knowledge, our lived reality, our sleek classical imagination—all the while refusing "to be defined by a language that has never been able to recognize [us]." In your hands language was handsome again. In your hands we saw how it was meant to be: neither bloodless nor bloody, and yet alive.[3]

Baldwin's funeral was a dramatic testament of his influence as a writer, thinker, friend, and social activist for the generation that followed him.

However, this funeral service, especially in its omissions, suggests the difficulties of interpreting Baldwin's legacy. Writing for the *Gay Community News*, Barbara Smith said: "Although Baldwin's funeral completely reinforced our Blackness, it tragically rendered his and our homosexuality completely invisible. In those two hours of remembrance and praise, not a syllable was breathed that this wonderful brother, this writer, this warrior, was also gay, that his being gay was indeed integral to his magnificence."[4] Baldwin wrote against a dominant strain of black nationalist thought which placed homosexuality in opposition to black resistance, an ideology that regarded homosexuality as a product of white oppression and evidence of internalized self-hatred. Given the homophobic climate, it is not surprising that interpretations of Baldwin's work that stress his contribution to representing black experience have, until quite recently, ignored or denied the importance of his homosexual themes and the homosexuality of his subjects, as if it were not possible to read his texts as expressions of both black and homosexual experience.[5]

Baldwin also wrote against an ideology that reified racial categories, insisting that "white" and "black" were inventions that oppressed blacks but also imprisoned whites in a false innocence that denied them self-knowledge. The only speaker at Baldwin's funeral who was not an African American was the French ambassador. Clyde Taylor found the irony inescapable: "Jimmy, like so many black artists, had been more fully honored and respected abroad than by his own society. France had given him its highest tribute, the Legion of Honor. By contrast, what had American society done?"[6] Perhaps the absence of an official honor from a representative of the American government was, finally, a testament to Baldwin's willingness to sharply criticize American institutions, and to his determination to be among the true poets who are "disturbers of the peace." Yet the absence of any American speaker of European descent is striking, given Baldwin's many white American friends and associates and the considerable impact Baldwin's writing had on the ways white Americans as well as black Americans think about race and sexuality.

Baldwin wrote that as a young man he left America in order to "prevent [himself] from becoming merely a Negro; or, even merely a Negro writer. [He] wanted to find out in what way the specialness of [his] experience could be made to connect [him] with other people instead of dividing [him] from them."[7] Later Baldwin would come to accept, even embrace, the designation of black writer and the enormous responsibility that went with it as part of the historical contingency within which he lived and worked. However, Baldwin never stopped exploring the "specialness" of his experience as it connected him to others. As an American, an African American, and a homosexual, Baldwin sought to provide a witness to overlapping but frequently incompatible experiences and communities. The challenge for writers who interpret his legacy is to find a language that doesn't reduce the complexity of Baldwin's art and vision. As Toni Morrison said in her funeral address: "The difficulty is your life refuses summation—it always did."[8]

At first glance it would seem that James Baldwin's life and work have received considerable attention. To date there have been eight biographies of Baldwin (four of which are for young readers);[9] eight book-length studies of Baldwin's work;[10] eight collections of critical essays; and three collections of tributes written shortly after Baldwin's death.[11] There has been significant bibliographic work done on Baldwin as well.[12] However, it becomes very clear after reviewing the critical output that comparatively little has been written on Baldwin's last three novels. The large majority of criticism has taken one or more of the first three novels as its focus or to a lesser extent the early essays through *The Fire Next Time*. Of the full-length studies only Carolyn Wedin Sylvander's discusses all of Baldwin's novels, and her book is primarily a reader's guide. Horace Porter's *Stealing the Fire* (1989) explores the influence of Henry James, Harriet Beecher Stowe, and Richard Wright on Baldwin's early essays and fiction, dismissing Baldwin's work after *The Fire Next Time* as unsuccessful. Porter's book is the most recent of the full length critical studies (not including Bobia's book on Baldwin's reception in France), yet it is over ten years old. Trudier Harris's *Black Women in the Fiction of James Baldwin* (1985) provides close readings of *If Beale Street Could Talk* and *Just Above My Head* but omits any discussion of *Tell Me How Long the Train's Been Gone* since it has no major black women characters. Macebuh's, Möller's, and Pratt's studies were written prior to the publication of Baldwin's last novel or novels.

The critical collections have emphasized Baldwin's earlier work as well. Even D. Quentin Miller's recent *Reviewing James Baldwin: Things Not Seen* (1999), which purports to give attention to Baldwin's neglected later work, has no discussion of *Tell Me How Long the Train's Been Gone* or *If Beale Street Could Talk* and only one essay on *Just Above My Head*. Miller's collection does, however, include important work on some of Baldwin's lesser-known writing, some of which was written during the seventies and eighties.[13] A number of the contributors to Dwight McBride's *James Baldwin Now* see Baldwin's work as a progenitor to theoretical developments in gender and gay studies as well as to the study of the cultural construction of whiteness. These essays, on the whole, do a much more sophisticated job of analyzing Baldwin's work as it complicates and interimplicates categories of race, gender, and sexuality than early essays were able to do.[14] They replace the old image of the fifties Baldwin as a liberal humanist with a much more complex figure, one who intervened in, rather than merely reflected, the liberal discourse of the period. However, the focus of this collection is Baldwin's early work, particularly *Giovanni's Room* and *Another Country,* in the context of post–World War II American culture. As a result there is little discussion of Baldwin's response to the changing culture and conditions of the sixties and seventies, and there is little discussion of Baldwin's representations of black families and of black communities, since there is nothing on *Go Tell It on the Mountain, Tell Me How Long the Train's Been Gone, If Beale Street Could Talk,* or *Just Above My Head.*[15]

In her introduction to *Black Women in the Fiction of James Baldwin* (1985), Trudier Harris wrote that she was "surprised to discover that a writer of Baldwin's reputation evoked such vague memories from individuals in the scholarly community" and found it "discouraging . . . that one of America's best-known writers, and certainly one of its best-known black writers, has not attained a more substantial place in the scholarship on Afro-American writers."[16] Although there was renewed interest in Baldwin's life and work in the late eighties following his death (as evidenced by the publication of James Campbell's and David Leeming's biographies, Quincy Troupe's *James Baldwin: The Legacy,* the published proceedings of a conference at the University of Massachusetts at Amherst, and the film *The Price of the Ticket*), the quantity of scholarship on Baldwin's writing has significantly lagged behind that of other well-known African American writers, such as Richard Wright, Ralph Ellison, or Toni Morrison. Moreover, Baldwin studies have not benefited from the presence of African American theory and scholarship in the academy. Craig Werner pointed out the extent to which Baldwin has been ignored:

> To be sure, Baldwin's name is occasionally invoked, generally as part of a trinity including Richard Wright and Ralph Ellison. But his work, much less his vision, is rarely discussed, even within the field of Afro-American

Studies. Baldwin is conspicuous by his absence from recent (and valuable) books on cultural theory (Henry Louis Gates Jr.'s *The Signifying Monkey*, Robert Stepto's *From Behind the Veil*, Houston Baker's *Blues, Ideology, and Afro-American Literature: A Vernacular Theory*); intellectual history (Sterling Stuckey's *Slave Culture: Nationalist Theory and the Foundations of Black America*, Harold Cruse's *Plural But Equal: Black and Minorities in America's Plural Society*); literary criticism (Keith Byerman's *Fingering the Jagged Grain: Tradition and Form in Recent Black Fiction*, John Callahan's *In the African-American Grain: The Pursuit of Voice in Twentieth-Century Black Fiction*); and period history (David Garrow's *Bearing the Cross*, Doug McAdam's *Freedom Summer*). There are to be sure occasional exceptions, mostly [sic] notably Michael Cooke's *Afro-American Literature in the Twentieth Century* and Melvin Dixon's *Ride Out the Wilderness: Geography and Identity in Afro-American Literature*. Still, given Baldwin's central importance to the development of issues raised in all of the above work, the general silence suggests that the larger changes of intellectual fashion have influenced the internal dynamics of discourse on Afro-American culture.[17]

Werner attributes Baldwin's marginalization in the academy to the dominance of a poststructuralist critique which "resurrected an ironic sensibility that renders Baldwin's moral seriousness and his political activism nearly incomprehensible to literary intellectuals."[18] While Baldwin's "concern with salvation" may have made him unfashionable, his incisive critique of racial and sexual categories in the formation of American identity certainly precede the poststructuralist critique of "identity." Eric Savoy has pointed out the limitation of a great deal of criticism that argues that Baldwin's main theme is "a search for identity." The direction of Baldwin's work is not toward the attainment of identity, but rather toward knowledge of self "as implicated, situated subject, but simultaneously as 'other' and therefore as resisting agent."[19] Baldwin's neglect by the academy may be explained by the dominance of an intellectual sensibility that rendered political activism and moral seriousness incomprehensible, as Werner claims. However, Baldwin's marginalization is also partly due to the pressures of canonizing black literature by defining a black difference. Baldwin's critique of racial representation—what Savoy has called his "double resist-ance" to both white, middle-class, heterosexual America and to the ways in which other black writers (especially Richard Wright) and gay writers (Andre Gide) brought their otherness to text—puts Baldwin at odds with at least some theories of black difference.

In Houston A. Baker Jr.'s influential *Blues, Ideology, and Afro-American Literature: A Vernacular Theory,* as well as in his earlier book *The Journey Back: Issues in Black Literature and Criticism,* Baldwin is not exactly ignored. He becomes the "other" in Baker's attempt to canonize Richard Wright as the writer whose work best reveals a distinctive and resistant African American discourse. Baker defends Wright from the neg-ative critique of *Native Son* and of "protest fiction" in Baldwin's "Everybody's Protest Novel" and "Many Thousands Gone." According to Baker, Baldwin's criticism of Wright is based on a bourgeois aesthetic in which the artist is perceived to be above or separate from society.[20] While Baker's deconstruction of the binary "art" versus "protest" is useful in revealing the political motivation of 1950s "aesthetic" criticism, he rein-states the binary by portraying Wright as the black writer with a political consciousness and Baldwin as the writer who advocates "a theology of art," whose writing is "poetic, analytical, asocial."[21] However, Baldwin's criticism of *Native Son* was as much politically motivated as it was aes-thetically motivated. His argument with Wright turned less on artistic flaws in the depiction of Bigger Thomas than on a racist representation of the black male in which Baldwin believed the novel to be implicated.[22]

One of the central problems of Baldwin's reception has been the way in which arguments over "art" and "politics" have misrepresented and marginalized his work. Baker's characterization of the difference between Wright and Baldwin mirrors and reverses the response of those New Critics who embraced Baldwin's criticism of Wright and read Baldwin's first novel as a vindication of their literary values, which emphasized formal structures over social criticism. Yet as Horace Porter, Craig Werner, and others have argued, Baldwin's early work, including *Go Tell It on the Mountain,* was not apolitical. As Werner points out, "Just as the original readers of *Native Son* simplified the work to accommodate their ideology, Baldwin's aesthetic defenders ignored major political elements of his novel."[23] Horace Porter's book (appropriately subtitled *The Art and Politics of James Baldwin*) makes this argument in detail by elaborating the intertexuality in Baldwin's early work with both Wright and Stowe.

While Baldwin has been criticized by some Marxist and some African American literary theorists for his alleged bourgeois aesthetics, with the publication of *Blues for Mister Charlie, Tell Me How Long the Train's Been Gone, No Name in the Street,* and *If Beale Street Could Talk* Baldwin came under attack in the liberal press by Mario Puzo, Pearl K. Bell, John Aldridge, and others for writing "propaganda." Using Baldwin's early statements on protest fiction against him, they argued that Baldwin was doing the very thing for which he had criticized Richard Wright: he was writing protest fiction with melodramatic plots and stereotypical characters. Moreover, taking offense at the occasional use of "street" language and the sharper, more militant tone, many of these critics argued that Baldwin's "bitterness" revealed that he was out of touch with American "progress" in race relations. Those who had embraced Baldwin's early work for aesthetic reasons felt betrayed.

To a large extent the scholarly community has agreed with the initial assessment of Baldwin's later novels. Horace Porter found Baldwin's later essays and fiction deeply disappointing:

> he moves from the promethean figure, the man who stole the fire of "Notes of a Native Son," the powerful writer of *The Fire Next Time,* to the embittered and self-indulgent nay-sayer of *No Name in the Street* and *Evidence of Things Not Seen.* None of Baldwin's later novels or essays rivals the narrative ingenuity and rhetorical power of *Go Tell It on the Mountain* and *Notes of a Native Son,* his first novel and his first collection of essays.[24]

Henry Louis Gates Jr. and Hilton Als concur with this evaluation of Baldwin's decline as an artist and place the blame on black militants (most notably Eldridge Cleaver), from whose criticism Baldwin allegedly never recovered. Gates views *No Name in the Street,* in particular, as a "capitulation" by a man who was desperate "to be loved by his own" and who "cared too much about what others wanted from him."[25] Reviewing the 1998 Library of America's two-volume selection of Baldwin's essays, early novels, and stories, Hilton Als reflects on "both [his] early infatuation and [his] later disaffection" with Baldwin's work. Because Baldwin "compromised" his unique perspective and "sacrificed his gifts to gain acceptance from the Black Power movement," Als sees Baldwin's career as "a cautionary tale . . . a warning as well as an inspiration."[26]

Clearly Baldwin has been in the crossfire of arguments that assume certain artistic and social values and set them in contradistinction. In fact, it remains very difficult to sort out aesthetic from political judgments when discussing Baldwin's reception because they are so deeply interconnected. One of the aims of this book is to interrogate the assumption that Baldwin's increased political activism and militancy in the sixties led to his decline as an artist. The reading of Baldwin's later work as lacking aesthetic value is as problematic as the reading of his earlier work as lacking political value. As Craig Werner has pointed out, James Baldwin "asserted the ultimately moral connection of political and cultural experience."[27] There is no doubt that Baldwin's later work was influenced by the turbulent political and racial environment of the sixties and early seventies, as well as by the decline in economic and social conditions for urban black youth and families in the seventies. I wish to argue that his response to the events of the sixties and seventies was more complex than has been acknowledged and that his last three novels should be read not as evidence of either a political capitulation or an artistic decline, but as evidence of the ways Baldwin creatively responded to a changing racial environment and discourse in an attempt to communicate the story he wanted to tell.

As the only major African American writer whose career spanned the pre- and post-civil rights and black power period, Baldwin's historical position was unique. Richard Wright died in 1960; Langston Hughes died in 1967; Ralph Ellison survived Baldwin, but stopped writing (or at least publishing) fiction. The sensibilities of prominent contemporary African American writers, including Toni Morrison, Alice Walker, and Amiri Baraka, were formed in the crucible of the civil rights era. Baldwin's work from the middle sixties on reflected the dramatic shift in American racial and political discourse, symbolized by the positive signification of "black" and the deployment of a resistant identity politics. His work also reflected a racial and political reality that Baldwin read as increasingly repressive, even genocidal, for the majority of black Americans, a reading that put him at sharp odds with a liberal rhetoric of black progress.

*Tell Me How Long the Train's Been Gone, If Beale Street Could Talk,* and *Just Above My Head* are not flawless novels. There are some over-written, even carelessly written passages and some inconsistencies in character and plot that are difficult to account for and that could have been corrected by more careful editing. Yet to focus solely on artistic faults (which the majority of reviewers did) is to ignore the power and vision present in these works. Moreover, what some reviewers described as artistic flaws were certainly aspects of Baldwin's intentional experimentation with voice and form. Baldwin took risks with his later work. He reframed his earlier stories to reflect his experience and, especially, his interest in reproducing in the novel a style of resistance that he found in African American music. Baldwin gave up the tighter, more formal structures of his earliest work. For example, the compartmentalized and isolated voices of the characters in *Go Tell It on the Mountain* give way to experiments in first-person narration. These novels demonstrate a relationship between author and character (i.e., Baldwin's relationship to Leo Proudhammer, Tish Rivers, and Hall Montana) that parallels a jazz musician's relationship to his instrument as an extension or elaboration of the performer's self.[28] Baldwin's narrators are instruments of self-expression who perform Baldwin's voice in different bodies—both male and female—and in different places—Harlem, the Village, Paris. They echo and revise the author's life. They suggest that "identity" is, indeed, a complex affair that involves a recognition of "others" and the presence of the "other" in the "self."

## II.

In 1988, shortly after Baldwin's death, a conference at the University of Massachusetts at Amherst brought several eminent writers and scholars together to pay tribute to James Baldwin. The published proceedings of this conference gave voice to a deep concern with the type of criticism Baldwin had been receiving. Describing literary criticism as an open letter to an author, John Edgar Wideman said, "We're getting a species of letter which endangers my relationship to James Baldwin and James Baldwin's relationship to the tradition and to you and to your children." In these "poison pen letters," Baldwin is cast as "a kind of villain" who "does not appreciate progress. He is enraged and bitter. He lost his footing as an artist and simply became a propagandist. And that version of Baldwin's career is very dangerously being promulgated and it's being pushed in a kind of surreptitious way by these letters."[29] Chinua Achebe sought to clarify Baldwin's accomplishment. Responding to the frequent charge that Baldwin failed to recognize America's progress, Achebe pointed out that for Baldwin progress was not a matter of more black mayors and generals. Baldwin's project was to "redefine the struggle" by seeing it "from a whole range of perspectives at once—the historical, the psychological, the philosophical, which are not present in a handful of statistics of recent advances." Baldwin's strength was in his ability "to lift from the backs of Black people the burden of their race" and "to unmask the face of the oppressor, to see his face and to call him by name." Achebe concluded that "Baldwin, belongs to mankind's ancient tradition of storytelling, to the tradition of prophets who had the dual role to fore-tell and to forth-tell."[30]

Although the proceedings of the Amherst conference offer a corrective to the white liberal dismissal of Baldwin's work after the middle sixties, they completely ignore Baldwin's homosexual themes and, more important, the extent to which black and white homophobia affected Baldwin's reception. There was more than one version of the "poison-pen letter." Around the same time Baldwin was being condemned by white liberals for his black militancy, he was being condemned by black militants for his homosexuality. The most notorious example was Eldridge Cleaver's attack on Baldwin in *Soul on Ice:* "There is in James Baldwin's work the most grueling, agonizing, total hatred of the blacks, particularly of himself, and the most shameful, fanatical, fawning, sycophantic love of the whites that one can find in the writings of any black American writer of note in our time."[31]

Cleaver argues that there is a "decisive quirk" in Baldwin's writing that caused him to "slander Rufus Scott in *Another Country*, venerate Andre Gide, repudiate [Norman Mailer's] *The White Negro*, and drive the blade of Brutus into the corpse of Richard Wright."[32] Charging Baldwin with waging "a despicable underground guerrilla war . . . against black masculinity" and calling "homosexuality a sickness, just as are baby-rape or wanting to become the head of General Motors,"[33] Cleaver expresses in virulent form a homophobia representative of some segments of the black community.

In Cleaver's analysis, which parallels that of conservative black critics such as Stanley Crouch, homosexuality is considered to be a remnant of slavery, a habit learned from whites and thus a symptom of internalized self-hatred. In this reading Baldwin's homosexuality necessarily negates any claim that Baldwin can speak to an authentic "black" experience. Of course homophobic responses to Baldwin's work are not limited to black critics. In writing about *Another Country*, Robert Bone said:

> Few will concede to a sense of reality, at least in the sexual realm, to one who regards heterosexual love as "a kind of superior calisthenics." To most, homosexuality will seem rather an evasion than an affirmation of human truth. Ostensibly the novel summons us to reality. Actually it substitutes for the illusions of white supremacy those of homosexual love.[34]

Although not exactly the same argument as Cleaver's, Bone's argument also links homosexuality with white supremacy as a travesty of truth. Numerous critics took the position that Baldwin's representations of bisexuality and homosexuality undermined his credibility as a novelist and as a spokesperson for blacks. In addition Baldwin's sexuality put him in a difficult relationship to other civil rights leaders; it was probably the main reason he was not invited to speak at the 1963 March on Washington.[35]

Emmanuel S. Nelson has effectively documented the homophobia in Baldwin's reception, in its silences as well as in its more obvious forms, and has suggested that the reason Baldwin has been more highly regarded as an essayist than as a novelist is related to the relative absence of homosexual themes in his essays compared with his novels.[36] Homophobia may also be at the center of the decline in Baldwin's reputation as a novelist since his later novels, with the exception of *If Beale Street Could Talk,* are increasingly positive and explicit in their representation of black homosexual relationships. Given this fact, the belief that Baldwin adapted his writing or "compromised" his vision to please critics such as Cleaver seems unfounded. In the face of black homophobia Baldwin responded by continuing to represent and even celebrate homosexuality in *Tell Me How Long the Train's Been Gone* and *Just Above My Head.* Nelson calls for an analysis of Baldwin's work that explores both his "racial awareness and his homosexual consciousness on his literary imagination" without privileging one over the other.[37] Bryan R. Washington expresses caution over "politically fashionable" but hollow efforts to "recanonize" Baldwin by avoiding his "homopoetics (politics)." He argues that such avoidance "proceeds from a desire to keep the recanonizing train on track—a train driven by theories of race and writing designed to minimize difference, to promote the academic institutionalization of blackness by homogenizing it."[38]

Although Baldwin has been underrepresented in the field of African American studies compared to other black writers of his stature, he has received substantial treatment in many studies on gay male writing, including Georges-Michel Sarotte's *Like a Brother, Like a Lover* (1976, translated into English, 1978), Stephen Adams's *The Homosexual as Hero in Contemporary Fiction* (1980), Claude J. Summers's *Gay Fictions: Wilde to Stonewall* (1990), David Bergman's *Gaiety Transfigured: Gay Self-Representation in America* (1991), Mark Lilly's *Gay Men's Literature in the Twentieth Century* (1993), and Wilfrid R. Koponen's *Embracing a Gay Identity: Gay Novels as Guides* (1993). Yet all of these studies ignore Baldwin's later fiction (and only Sarotte's book was published before Baldwin's last novel). None discuss *Just Above My Head,* and *Tell Me How Long the Train's Been Gone* receives only passing mention, if any at all. Summers and Koponen work strictly with *Giovanni's Room,* while Adams and Lilly work with both *Giovanni's Room* and *Another Country.*

In his substantial chapter on Baldwin, Stephen Adams argues that "the knowledge Baldwin claims of American masculinity—as one who has been menaced by it—has an authority which in turn menaces preferred images of manhood, both black and white. He puzzles over his own definitions in ways which explode the notions of narrowness in the experience of a racial or sexual minority."[39] Adams takes several of Baldwin's critics to task, including Irving Howe, who charges Baldwin with "whipped cream sentimentalism" in the portrayal of homosexual love in *Giovanni's Room,* and Sarotte, who reads *Giovanni's Room* as memoir and identifies David's position as a homophobic homophile with Baldwin's. While Adams develops careful and sympathetic readings of *Giovanni's Room* and *Another Country,* he dismisses *Tell Me How Long the Train's Been Gone* in the last paragraph, calling it Baldwin's endorsement of black militancy and describing the Leo-Christopher relationship as a product of Baldwin's "wishful thinking" that "rings false."[40] David Bergman's treatment of Baldwin occurs within a broad discussion of black discourse on racism and sexuality, evangelical Protestantism, Africa as racial homeland, and the coded discourse of earlier black homosexual writers, especially Alain Locke. What could be a promising approach to the intersection of race and homosexuality in Baldwin's writing is marred by Bergman's uninformed statements about Baldwin's work. For example, Bergman is seemingly unaware of Baldwin's theoretical and personal essays on homosexuality—"The Preservation of Innocence" and "There Be Dragons"—when he claims that Baldwin's only nonfiction on homosexuality is "The Male Prison."[41] In addition, Bergman's assertion that "after Cleaver's attack, Baldwin emphasized racial much more than sexual issues" is simply not supported by Baldwin's later work.[42]

That most gay studies ignore Baldwin's later novels adds weight to Nelson's observation that analyses which privilege Baldwin's homosexuality tend to ignore his blackness. Unlike *Giovanni's Room* and *Another Country,* the homosexuality of *Tell Me How Long the Train's Been Gone* and of *Just Above My Head* occurs within a specifically black context, making it impossible to explore the representation of homosexuality in these novels without also addressing the representation of race. Melvin

Dixon's chapter on Baldwin in *Ride out the Wilderness* and Lee Edelman's essay, "The Part for the (W)hole: Baldwin, Homophobia, and the Fantasmatics of 'Race,'" in *Homographesis* are important exceptions to the tendency to privilege either "blackness" or "homosexuality" when reading Baldwin's texts, and both produce very interesting, although quite different, readings of *Just Above My Head*.[43]

In the history of twentieth-century American letters it would be hard to find another figure more simultaneously praised and damned, often by the same critic in the same essay, than James Baldwin. A remarkable aspect of Cleaver's response to Baldwin is its initial adulation of Baldwin's work and the way this adulation is expressed in clearly sexual terms. From the beginning tone of Cleaver's essay, one would not expect the coming attack. Cleaver describes the "continuous delight" he felt reading "a couple of James Baldwin's books." He describes Baldwin's talent as "penetrating" and says he "lusted for anything Baldwin had written. It would have been a gas for [him] to sit on a pillow beneath the womb of Baldwin's typewriter and catch each newborn page as it entered this world of ours."[44] However, Cleaver begins to feel "an aversion in [his] heart to part of the song [Baldwin] sang" and after reading *Another Country* he "knew why [his] love for Baldwin's vision had become ambivalent."[45] This movement from praise and identification with Baldwin's work to ambivalence, disappointment, and rejection is the single most common characteristic of Baldwin criticism, regardless of the particular ideological, racial, or sexual orientation of the critic. (Noting the irony, Craig Werner has pointed out that "it is perhaps not surprising that Baldwin's blackness has never been clearer than in his rejection."[46])

Baldwin's work has presented problems to readers from almost every perspective—liberal, black nationalist, feminist, and homosexual—and to some extent each of these constituencies in their inability to accommodate Baldwin's complexity has helped to marginalize him. In addition to the previously discussed challenges he presents to both liberal and nationalist discourses, Baldwin's work gets an ambivalent response from feminist and gay criticism as well. Although Baldwin's female characters are numerous, varied, and complex, especially when compared to other black male writers of his generation, Trudier Harris, Hortense Spillers, and others have critiqued

Baldwin's discourse for essentializing gender, and his female characters for their dependence on men and male values. While acknowledging Baldwin's tremendous contribution to making the representation of a gay black male sexuality possible, some pro-gay critics are uncomfortable with Baldwin's reluctance to discuss gay issues in his nonfiction or to assert a gay identity. (Baldwin insisted that "homosexual" was not a noun.) The predominance of bisexual characters in Baldwin's fiction and his use of a heterosexual narrator to describe homosexual experience in *Just Above My Head* is taken by some as evidence of the extent to which Baldwin is, himself, implicated by the homophobia he so trenchantly critiques.

What these narratives of disappointment suggest is that James Baldwin did not tell the story that various critical constituencies wanted him to tell. For the white liberal he did not confirm that the "success" of a talented black individual represented the "progress" of the race; for black and white integrationists he seemed to lose faith in the dream of interracial understanding; for the black nationalist his stories did not evoke masculine-individualist heroics (and thus were judged as stories of complicity rather than resistance); for the feminist his women characters were too traditional in their relationships to men, and his concern with reinventing "masculinity" appeared to construct the feminine as other; for the gay activist he did not assert a separate homosexual identity. The critical narratives of Baldwin's "unfulfilled potential" must be understood in terms of the critics' own desire for a particular kind of spokesperson, but they also must be understood in relationship to the "promise" that Baldwin presents to his readership and to his politics of "salvation." (As Baldwin said in a 1987 interview, "I am working toward the New Jerusalem. That's true. I'm not joking. I won't live to see it but I do believe in it. I think we're going to be better than we are."[47]) While Baldwin's concern for salvation may make him incomprehensible to a certain poststructuralist sensibility, as Werner claims, it also raises expectations in readers who would probably not agree on just what the New Jerusalem should look like. Baldwin did not leave a map of his heavenly city, only a few trail markers to indicate the way.

Baldwin's work is wedded to the tradition of realistic fiction as well as to the tradition of the jeremiad, which seeks to call people to their better selves while warning them of the failings and the dangers of their current course. His work is driven by two traditions, which are not always compatible: the tradition of mimetic truth telling and the tradition of religious truth telling. The first called Baldwin to testify to the sorrows, joys, contingencies, and interruptions of everyday experience, while the second called him to exhort, to promise, and to create a vision of a new and better order out of the old, corrupt one. It is the balance Baldwin creates between these two impulses that make up his distinctive voice. His fidelity to lived experience and to representing human relationships in all their complexity signifies on what Baldwin called "the protest novel." His commitment to a moral vision also signifies on "the protest novel," requiring that he, too, protest, but in a different key.

# 2 The Celebrity's Return: *Tell Me How Long the Train's Been Gone*

All I can do is work out the terms on which I can work, and for me that means being a transatlantic commuter.

—James Baldwin, *Conversations with James Baldwin*

A t the end of *Tell Me How Long the Train's Been Gone* James Baldwin signs his work by listing the places and dates where it was written: "New York, Istanbul, San Francisco, 1965–1967." This journalistic signature draws attention to the autobiographical element of the novel and invites readers to understand it in its historical and political context as the most recent chapter of Baldwin's ongoing chronicle of his experience in a racially divided American landscape. The list of cities suggests the author's status as an international celebrity, but it also suggests his displacement and the difficulty he had finding time to work and a place to call home. Baldwin's political activism, his celebrity, and his final breakup with his lover, Lucien Happersberger, both interrupted and informed this novel.[1] The dates 1965–1967 correspond to the increasing polarization of American society over race, the radicalization of the Civil Rights movement, and the increased repression of activists by local and federal authorities. The novel's closing signature authenticates the crisis in the life of the protagonist, Leo Proudhammer, with the author's own experience of personally and politically turbulent times. *Tell Me How Long the Train's Been Gone* was released in 1968 about two months after the assassination of Dr. Martin Luther King, a fact which added credence to Leo Proudhammer's apocalyptic prophecy at the end of the novel.

Yet Leo's story suffered the fate of prophecies of old. One of Baldwin's biographers finds a "morbid congruity" in the death of King and the release of Baldwin's fourth novel, stating that "the novel's publication signaled the second assassination of the year."[2] With few exceptions the novel received negative reviews, including hostile reviews from prominent critics and writers Granville Hicks, Irving Howe, Nelson Algren, and Mario Puzo.[3] Each claimed that the novel was an "artistic failure," yet the real animus of these early reviews, as well as some of the later critiques, was directed at the novel's racial and sexual politics. Several critics eschewed what they perceived to be Baldwin's turn to militancy and charged *Train* with being outdated protest realism at best and propaganda at worst. Nelson Algren complained that all the good guys were white and all the bad guys were black. Irving Howe accused Baldwin of "whipping himself into postures of militancy and declarations of racial metaphysics." Mario Puzo advised Baldwin "to forget the black revolution and start worrying about himself as an artist." The argument put forth by mostly white male critics was that Baldwin's racial anger (which they had a hard time taking seriously) compromised his artistic talent.[4]

In fact, *Tell Me How Long the Train's Been Gone* is about, among other things, the problem and uses of racial anger rather than the unmediated expression of anger that these critics interpreted it to be. The complete breakdown in understanding between Baldwin and the majority of his critics was, indeed, a sign of the times. It corresponded to sharply differing views on the state of America and the gains of the Civil Rights movement. Baldwin often referred to the Civil Rights movement as the "latest slave rebellion," not only to emphasize the historical continuity of the conditions of American blacks, but to deconstruct the myth that "civil rights" had made blacks and whites equal. The physical conditions and lack of opportunities for young blacks in Harlem, where Baldwin had grown up some thirty years before, were certainly not better and were, in many respects, worse by the late sixties.[5] An addition to the problems of continuing discrimination and poverty was the ongoing destruction of black leadership. Baldwin, an active participant and public speaker in the Civil Rights movement, had met and worked with Medgar Evers, Malcolm X, and Martin Luther King. When King was murdered, Baldwin experienced a severe depression, believing that he could also be a target for an assassin's bullet.[6] Baldwin was also friendly with the Black Panthers, who were being systematically targeted by the FBI and the local police forces.[7] Meanwhile a large segment of the liberal middle class believed that the Civil Rights movement had accomplished its goals and that militant blacks were either "going too far" or endangering the progress that had been made. According to this view, laws against segregation had lifted the remaining barriers to black progress. The stridency of black militant rhetoric angered and frightened many who had been sympathetic to the Civil Rights movement, but who viewed assertions of "black power" as a threat to their own cultural, economic, and political hegemony. Where many whites saw "progress," many blacks felt "betrayal." While Baldwin became increasingly disillusioned over America's willingness to change its structure of racial inequalities, much of the liberal press portrayed Baldwin as "bitter" and "out of touch." This is the context that must be brought to an understanding of the reception of *Train*.

The reception of *Train* was not only marked by an outraged liberalism, but by a somewhat quieter, though not always subtle, homophobia. Overall, the novel's sexual themes were either ignored or treated with dismissal and sarcasm, while a few critics expressed outright distaste or offense.[8] Most reviews did not make any direct reference to the sexual relationship between Leo Proudhammer and his brother Caleb or even to the later sexual relationship between Leo and Black Christopher. Yet these relationships carry a great deal of symbolic weight and are key to any meaningful reading of the text. Emmanuel S. Nelson has explored the role of homophobia in the reception of Baldwin's fiction from *Giovanni's Room* to *Just Above My Head* and in doing so challenges the critical consensus that Baldwin was a better essay writer than fiction writer. As Nelson points out, Baldwin rarely wrote about homosexuality or bisexuality in his essays but wrote about the subject with increasing directness in most of his fiction. If we acknowledge the considerable degree of homophobic response to Baldwin's fiction from *Giovanni's Room* on, then we must agree with Nelson's assertion that "it would be naive . . . to assume that the gay content of his fiction is not at least partly responsible for the mixed criticism it has provoked."[9]

With the distance of thirty years, the absolute inadequacy and overall misguided nature of the initial response to *Train* becomes obvious. What the reviewers missed was the extraordinary way that Baldwin's fourth novel engaged with and challenged the changing racial and sexual politics of the sixties. *Tell Me How Long the Train's Been Gone* explores the failure of liberalism to end racism, while simultaneously exposing the limits of an old and new black nationalism (represented by Leo's father, a follower of Marcus Garvey, and Leo's young lover, a militant black activist). The symbolic structure of *Train* suggests that both liberalism and black nationalism as strategies of resistance to racial oppression are limited to the extent that each relies on essentialist conceptions of personal and political identity and fail to accommodate difference in the construction of those identities. In *Train* Baldwin affirms the revolutionary impulse of "black power" to transform American society and end white supremacy, while refusing a genetic and romanticized ethos of "blackness." Through the character Christopher Hall, referred to by Leo as "Black Christopher," Baldwin makes visible the repressed elements of the black nationalist ethos: its interracial origins and its homoerotic desires. Leo's bisexuality, his self-acknowledged "ambiguity," and his interracial love affairs are Baldwin's challenge to the emergent identity politics of the sixties and represent his continued insistence on deconstructing categories of race and sexual orientation in a political climate that was hostile to such efforts. Leo's lifelong friendship, once love affair, with the white, Barbara King, and his more recent love affair and passion for Black Christopher, the novel's young black nationalist revolutionary, provide the symbolic ground for Baldwin's explorations of the ways in which race and sexuality are linked in American identity formation. If Black Christopher is Baldwin's challenge to American liberalism, he is also Baldwin's challenge to the black power movement's homo-phobia. To this end Baldwin gives Black Christopher a sexual history and a symbolic family genealogy that violate American sexual and racial taboos and place him in a dramatically revised oedipal drama, forever linking him to America's interracial family.[10]

# I.

*Train's* critique of American liberalism is most evident in its revision of the American success story and its revision of black autobiographical narratives that celebrate individual achievement as representations of racial progress.[11] James Baldwin told an interviewer from the *LA Times* that *Tell Me How Long the Train's Been Gone* is a novel about the problems of "surviving success" in America.[12] Prior to writing *Train* Baldwin's lawyer, Theodore Kupferman, told Baldwin that his "rage period should be over and he should surprise everybody and do a book about a black who made it" because "the whole system was changing and it was possible for a qualified black not to be restricted in any way."[13] Baldwin not only disliked the idea but was annoyed to the point of firing his lawyer. A fictionalized version of this interchange between Kuperfman and Baldwin is represented in *Train* in the con-versation that Leo Proudhammer has with Ken, Barbara's brother, and another white character, Bennett.

> "And you made it, all right, didn't you?" Bennett asked. "Why, I bet you make more money than I do—I know you make more money than I do," and he chuckled. "And I bet you didn't do it sitting around, feeling sorry for yourself, did you?"
>
> "Hell, no" Ken said. "He just made his own way. And anybody can make his way in this country, no matter what color he is.". . .
>
> [Leo responds] "But there's no point in pretending that Negroes are treated like white people in this country because they're not, and we all know that."

"But look at you," said Ken. "I don't know what you make a year, but I can make a pretty shrewd guess. What have you got to complain about? It seems to me that this country's treated you pretty well. I know a whole lot of white people couldn't afford to live in this apartment, for example—. . . .

[Leo responds] "You can't imagine my life, and I won't discuss it. I don't make as much money as you think I do, and I don't work as often as I would if I were white. Those are just facts. The point is that the Negroes of this country are treated as none of you would dream of treating a dog or a cat. What Christopher's trying to tell you is perfectly true. If you don't want to believe it, well, that's your problem. And I don't feel like talking about it anymore, and I won't." I looked at Ken. "This is my house."[14]

Leo (like Baldwin) is outraged by the idea that his individual success can be used to reassure whites that America has no significant or structural racial injustice. Although Baldwin rejected Kupferman's idea of writing about a black who had "made it," *Tell Me How Long the Train's Been Gone* could have been conceived as a response to such a suggestion. *Train* is a "success" story that could not be used as a salve for the white conscience; it does not equate the "success" of an individual with the progress of a nation, and it emphasizes the obligations of success as well as its personal and spiritual price. Leo tells a reporter, "I did not make myself—I do not belong to me."[15]

In writing Leo's success story Baldwin not only deconstructs Kupferman's assumptions about the meaning of individual success stories but revises African American narrative patterns as well. One indication that Baldwin is specifically working within the form of the black autobiographical narrative in *Train* is his choice of a particular type of first-person point of view, one that is almost unique in Baldwin's fiction. Although Baldwin used the first person in four of his six novels and several stories, *Tell Me How Long the Train's Been Gone* represents a departure. It is the only Baldwin novel in which the narrator sets out to tell his own story rather than the story of another. (David tells the story of Giovanni in *Giovanni's Room*, Tish tells the story of Fonny in *If Beale Street Could Talk*, and Hall tells the story of Arthur in *Just Above My Head*.) While all of Baldwin's first-person protagonists function as witnesses, combining the roles of participant and observer, Leo Proudhammer's relationship to his narrative most closely resembles the point of view associated with a long tradition of African American autobiography, the point of view of the "literate survivor." A number of early critics found fault with the novel's point of view, including Mario Puzo, who objected to Leo as a "moralist" who tells the story "in a straight-out polemical way." Puzo went on to claim that the first person is only effective in fiction when it is used to narrow the focus of the story or to filter the story through an eccentric or minor character.[16] Assessments like Puzo's reveal a particular aesthetic bias, but even more they reveal a lack of awareness of the literary forms upon which Baldwin signifies. Hortatory and moral persuasion are essential characteristics of the literate survivor, a first-person point of view designed not to narrow the focus of the story but to position the narrator's life as both representative of his people and as a model for survival. To accomplish this goal the narrator typically intertwines the stories of others with his own, speaks directly to the reader on the authority of his or her experience, and aims for a relationship of sympathy rather than ironic distance. All too often complaints of artistic failure in the criticism of Baldwin's work, like Puzo's, are the result of applying inappropriate aesthetic measures.[17] A more interesting line of inquiry would be the relationship between Baldwin's point of view and those adopted by earlier African American writers, from Frederick Douglass, Booker T. Washington, and W. E. B. Du Bois to James Weldon Johnson, Richard Wright, and Ralph Ellison.

In *From behind the Veil: A Study of Afro-American Narrative* Robert B. Stepto maps out two basic trajectories of the tradition of black autobiography (and autobiographical fiction): the ascent narrative and the immersion narrative.[18] I wish to argue that *Train* incorporates both kinetic patterns of ascent and immersion in its structure, signifying on the "success" story that is part of the ascent narrative, and on the story of cultural renewal and homecoming that is part of the immersion narrative. The ascent narrative, the earliest of which were slave narratives, is characterized by the narrator's physical and spiritual movement upward—from South to North, from slavery to freedom, and from illiteracy to literacy.

The narrator's development or self-mastery is the primary subject of the work. Self-mastery implies becoming a more acute observer and interpreter of society, particularly of the ways racial oppression is manifested in political, social, educational, and religious institutions. The narrator's personal development works in tandem with the theme of a broader responsibility. Typically slave narratives and neoslave narratives use exhortation and are aimed at both educating white audiences about racism and providing models of hope for black audiences. In Robert B. Stepto's words, the persona of an ascent narrative becomes a "definitive historian" who progresses from "muteness to voice" and "from formless forms to highly formal forms." A classic example of the ascent narrative is *Narrative of the Life of Frederick Douglass*. Twentieth-century examples would include Richard Wright's *Black Boy* and Alex Haley's *The Autobiography of Malcolm X*.

*Tell Me How Long the Train's Been Gone* appears to be an ascent narrative: Leo journeys from anonymity to fame, from childhood confinement in an urban ghetto to adulthood freedom as an international celebrity. He is on a quest for spiritual wholeness, which involves his responsibility, especially to the young of his community. His celebrity status gives him both the opportunity and the duty to exercise his public voice in support of the struggle for black freedom. However, *Train* revises important elements of the ascent narrative. In particular it proposes a conception of the self that is quite different from the persona of an ascent narrative; it does not employ chronology as the primary method of structuring plot; and it refigures the relationship between self and time that is central to the structure of the ascent narrative.

The narrator in a classic tale of ascent emphasizes the positive difference between the self who tells the story in the present moment and the self who makes up the subject of the story. Robert B. Stepto describes Frederick Douglass's and Richard Wright's autobiographies as examples of the "essential retrospective voice" which "[exploits] the reach between past and present."[19] The retrospective voice emerges when the narrator invokes the present to measure the distance he has come from the past. An example of this voice occurs at the end of chapter 5 in *Narrative of the Life of Frederick Douglass* where Douglass describes the importance of his removal from Colonel Lloyd's plantation to Baltimore. His language sets up a clear juxtaposition between past and present. If it were not for this providential removal, Douglass speculates, "I should have to-day, instead of being here seated by my own table, in the enjoyment of freedom and the happiness of home, writing this Narrative, been confined to the galling chains of slavery."[20] This image of the present self foregrounds both "writing" and "home" as achievements which mark his distance from the illiteracy and homelessness of slavery.

An example of the retrospective voice in Wright's *Black Boy* occurs at the end of chapter 1 when the narrator moves ahead twenty-five years to describe his visit to the father he had not seen since he was a young child. The father represents an incomprehensible "crude and raw past" from which Wright's persona measures his achievement:

> a quarter of a century during which my mind and consciousness had become so greatly and violently altered that when I tried to talk to him I realized that, though ties of blood made us kin, though I could see a shadow of my face in his face, though there was an echo of my voice in his voice, we were forever strangers, speaking a different language, living on vastly distant planes of reality.[21]

While Wright's father is a "creature of the earth" who did not have "a chance to learn the meaning of loyalty, of sentiment, of tradition," the son, Wright's adult persona, is a man who "forgave him and pitied him." While the father is a "black peasant whose life had been hopelessly snarled in the city," the son has been rescued by the city that bore him "toward alien and undreamed-of-shores of knowing."[22]

The conception of the self in the ascent narrative is one of progressive development. The self in both the *Narrative of the Life of Frederick Douglass* and *Black Boy* gains stature through acts of intellectual and physical revolt and through the act of telling and writing his story. Becoming a public voice for the cause of black freedom represents a culmination in the narrator's depiction of self-achievement. For example, Douglass concludes his narrative by showing himself at the 1841 antislavery convention in Nantucket where he made his first speech in front of white people: "I spoke but a few moments, when I felt a degree of freedom, and said what I desired with considerable ease."[23] William Andrews has described Douglass's *Narrative* as a "Franklinesque" autobiography because of the construction of a self whose development from obscure origins to a historical public self reflects on and provides a model for his community.[24] However, an important variation from Franklin's autobiography should be noted. For Douglass, who wishes to emphasize the dehumanizing aspects of slavery, the journey of the "self-made" man takes on a very literal meaning. Rather than the story of a poor boy who makes good, the *Narrative of the Life of Frederick Douglass* is the story of a nonman (slave) who becomes a man; thus Douglass argues for the humanity of the slave by paradoxically suggesting that one's humanity is not a given, but must be struggled for.

Wright extends this theme in his depiction of southern life as unremittingly oppressive. While Douglass contrasts the dehumanized condition of most slaves with the existence of a positive slave community, where "noble souls" and "brave ones" together attempt to resist their condition, Wright offers no such image of communal solidarity.[25] As Charles T. Davis has noted, the narrator of *Black Boy* assumes "the posture of the isolated hero, cut off from family, peer or community support."[26] All the qualities that support the narrator's imagination—his curiosity, his intellect, and the development of his artistic talent —are drawn in conflict with the demands of his family and with adjustment to southern life. His survival as a writer requires that he resist the pressures to conform to family and community expectations. Conflict is structured within Wright's narrative so that the persona's isolation is a necessary condition of his personal and artistic growth and of his final posture as a "definitive historian" of American race relations.

*Tell Me How Long the Train's Been Gone* revises the posture of the isolated hero. Leo Proudhammer is isolated, but his isolation is presented as a problem, even as a handicap, which limits rather than increases his authority as a representative spokesman. By emphasizing the personal price of success, *Train* does not conflate the process of a developing self with the achievement of a public voice. Instead, the public self is a mask that hides the private self from itself, and others, and increases the protagonist's isolation. Early in the novel Leo describes his self as a "treacherous labyrinth."[27] The only escape from this maze is the intersubjective experience of love, which allows the self to momentarily experience recognition, to "see" itself in another. If the self in Douglass's and Wright's narratives resembles the Franklinesque "self-made man," the model of the self in *Train* is the actor who seeks to reinvent himself and others. The retrospective voice in *Train* is not that of a "definitive historian" who narrates a story of self-mastery and a mastery over the past. It is the voice of a middle-aged man in crisis whose memories unmask the safety and authority of success. Rather than a "definitive historian," Leo is an "archeologist" who seeks a new wholeness in the discontinuities and division of memory.

Leo is self-conscious about the "constructed" nature of his identity. He deromanticizes the idea of the "self-made man" by emphasizing the cost of all successful "self-inventions." His name, Leo Proudhammer, and his career, acting, are important to the complex idea of self that is developed in the novel. Given his small size and what he describes as his "strangeness, [his] helpless ambiguity,"[28] Leo's first name appears inappropriate, if not ironic. However, Leo learns early to live up to the name of the lion, precisely because he is not the king of the jungle, but is surrounded by other lions: "I became tyrannical. I had no choice. . . . To run meant to turn my back on—lions; to run meant the flying tackle which would bring me down; and anyway, run where?"[29] Leo becomes a "tyrant" out of necessity, but this tyranny is hidden by vulnerability, the very quality that caused him to become a tyrant in the first place. As Leo explores the contradictory sense of himself as both tyrannical and vulnerable, he suggests that the "mask" is not less real than the state that is "masked":

> But this absolutely single-minded and terrified ruthlessness was masked by my obvious vulnerability, my paradoxical and very real helplessness, and it covered my terrible need to lie down, to breathe deep, to weep long and loud, to be held in human arms, almost any human arms, to hide my face in any human breast, to tell it all, to let it out, to be born again. What a dream: is it a dream? I don't know. I know only what happened—if, indeed, I can claim to know that. My pride became my affliction. I found myself imprisoned in the stronghold I had built. The day came when I wished to break my silence and found that I could not speak: the actor could no longer be distinguished from his role.[30]

This passage captures Leo's extreme sense of isolation early in the novel and explores the role of "pride" in the "treacherous labyrinth" of the self. Leo's prison is the loss of an authentic language that will connect him to others. Pride is a stronghold created by necessity, but like all self-inventions it has its price. Leo is trapped within the very self-constructions he created for survival.

Leo's last name, Proudhammer, extends this meditation on the nature of pride by linking him to the African American folk hero, John Henry, who proved his manhood through a feat of strength that costs him his life. The first verse of the folk song establishes the "hammer" as a symbol of manhood and pride: "John Henry told his captain, 'Well a man ain't nothin' but a man, / But before I let your steam drill beat me down, I'll die with a hammer in my hand.'"[31] While the small, wiry Leo may appear to have little in common with this working-class hero of fabled strength, their conditions are parallel. Leo's more nuanced story of heroic achievement suggests the problem with the John Henry model of manhood and pride. Like John Henry, Leo becomes an American cultural hero by achieving an extraordinary feat (as his doctor comments, "I should guess that the odds against you were fantastic").[32] Like John Henry, Leo is an "obsessional type," and his heart attack, like Henry's, is due to "nervous exhaustion and overwork."[33] Both represent the end of an era. The folk hero represents the eclipse of a preindustrial America. Based on a work ethic of individual strength and competition in an age when workingmen were being replaced by machines, John Henry's heroism is more of an anachronism than a model for future generations. He beats the machine, but only at the cost of his life, a one-time victory. Leo's position is analogous in that his success is also bittersweet and not represented as a model for future generations. Leo represents an earlier type of black spokesperson, one who has been supplanted by a younger generation that views him with some suspicion.

Black Christopher's assertion of pride in a racial and cultural group identity is a foil to Leo's individual struggle with pride. While Leo's pride has become his "affliction" by separating him from others, Christopher's black pride inspires Leo's love and reconnects him to the memory of his brother, to his father, and to an earlier self. Yet the foil works both ways.

If Christopher's pride in the group suggests the limits of pride based on individual success, Leo's heightened awareness of pride's pitfalls, his early experience with his father's pride in the lost kingdoms of Barbados, and his concern that Christopher's proud militancy will cause his death all suggest the limits of a nationalistic pride. For both the individual and the nation, pride has its price. Those critics who read *Tell Me How Long the Train's Been Gone* as a simple endorsement of black militancy missed the ways that the novel speaks to and signifies on the black power movement of the 1960s. Black Christopher's bisexuality challenges the movement's well-documented homophobic conception of manhood, and the complex meditations on pride suggest its limitations as a value of liberation, especially when it gets in the way of life and love.

In addition to his name, Leo's complex self is represented by his acting career. Acting becomes a metaphor for the possibilities and the limitations of African American creative expression in racially proscribed contexts. Leo's career as an actor suggests a tension between empowerment and entrapment similar to that developed in the pride theme. This tension is first captured in the party that Leo and Barbara attend in book 1. Young and completely unknown, they are surrounded by famous actors, directors, and playwrights. Leo discovers that in real life the actors are not nearly as tall or as beautiful as they had appeared in their roles. The observation increases Leo's commitment to acting, because of what he sees as its power to test the boundaries of reality, to transform the perceptions of others, and thus to transform the self: "If a dwarf could be a queen and make me believe that she was six feet tall, then why was it not possible that I, brief, wiry, dull dark me, could become an emperor—The Emperor Jones, say why not?"[34] A more ambiguous image of the power of acting is developed as Leo and Barbara become performers at this party of actors. Knowing that a southern white girl and a black boy would, by definition, each invest the other with an aura of sexuality, danger, and intrigue, they pretend to be lovers (which they will later become) and play to racial stereotypes by consciously manipulating others' presumptions in order to gain an entrance into the theatrical world. They succeed in gaining the attention of the San-Marquands, who direct The Actors' Means Workshop, but Leo soon finds himself enraged by Saul San-Marquand's condescending query about Leo's "qualifications" to be an actor. The end result of Leo's rage results in a blues performance. Angry, mostly at himself for allowing anger to be his master, and determined not to allow the world's response to "the fact of [his] color to become [his] own,"[35] Leo reflects on the relationship between his race, his pain, and his rage. He concludes that he won't be able to master his rage until he "assesses" his pain. Out of his pain is the possibility of creating a "language" and a "self."[36] This realization leads to Leo's performance of a blues song that he remembered Caleb singing, a performance which immediately receives the approbation of his white audience, proves his "qualifications" to the San-Marquands, and gains him an invitation to the workshop. Leo's performances at the actors' party delineate both the power and the limits of self-invention in a racially demarcated society by stressing the power of the audience (the white world in this case) to shape the field in which the black actor creates his role.

Leo comes to understand acting as a dynamic process between the actor and the audience. Leo is nineteen when he attends The Actors' Means Workshop, and throughout most of the summer he runs errands for the outfit, being assigned the role in life that blacks were most often assigned on stage. At one point he finds himself alone on the stage in an empty theater; the rain is "drumming on the roof like all Africa," and for the first time he imagines his "desire [to become an actor] as a reality involving others."[37] It is this "coupling" that will define Leo's destiny. Unlike Douglass's and Wright's narratives, the retrospective voice that looks back on a defining moment does not emphasize the narrator's mastery of experience but suggests the difficulties in re-creating significant moments from the past:

> I was young. Perhaps it is hard, now, to credit, still less to sound, the depth of my bewilderment. I merely suspected in the chilling height, the dusty, roaring darkness, the presence of others, each of whom was myself. But these others could not know it, and neither could I, unless I was able, being filled by them, to fill this theater with our lives. This was, perhaps, my highest possibility of the act of love. But I did not say it that way to myself that afternoon."[38]

In remembering this scene from his youth, Leo articulates an idea of the artist and audience as lovers involved in a mutual act of creation. That this creation is only a potential is evoked by the image of invisibility. Leo, alone in a dark theater, senses "the presence of others, each of whom was [himself]." The invisible audience (or community) contains, in its members, the invisible actor (or individual), who is in turn "filled by them."

The promise of Leo's vision in the empty theater is fulfilled with his performance in an experimental version of *The Corn Is Green*. Although this event occurs when Leo is 26, about thirteen years before the present time of the novel, it is retold close to the end of the text, making the true climax of Leo's story the very beginning of his career as a serious actor. Leo plays the main character, Morgan, who in this version is a poor American black boy rather than a poor Welsh boy. A white schoolteacher provides Morgan with a sense of his potential to be a great writer:

> I played that scene for all that was in it, for all that was in me, and for all the colored kids in the audience—who held their breath, they really did, it was the unmistakable silence in which you and the audience re-create each other—and for the vanished Little Leo, and for my mother and father, and all the hope and pain that were in me. For the very first time, the very first time, I realized the fabulous extent of my luck: I could, I *could,* if I kept the faith, transform my sorrow into life and joy.[39]

The invisible "presence of others, each of whom was [himself]" that Leo had sensed years before takes form as "all the colored kids in the audience" who are "the vanished Little Leo." This episode represents the culmination of Leo's vision of artistic performance as a potentially liberating communal process in which new subjectivities emerge for both the artist and the audience. It also represents a culmination of the blues theme begun at the actors' party when Leo first considers creating a "language" and a "self" out of his pain.

Leo's performance in *The Corn Is Green* symbolizes an ideal relationship between the artist and his audience, one that Leo has not been able to sustain as a celebrity actor and political spokesman who has become "trapped in his role." The classic ascent narrative culminates in the narrator's achievement of a public voice (as in Douglass's Nantucket speech) or at least presents the public speech as a defining moment in the narrator's quest for freedom (as in Wright's graduation speech in *Black Boy*). In contrast, the public address scene in *Tell Me How Long the Train's Been Gone* occurs relatively early in the novel, rather than late, and reveals Leo's deep ambivalence about his public role. Leo speaks at a rally in downtown New York with thousands in attendance. He is not at ease with the other luminaries who will also speak, suspecting "the mighty gentlemen" are "unable to imagine such a journey as [his] own," and that they disapprove of him as he does of them. He attributes his difference to his "condition" as an "artist," a condition that is not desired, but only "with difficulty . . . supported."[40] However, Leo joins the others on the public platform out of a responsibility to the young. Leo cares deeply about not failing the next generation, who are represented at the rally by Christopher and a young black girl who sings "deliverance will come."[41] But at the same time, Leo notes that nothing he nor the other speakers (who are even older than he) have done or not done has succeeded in saving them. As one of the elders, Leo believes it his duty to help make the world a home for the children, and yet he cannot help but reflect on the paradox of his position:

I had never been at home in the world and had become incapable of imagining that I ever would be. I did not want others to endure my estrangement, that was why I was on the platform; yet was it not, at the least, paradoxical that it was only my estrangement which had placed me there? And I could not flatten out this paradox, I could not hammer it into any usable shape.[42]

At the end of the rally scene Leo is rushed to a waiting vehicle by Christopher, whose concern for Leo's safety in this "time of assassins" makes the actor see himself as "the Leo who certainly did not belong to himself and who belonged to the people only on condition that the people were kept away from him."[43] The rally scene, early in the novel, juxtaposed to Leo's first major performance in *The Corn Is Green,* late in the novel, shows a textual trajectory from alienation to fulfilled selfhood, from being apart from to being in communion with others. Leo's success with *The Corn Is Green* is the success of having kept faith with self and others: "I had not betrayed [the director]. I had not betrayed the play. I had not betrayed myself and all those people whom I would always love, and I had not betrayed all that history which held me like a lover and which would hold me forever like that."[44]

Although the middle-aged Leo Proudhammer describes himself as a "double-minded" man, an actor "trapped in his role," the process of remembering his early life serves to remind him that the origins of his success were in a profound moment of faith and loyalty, a moment when actor and audience successfully "re-created" each other. This memory is connected to the present by Leo's desire to keep faith with Christopher, and with his family and community and their struggle for physical as well as spiritual survival.[45] Leo's recovery from his heart attack is facilitated by recovering the memories of his divided life, a life redeemed by its moments of integration and recognition. The trajectory of the text, from alienation to selfhood, repeats the pattern of the ascent narrative while revising it. The trajectory of the text reverses the actual history of Leo's professional life, allowing Leo to mine personal and cultural memory to redeem the present crisis. *Tell Me How Long the Train's Been Gone* is a blues performance analogous to Leo's performance of Caleb's blues at the actor's party.

Although the subject of *Tell Me How Long the Train's Been Gone,* the narrator's struggle to rise from conditions of neoslavery to freedom, from anonymity to public prominence, is the subject of the "ascent narrative," the structure and sensibility of the novel resemble what Robert B. Stepto has described as an "immersion narrative." Immersion is a response to the loss of cultural identity entailed by ascent. The protagonist of the immersion narrative finds spiritual sustenance by a return to cultural roots, represented by the South, the family and community, and by African American musical traditions or historical discovery. As Stepto states,

> The immersion narrative is fundamentally an expression of a ritualized journey
> into a symbolic South, in which the protagonist seeks those aspects of tribal

literacy that ameliorate, if not obliterate, the conditions imposed by solitude. The conventional immersion narrative ends almost paradoxically, with the questing figure located in or near the narrative's most oppressive social structure but free in the sense that he has gained or regained sufficient tribal literacy to assume the mantle of an articulate kinsman.[46]

Both narrative types imply a journey and a quest, but the journey ends in radically different geographical, social, and psychological spaces for the protagonists, and the difference in the corresponding knowledge that they pass on is the difference between "the articulate survivor" and "the articulate kinsman."

Stepto identifies W. E. B. Du Bois's *The Souls of Black Folks* as the first narrative expression of the immersion ritual and views it as a predecessor to such texts as James Weldon Johnson's *The Autobiography of an Ex-coloured Man* and Jean Toomer's *Cane*. Central to these narratives is the struggle to reconcile a "double consciousness," the term Du Bois used to characterize black subjectivity in America as a problem of reconciling two "warring" selves and ideals:

> After the Egyptian and the Indian, the Greek and Roman, the Teuton and Mongolian, the Negro is a sort of seventh son, born with a veil, and gifted with second-sight in this American world,—a world which yields him no true self-consciousness, but only lets him see himself through the revelation of the other world. It is a peculiar sensation, this double-consciousness, this sense of always looking at one's self through the eyes of others, of measuring one's soul by the tape of a world that looks on in amused contempt and pity. One ever feels his twoness,—an American, a Negro.[47]

For Du Bois the dream of reconciliation involves a merger which sacrifices neither self, but allows one to "be both a Negro and an American, without being cursed and spit upon by his fellows, without having the doors of Opportunity closed roughly in his face." Thus, this "true self-consciousness" implies not only a new subjectivity, but a new nation where the Negro can "be a co-worker in the kingdom of culture."[48]

Several qualities that Robert B. Stepto identifies with the immersion narrative can be found in *Tell Me How Long the Train's Been Gone,* including the prophetic tone, the construction of a public and private history with little reference to chronology, the dual concern with black leadership and black spiritual expression, an examination of the pervasive color line in American society, and the archetype of the "weary traveler," whose journey to the "deeper recesses" is a call for a new, culturally plural America. (Leo is, indeed, a weary traveler, as he says: "A day may come, but not for me, when the American South will be habitable. Till then—well, I am wandering."[49]) Some of these elements in *Train* have already been discussed, but clearly the most obvious reference to Du Bois, in particular, is Leo's description of himself as a "double-minded" man. The narrative structure of *Train,* which many readers have found problematic, is appropriate as a function of Leo's character. It is the textual representation of Leo's struggle with the split self. Events are ordered by the associations of dream and memory; juxtaposition rather than chronology dramatizes Leo's bifurcated story. Thus, memories of Caleb and Harlem are interrupted by memories of Barbara and the East Village or The Actors' Means Workshop and vice versa.

The double-consciousness theme is powerfully dramatized in book 2 of *Train* in its structure, setting, and language. The title, "Is There Anybody There," immediately suggests the problem of finding a mirror in which one can reflect, in Du Bois's words, a "true self-consciousness." Book 2 covers Leo's development, between the years of fourteen and nineteen, when he first experiences sex and love. Rather than presenting a continuum of past experience, book 2 is structured around two separate stories, one of which is embedded in the other. The story of Caleb's return from prison, and Leo and Caleb's love, interrupts the longer story of Leo's summer at the Actor Means Workshop, his bitter experiences with racial prejudice in the adjacent, small New Jersey town, and his romance with Barbara King. The two stories are linked in the text by a dream which awakens Leo to intense feelings of sexual and racial guilt. Not yet admitting his love for Barbara, Leo sleeps with a white actress, Madeleine, but dreams he is in Caleb's arms, then wakes up feeling like "Judas" in a "white cunt's bed."[50] What follows is the story of Caleb's brief return home five years earlier and the sexual consummation of Leo and Caleb's love. Over thirty pages later the narrative picks up where it left off in Madeleine's apartment. This dream and waking memory suggest the psychological cost of Leo's later love for Barbara. That Leo has not resolved these feelings of racial and sexual betrayal is revealed earlier, near the end of book 1, when the middle-aged Leo wakes in his hospital bed from a nightmare in which Caleb has been relentlessly pursuing Leo and Barbara with a great wooden Bible. An image of this present nightmare, in which he and Barbara are painting signs in a wooden shed, evokes the past and provides a segue to book 2 and the story of the summer, twenty years before, at The Actors' Means Workshop. Thus, dreams are avenues into the past and provide important structural links in the text, as well as suggest the problem of Leo's split self.

The settings in book 2 are a symbolic geography of racial segregation. The unnamed New England small town, the Italian restaurant, and Lucy's juke joint each provides the narrator the occasion to examine American race rituals and the prevalence of the color line. Leo and his white friends, Jerry and Barbara (whose skin has become darker in the summer sun), call themselves "the Negro color problem" as they stroll through town, but the joke becomes grimmer when Leo is jailed after an elderly couple sees him coming out of Madeleine's apartment, and Leo and Barbara feel the full force of the town's animosity toward interracial couples when they appear in public without Jerry. The town becomes a "gauntlet" of racial epithets, threats, and hate that the young lovers must walk through.[51] The restaurant scene underscores Leo's sense of displacement by contrasting the white immigrant experience in America with the black experience. Leo observes the way the Sicilian proprietor, who has never met any of them before, treats Jerry, another Italian, like a son. By contrast Leo feels painfully estranged from the town's small black community. Leo's reflection on the importance of communal bonds in creating individual consciousness is suggestive of Du Bois's language: "[Salvatore] found the key to Jerry in the life he himself had lived. But he had no key for me: my life, in effect, had not yet happened in anybody's consciousness. And I did not know why. Sometimes, alone, I fled to the Negro part of town. . . . But my connections all were broken."[52]

Leo examines his displacement from the other side of the color line when he visits Lucy's with his white friends. The drive from the Italian restaurant to the juke joint causes Leo to reflect on "the most dramatic, the most appalling . . . invisible frontier which divides American towns, white from black."[53] Lucy's juke joint represents what Robert B. Stepto calls a "ritual ground," an African American spacial configuration (like Harlem or the Black Belt) which both responds to and is subsumed by the dominant social structure; it is a place that suggests the "double life" and gives rise to the burden of the "double-consciousness."[54] Leo's double-consciousness is revealed by his tendency to interpret the meaning of Lucy's from conflicting perspectives. The ambience of the dance hall appears to confirm a white fantasy of black life (the "tenacious American folk-lore concerning the happy, prancing niggers").[55] As such, Lucy's is a "particular reproach" to Leo. Leo also experiences his presence and that of his white friends through the black gaze of Lucy's patrons. He sees Madeleine through their "speculative, lewd contempt" and must force himself not to let go of her hand. Leo tries to manage his discomfort by historicizing this double vision. His analysis of the music and dancing echoes and revises Frederick Douglass's famous comments on white misinterpretation of Negro spirituals.[56] Whereas Douglass revealed the pain and sorrow of the spirituals, Leo-Baldwin reveals the rage and arrogant passion of black secular music. The black gaze, as well as the white gaze, is a construction of the racial divide. The blacks "saw themselves as others had seen them. They had been formed by the images made of them by those who had had the deepest necessity to despise them. . . . they saw what their history had taught them to see."[57] Whether in white town or in black town, by crossing the color line, Leo finds himself in a "false position" vis-à-vis others' assumptions and expectations. Yet his "false position" yields him a heightened awareness, a place from which to view the forms of consciousness created by the racial divide.

While book 2 of *Tell Me How Long the Train's Been Gone* examines the color line and double-consciousness, book 3 opens possibilities of "*communitas.*" Robert B. Stepto borrows the term "*communitas*" from Victor Turner and adapts it to his idea of symbolic geographies in African

American literature. Turner views human history in terms of a tension between structure and *communitas*. *Communitas* (the Latin word for community) describes social bonds that are in transition and are essentially nonstructural, nonrational, and egalitarian. Such bonds are immediate, not shaped by institutions, and tend to exist outside time. They represent "the desire for a total, unmediated relationship between person and person," a relationship which "does not merge identities" but "liberates them from conformity to general norms."[58] Stepto argues that the experience of "*communitas*" is vital to the immersion narrative. He also argues that in African American literature the expression of *communitas* is group oriented as opposed to individual oriented, suggesting a "We-They" rather than an "I-Thou" relationship. Such group orientation is suggested by the spatial geography of *communitas* in African American literature, which can be the same as a "ritual ground" but on different terms. Thus Harlem, the Black Belt, and other ritual grounds of black confinement can also be spaces of *communitas*. The "weary traveler's" perception of the spirit of the place, the *genius locus,* is the goal of the immersion narrative.

The movement of *Tell Me How Long the Train's Been Gone* is toward increasingly public and inclusive (if not unproblematic) expressions of *communitas*. The first such expression is intensely individual and personal. Leo's incestuous love for Caleb fits the definition of *communitas* as a relationship which occurs in opposition to a prescribed structure (in this case the structure of family relationships) and fulfills the desire for a total unmediated relationship where the participants realize their commonness without losing their identities. This first experience of *communitas* occurs in the middle of the novel and in the middle of book 2, which, as I have argued, is largely devoted to expressions of race ritual and double-consciousness. The second and third expressions of *communitas* occur in book 3. The previously described performance of *The Corn Is Green* provides Leo with a primarily (although not exclusively) intraracial experience of *communitas*. The locale, a public theater, becomes a transformed symbolic space. Up to this point Leo has found himself playing servants and chauffeurs, reenacting the race rituals of American society on stage. With the performance of *The Corn Is Green,* actors and audience re-create each other in a moment of ritual transition, liberating themselves from stereo-types. The performance links Leo to the black community, to his own child-hood, and redeems past suffering.

In the last few pages of the novel paired scenes represent Leo's contin-ued quest for spaces of *communitas* in America. For the first time since his heart attack Leo is able to go outside. His return to the world is represented by sharply contrasting symbolic geographies which reveal the unfinished nature of Leo's quest. The first scene takes place in an expensive Chinese restaurant where Leo enjoys a last supper in San Francisco with his closest friends—Christopher, Barbara, and Pete. This group, which crosses racial and economic lines, suggests an ideal, and Leo feels "recalled to life." The atmosphere of comfort and wealth creates "an astounding illusion of safety, order and civilization. Evil did not seem to exist here."[59] Yet Leo is all too aware that this upscale restaurant is not the site of the "welcome table" about which his mother sang: "Beneath this table, deep in the bowels of the earth, as far away as China, as close as the streets outside, an energy moved and gathered and it would, one day, overturn this table."[60] The privileged "order and civilization" of the restaurant scene contrasts with the final image of an interracial *communitas* located in the energy of those "streets outside." The scenes are linked by the language and images of apocalypse.

After leaving the restaurant, Christopher takes Leo to a street in San Francisco, where black and white youth dressed in the clothes of the six-ties counterculture suggest that something new is emerging in the American landscape. They enter a dark building that had once been a movie theater, where the music is so loud it assaults the senses, and hundreds of youth are milling, embracing, and dancing in a flickering violent light. On all four walls, screens show images of writhing figures and faces. In place of reas-suring order is the energy of chaos. Describing the dancing figures in apoc-alyptic images of the dead arising, Leo finds himself "witnessing, not sharing" a "rite" that reminds him of the rites in black churches and "older than that, in forests irrecoverable."[61] The images on the screen move in "a tremendous sexual rhythm," making Leo think of "nameless creatures, blindly coupling in all the slime of the world." He even thinks he sees his own face flit across the screen.[62] Leo, who must leave before the people start to recognize him, remains more observer than participant in the novel's final expression of *communitas*. But even though the flesh and blood Leo cannot participate, Leo's image within this mass media version of a primordial soup indicates that his identity has been appropriated by the young for a new symbolic space where blacks and whites can create bonds outside confining race rituals. This splitting between the image on the screen and the flesh and blood man, who stands apart "try[ing] to understand what was happening,"[63] is characteristic of Leo's position as both outsider and insider, implicated in and affected by the events which whirl around him, but ultimately unable to control or even sufficiently interpret them. The closing scenes suggest the continued distance between the dream of *communitas* and its actualization. In an America defined by its sharp racial and economic divisions, the dream of *communitas* is largely unfulfilled; it is a rumble in the streets, the noise and chaos of a dance hall.[64]

*Tell Me How Long the Train's Been Gone* incorporates and revises patterns of ascent and immersion in its thematic and formal development. As such, it speaks to the modernist theme of the relationship between the individual and the community within the particular context of American and African American social and literary history. Published sixteen years after Ralph Ellison's *Invisible Man*, *Train* takes up and revises that novel's figuration of public and private and its relationship between individual and social identity. Both *Invisible Man* and *Tell Me How Long the Train's Been Gone* depict the challenges of black leadership in the twentieth century, both are suspicious of the rhetoric of progress and heroic self-portraiture (one inheritance of the ascent narrative), and, perhaps most important, both are concerned with the position of the black artist in America vis-à-vis his dual audience (black and white) and the dual demands of expressing individual and communal experience. *Train* revoices some of the central tropes in *Invisible Man*, including visibility-invisibility, running, and hibernation. Through revoicing these tropes, Baldwin suggests a different vision of the artist and his role from that of Ellison.

An early passage in *Train*, just after Leo's heart attack, brings into play images of visibility-invisibility and of running and suggests Baldwin's engagement with Ellison's novel:

The door to my maturity. This phrase floated to the top of my mind. The light that fell backward on that life of mine revealed a very frightened man—a frightened boy. The light did not fall on me, on me where I lay now. I was left in darkness, my face could not be seen. In that darkness I encountered a scene from another nightmare, a nightmare I had had as a child. In this nightmare there is a book—a great, heavy book with an illustrated cover. The cover shows a dark, squalid alley, all garbage cans and dying cats, and windows like empty eyesockets. The beam of a flashlight shines down the alley, at the end of which I am fleeing, clutching something. The title of the book in my nightmare is, *We Must Not Find Him, For He Is Lost.*[65]

As Leo lies in wait for the doctor he is an invisible man; his face "could not be seen in the darkness." By contrast his youth—as it exists in the memory of his nightmare—is well lit. Thus Baldwin-Leo reproduces the tropes through which Ellison's protagonist comes to define himself. The Invisible Man's maturity (or self-knowledge) is linked to the discovery of his invisibility, which in turn allows him to illuminate his story, literally and figuratively. Leo's childhood nightmare, and especially its title, *We Must Not Find Him, For He Is Lost,* echoes the Invisible Man's own nightmare at the end of the first chapter when he discovers an engraved document in his briefcase that reads "Keep this nigger boy running."[66] The tableau of the black boy fleeing, clutching something, is a classic image echoing back to handbills of escaped slaves, and is particularly suggestive of the flight scene near the end of Ellison's novel during the Harlem riot when the protagonist, clutching his brief case, is chased down a manhole.[67] But most important, this passage illustrates that memory and identity are mediated through layers of representation. First, Leo's memory is of a nightmare, rather than an actual childhood event, and second, the nightmare itself is about a book in which Leo discovers his own frightened self on the cover.

Leo's fear of being trapped in fictional representations of black experience introduces *Train* as a metanarrative. By suggesting that the artist is implicated in the trap of history, *Train* may be read as a response to *Invisible Man,* another metanarrative, one which (unlike *Train*) poses art as a solution to history.[68] Robert B. Stepto has argued that *Invisible Man* creates a new narrative arc and a new voice out of the dialectic of ascent and immersion in African American literature.[69] As Stepto has pointed out, much of the burden of the novel's ability to synthesize the patterns of ascent and immersion lie in its frame, which formalizes the "fiction" of history and suggests that "art may impose upon event."[70] Ellison's narrator speaks to his audience from the position of the solitary artist as saboteur who exists in a state of creative hibernation. As an artist he is able to interpret the events that have driven him into the manhole, to transform blindness into sight, invisibility into visibility, and running into hibernation. As an artist he is able to create his individual form (and, by extension, the form of a larger American experience—"Who knows but that, on the lower frequencies, I speak for you").[71]

In many respects the role of the artist-protagonist in Ellison's novel is conventionally American. He represents the value of American self-reliance and individualism and the paradox that only by separating himself from society can the artist become a universal voice that effectively speaks for others. The idea that individualism can provide redemption for the group is voiced in the words of the protagonist's English teacher as he analyzes James Joyce's *Portrait of an Artist as a Young Man*:

> Stephen's problem, like ours, was not actually one of creating the uncreated conscience of his race, but of creating the uncreated features of his face. Our task is that of making ourselves individuals. The conscience of the race is the gift of its individuals who see, evaluate, record. . . . We create the race by creating ourselves and then to our great astonishment we will have created something far more important: We will have created a culture.[72]

This passage sums up an important thesis of Ellison's novel. The protagonist's struggle during the course of the novel is to form an identity separate from the ideologies and institutions that have defined him. The novel juxtaposes the socially constructed identities ("invisibility") that the narrator passively assumes during the body of the narrative—the student in the southern black college, the northern industrial worker, and the spokesman for a radical organization—with the narrator's active self-formation ("visibility") taking place in the frame of the narrative. By positing a new territory, a warm hole outside history, *Invisible Man* argues that the individual as artist can transcend limiting, socially constructed identities. However, a return to the surface (to history) will mean a return to the narrator's invisibility. Presumably, when the narrator surfaces, his new (in)sight into the "possibility" of invisibility will bring him some advantage, but this is beyond the scope of the novel, as it ends with the Invisible Man's promise to end his hibernation, "since there's a possibility that even an invisible man has a socially responsible role to play."[73]

*Tell Me How Long the Train's Been Gone* breaks the frame of *Invisible Man* and reinserts the artist into society and history. In a sense it takes up where *Invisible Man* leaves off by posing a self-conscious protagonist-artist who seeks a socially responsible role. By making Leo Proudhammer a famous professional black actor as well as a spokesman for black freedom, Baldwin suggests that art is not a solitary activity, a separate territory, or a solution to the problem of individual identity. The artist's life is embedded in a social context that cannot be escaped. At one point Leo remarks that the actor, like the preacher, got his start in the pulpit. The actor is an engaged artist whose identity represents a process of social interaction rather than individual transcendence. The actor needs a script, a director, other actors, and an audience, and his success depends upon the relationship that is established between these elements. The actor works within a set of socially constructed roles, but if he is good and lucky, he may contribute to their transformation, as Leo does in his performance of *The Corn Is Green*. When Leo first imagines the alchemy that must occur between the actor and his audience, he evokes and revises Ellison's trope of invisibility as possibility: "I merely suspected in the chilling height, the dusty, roaring darkness, the presence of others, each of whom was myself. But these others could not know it, and neither could I, unless I was able, being filled by them to fill this theater with our lives."[74]

The surface similarities between *Invisible Man* and *Train* work to underscore Baldwin's signifying relationship to the earlier novel. Indeed both protagonists are forced by a traumatic event to temporarily retreat from their social roles and the work of daily life. Leo's heart attack, the

opening event in the novel, is a symbolic hole which forces him off the stage
of life and provides the catalyst for his reflections:

> I was chilled by the fear of what I might find in myself with all my harness off,
> my obligations canceled, no lawyers, no agents, no producers, no television
> appearances, no civil-rights speeches, no reason to be here or there, no lunches
> at the Plaza, no dinners at Sardi's, no opening nights, no gossip columnists, no
> predatory reporters . . . no need to smile when I did not want to smile, no need,
> indeed, to do anything but be myself. But who was this self? Had he left for-
> ever the house of my endeavor and my fame? Or was he merely having a hard
> time breathing beneath the rags and the rubble of the closets I had not opened
> in so long?[75]

Yet the protagonists' forced disengagement from the world is treated quite
differently. While the Invisible Man is catapulted into a creative world of
his own making, into art, Leo Proudhammer, in his seclusion, is forced to
face the world without a role and without the consolations of art.
Moreover, the hospital where Leo recovers, unlike the Invisible Man's
warm hole, does not frame the novel, nor is the hospital a place from where
Leo gains a new identity or narrative authority. While Ellison proposes a
state of creative hibernation to suggest progress (blindness to sight, invisibility to visibility), Baldwin does not. As a young man Leo discovers that
he can not run, because there is no place to run, and as a mature man Leo
learns that he can not hibernate, because the demands of the present require
the actor to find his role. Like his creator, James Baldwin, the "transatlantic
commuter," Leo remains above ground, and at the end of the novel he is
as he was before his heart attack, once more "standing in the wings again,
waiting for [his] cue."[76] The critics that charged *Train* with "artistic failure" failed to comprehend the relationship between the novel's complex
narrative structure and its deployment of the author-witness point of view,
with the long tradition of black male autobiography and autobiographical
fiction that informs it.

# II.

It is also important to read *Train* in the context of Baldwin's own earlier texts and to understand its significance to his oeuvre. Several reviewers dismissed the novel as merely repetitive of Baldwin's earlier fiction.[77] However, it would be more accurate to view *Train* as a critical link between his first and third novels, *Go Tell It on the Mountain* and *Another Country*, and his last two novels, *If Beale Street Could Talk* and *Just Above My Head*. *Train* brings together the geographies of *Go Tell* (Harlem) and *Another Country* (the Village) in one novel, it continues the story of the young John Grimes in the story of the middle-aged Leo Proudhammer, and it is Baldwin's first rendering of sexual love between black men. Baldwin continues his exploration into the interrelationship between race and sex in American identity formation but pitches his representation to a new generation and a newly forming discourse of racial resistance. He is less concerned with delineating the processes of internalized racism, misogyny, and homophobia that dominate *Go Tell, Giovanni's Room*, and *Another Country* (although these remain givens) and is more concerned with representing the processes of conscious resistance to racial and sexual oppression in the lives of his three main characters, Leo Proudhammer, Barbara King, and Black Christopher.

In fact, *Tell Me How Long the Train's Been Gone* sharply revises several figures from Baldwin's earlier novels and stories, including the figure of the black artist and the representation of interracial love in *Another Country*. As Baldwin told a French interviewer, Leo was "Rufus qui n'est pas un suicide."[78] In *Train* Baldwin recreates the black artist as a survivor and successful public figure in the character of Leo Proudhammer. Similarly, the Leo and Barbara relationship is a revised version of the relationship between Rufus and Leona (Barbara like Leona is a southern white girl, but unlike Leona, Barbara comes from a wealthy family). While Rufus and Leona have internalized their victimization so thoroughly that they destroy each other in an intensely sadomasochistic relationship (Rufus takes his revenge on the white world by abusing Leona, who goes mad, and then kills himself by jumping off the George Washington Bridge), Leo and

Barbara resist the culturally scripted racial drama that punishes miscegenation. Their theatrical vocation is both the means and symbol by which they attempt to redefine their roles as a black man and a white woman. This redefinition is dramatized by the first scene they perform together for The Actors' Means Workshop. Leo "refused to consider doing anything from *All God's Chillun Got Wings*," Eugene O'Neill's play about a tragic interracial marriage destroyed by the couple's inability to resist internalizing racist definitions. Instead they choose to perform the concluding scene from Clifford Odets's *Waiting for Lefty* to "put the liberal San-Marquands to a crucial test."[79] While race is not a subject in Odets's play, Leo and Barbara can easily identify with the young lovers, Sid and Florrie, whose poverty during the Great Depression prevents them from marrying. The denial of domestic happiness is a radicalizing experience for Sid, who devotes himself to the struggle for economic and social justice.

The Leo-Barbara relationship represents the possibility of interracial love and the social barriers to its fulfillment in America. From the beginning Leo and Barbara recognize that the social inequalities of race and class, as well as their own ambitious natures (and, one might suppose, Leo's bisexuality) would be formidable obstacles to a happy marriage. As Barbara says,

> If we were different people, and very, very lucky, we might beat the first hurdle, the black-white thing. If we weren't who we are, we could always just leave this—unfriendly—country, and go somewhere else. But we're as we are. I knew, when I thought about it, that we couldn't beat the two of them together. I don't think you'd care much that your wife was white—but a wife who was both white and rich! It would be horrible. We'd soon stop loving each other.[80]

The terms of their relationship are set; they will focus on advancing their theatrical careers: "We must be great. That's all we'll have. That's the only way we won't lose each other."[81] Leo and Barbara, resilient and smart, represent the possibility of interracial love. As Houston A. Baker Jr. has suggested, they are the fictional embodiment of Baldwin's call at the end of *The Fire Next Time* for "the relatively conscious whites and the relatively conscious blacks, who must, like lovers, insist on, or create the consciousness of the others."[82] But their relationship suggests the limits of such idealism as well. Paradoxically their love endures because it is based on their early renunciation of the dream of domestic happiness, which appeared totally out of reach (as it did to Sid and Florrie in Odets's play). The public success which enables their relationship to endure comes at the cost of their private lives. At the end of *Tell Me How Long the Train's Been Gone* the job of consciousness raising does not go to Barbara and Leo but to their symbolic "child," Christopher Hall, whose black nationalism suggests Leo and Barbara's failure to reproduce an interracial model of political resistance.

*Tell Me How Long the Train's Been Gone* also revisits and revises *Go Tell It on the Mountain,* initiating new directions that Baldwin will further explore in his later work as he looks to his familial, religious, and cultural heritage as resources of resistance and modes of expressing his wider vision. The rich intertextual relationship between *Tell Me How Long the Train's Been Gone* and *Go Tell It on the Mountain* offers readers important insight into Baldwin's development as an autobiographer, moral spokesman, and artist. The very title of Baldwin's fourth novel signals a revisionary relationship to his first. Both titles are from African American religious songs. "Go Tell It on the Mountain" is the first line of the spiritual announcing the "good news" that Jesus Christ is born.[83] The title points toward the culminating event of *Go Tell,* John's experience of salvation on the threshing floor in the Temple of the Fire Baptized, and is one of several allusions linking John Grimes to the biblical John of Revelation. "Tell Me How Long the Train's Been Gone" is the refrain of a gospel song which warns those who have fallen away from righteousness that Judgment Day will come. The "train," God's followers, have left the temple and are living among the "unclean," oblivious that their days are numbered: "While everything you think is going on well / your poor soul is burning in hell / Tell me how long / the train's been gone."[84] The title of Baldwin's fourth novel points toward Leo's fearful speculations of a coming apocalypse suggested by Black Christopher's call for guns near the end of the novel. The titles mark the transition from innocence (John's salvation) to experience (Leo's fallen condition), from youth to maturity, signaling the autobiographical relationship between the novels.

The titles reflect the Manichean structure of a religious imagination suspended between the poles of salvation and damnation, but they also suggest the ambiguity characteristic of Baldwin's treatment of such dualism. Neither John's salvation in the church nor Leo's regard for Black Christopher's political militancy should be read as uncomplicated acts or final solutions to the conflicts the novels depict. Both outsiders who want to be insiders, John and Leo remain in an ambiguous relationship to the religious and political frameworks of the communities they claim. While John Grimes is "saved," he continues to be in bondage not only to poverty and racism, but to his own lack of knowledge of his history: at the end of the novel, the truth of his origins remains in an undisclosed letter held by his aunt. Moreover, as Shirley Allen notes, the title, "Go Tell It on the Mountain," is ambiguous in its religious reference: "'Go tell it,' refers to the good news (gospel) that 'Jesus Christ is born' or to the message of Moses to the Pharaoh, 'Let my people go.' The ambiguity of the allusion in the title is intentional and also suggests the unity of Old Testament and New Testament faith that is characteristic of the Christian belief described in the novel."[85] The title of Baldwin's novel captures the paradox of John's condition as saved but still in bondage as a member of a group who continues to be oppressed.

Similarly Leo's complex situation is suggested in the mix of secular and religious associations in the title, *Tell Me How Long the Train's Been Gone*. As the main transportation north in the early twentieth century, the train came to represent escape, change, opportunity, and freedom. From the early blues, to Richard Wright's "Big Boy Leaves Home," to the movie *Clockers*, directed by Spike Lee (based on Richard Price's novel by the same name), the train carries a great deal of symbolic resonance in African American cultural expression. Indeed, the train plays a prominent role in Houston A. Baker Jr.'s blues theory of American literature, which he figures as the train at the crossroads.[86] The epigraph of *Tell Me How Long the Train's Been Gone*, which is the refrain of the spiritual, "Mary Had a Baby," also evokes the image of a departed train: "Never seen the like since

I been born, / The people keep a-coming, / and the train's done gone." In its allusion to the story of Christ's birth, the subtitle signifies on the title of *Go Tell It on the Mountain,* suggesting the promise of "salvation" is yet to be fulfilled.[87] The title of *Tell Me how Long the Train's Been Gone* and the epigraph conflate secular and sacred meanings of train, as a vehicle of transportation and as a group of loyal disciples. Leo has clearly ridden the train of opportunity. He has been successful "against all the odds," but along the track he has lost his "train" (his followers); he is a prophet separated from the community. Success is a trap, as suggested by the title of book 1, "The House Nigger." As a spokesman for the Civil Rights movement, Leo has become superannuated by the younger, more militant generation, and he now finds himself under a double surveillance by the people and the police.[88] The title *Tell Me How Long the Train's Been Gone* suggests Leo's difficult and divided relation to the black and white communities.

The two implied meanings of "train," as religious acolytes and as a vehicle for the pursuit of worldly opportunity, also represent a thematic movement from *Go Tell It on the Mountain* to *Tell Me How Long the Train's Been Gone* as Baldwin returns to an exploration of the black family and community in a more secular key. In many respects the story of the middle-aged Leo Proudhammer continues the story of the young John Grimes. From the innocence of youthful revelation to the experience of reaching maturity in a fallen world, John Grimes's dreams of the future become the reality of Leo Proudhammer's life. In part 1 of *Go Tell* John imagines himself to be a powerfully successful adult with a "Great Future." John's reflections are qualified by the narrator's quiet irony: "He might become a Great Leader of His People. John was not much interested in his people and still less in leading them anywhere, but the phrase so often repeated rose in his mind like a great brass gate, opening outward for him on a world where people did not live in the darkness of his father's house."[89] John imagines himself in various roles, as "a poet, or a college president, or a movie star,"[90] and later he climbs a hill in Central Park and imagines himself a "tyrant" conquering the city.[91] All of these images have intertextual referents in *Train.* Leo Proudhammer is fourteen, the same age as John Grimes, when he tells his older brother that he is going to be an actor.[92] Later in the day as the brothers walk along Broadway, Caleb asks if Leo will have his name on the great marquees:

"Yes," I said. "I will. You wait and see."

"Little Leo," said Caleb, "on the great white way."

"It won't be so white," I said, "when I get through with it."[93]

About ten years later, Leo has his break in the experimental production of *The Corn Is Green* and is on his way to stardom: Leo becomes the movie star that John dreams of becoming. While Leo does not become a poet or a college president, he does become the combination of artist and public figure that John's fantasy suggests, and he does become a "leader of his people," albeit a reluctant and rather powerless one. The irony that one can somehow simultaneously "escape" and lead his people goes unrecognized by John Grimes, but not by Leo Proudhammer, who is acutely aware of the ways that success has distanced him from the people. Even as a young man Leo is a more politically astute version of John. Leo understands his family's problems as a result of racial and economic oppression, and, unlike John, he directs his anger outward at the landlords and the justice system.

The most striking intertextual moment linking Leo Proudhammer to John Grimes occurs near the end of *Tell Me How Long the Train's Been Gone.* Leo looks down at a panoramic view of San Francisco and reflects on his success in language that explicitly refigures John's vision of his future in part 1 of *Go Tell.* Standing on a hill in Central Park and looking down on opulent Fifth Avenue, John's vision of the city and his future role there is deeply divided. In his imagination the landscape takes on the shape of Christian myth. Is it the New Jerusalem beckoning or is it the City of Destruction?

he felt like a long-awaited conqueror at whose feet flowers would be thrown, and before whom multitudes cried, Hosanna! He would be, of all, the mightiest, the most beloved, the Lord's anointed; and he would live in this shining city which his ancestors had seen with longing from far away. For it was his . . .

And still, on the summit of that hill he paused. He remembered the people he had seen in that city, whose eyes held no love for him. . . . Then he remembered his father and his mother, and all the arms stretched out to hold him back, to save him from this city where they said, his soul would find perdition.[94]

Midtown and Harlem: white and black; rich and poor; light and dark; broad and narrow; lost and saved; these are the boundaries of a physical and spiritual landscape that John must negotiate. For John the question is not will he conquer the city, but "what would his conquest of the city profit him on [judgment] day?"[95]

At the end of *Tell Me How Long the Train's Been Gone*, Leo Proudhammer, separated from John by a continent and a generation, answers the question:

> It was a beautiful, dark-blue, chilly night. We were on a height, and San Francisco unfurled beneath us, at our feet, like a many-colored scroll. I was leaving soon. I wished it were possible to stay. I had worked hard, hard, it certainly should have been possible by now for me to have a safe, quiet, comfortable life, a life I could devote to my work and to those I loved, without being bugged to death. But I knew it wasn't possible. There was a sense in which it certainly could be said that my endeavor had been for nothing. Indeed, I had conquered the city: but the city was stricken with the plague. Not in my lifetime would this plague end, and now, all that I most treasured, wine, talk, laughter, love, the embrace of a friend, the light in the eyes of a lover, the touch of a lover, that smell, that contest, that beautiful torment, and the mighty joy of a good day's work, would have to be stolen, each moment lived as though it were the last, for my own mortality was not more certain than the storm that was rising to engulf us all.[96]

Leo at almost forty has conquered the city, but his conquest has profited him much less than he had hoped. Because the city is "stricken with the plague," he cannot enjoy the fruits of his labor, especially the domestic comforts of a stable private life that John Grimes imagined would result from worldly success. For Leo Proudhammer, who does not share (and explicitly rejects) John's evangelical tradition, the apocalyptic imagery is a metaphor for the escalating social and political turmoil resulting from the nation's continuing failure to address racism and its effects. Leo's apocalypse does not discriminate between the saved and the damned, but will "engulf us all." Leo may have "conquered" the city, but he is powerless to save it.

Just as Leo Proudhammer's story continues and revises the story of John Grimes, the Proudhammer family bears a revisionary relationship to the Grimes family. The initial description of the father, Mr. Proudhammer, in the opening pages of *Train* immediately reminds Baldwin's readers of Gabriel Grimes. Both men are characterized by a fierce pride at odds with their truly desperate and humiliating circumstances. Their pride, which isolates them from others in their community, is inherited as a burden and a challenge by their sons. Leo's father is "a ruined Barbados peasant, exiled in Harlem."

[He] brought with him from Barbados only black rum and a blacker pride, and magic incantations which neither healed nor saved. He did not understand the people among whom he found himself, for him they had no coherence, no stature and no pride. He came from a race which had been flourishing at the very dawn of the world—a race greater than Rome or Judea, mightier than Egypt—he came from a race of kings, kings who had never been taken in battle, kings who had never been slaves. He spoke to us of tribes and empires, battles, victories, and monarchs of whom we had never heard—they were not mentioned in our schoolbooks—and invested us with glories in which we felt more awkward than in the secondhand shoes we wore. . . . If our father was of royal blood and we were royal children, our father was certainly the only person in the world who knew it.[97]

Like Mr. Proudhammer, Gabriel Grimes also believed he was of "royal blood," although Gabriel received his authority from God. Gabriel believed that he was chosen, like Abraham, to father a line of royal descendants. It is this conviction which causes him to reject his stepson, since John is not of his seed, and to name his biological son "Royal." Mr. Proudhammer is clearly a secular version of Gabriel Grimes; his pride and rage are based on a myth of lost historical grandeur instead of the religious conviction that he is one of God's elect. In fact, the Proudhammer family "had never gone to church, for our father could not bear the sight of people on their knees."[98] While John's illegitimate birth excludes him from his father's "royal" line, Leo is biologically and, as his first name suggests, spiritually a Proudhammer. The difference between the two fathers is important. By reconstructing Gabriel as the secular Mr. Proudhammer, Baldwin writes a novel in which the son is able to put the father's failures into perspective and finally bridge the chasm that separates father and son.[99]

Throughout *Train* Mr. Proudhammer is never given a first name, which suggests the diminished role he plays in Leo's life and in the text itself compared to the role of Gabriel in John's life. In *Go Tell* the overwhelming impact that Gabriel has on John is matched by the prominence of Gabriel's story, which is the longest chapter, located in the center of the text. In contrast Mr. Proudhammer is described briefly at a few key points in the novel. Often drunk, angry, and emotionally absent, Proudhammer seems to have been supplanted by his eldest son, Caleb, to whom Leo is fiercely attached. David Leeming has argued that the Proudhammer family has autobiographical significance, but, unlike the Grimes family, it is more "idealized than real."[100] While it is true that the Proudhammers do have "rare joyful moments" (one such moment occurs when Caleb and his mother waltz to a Calypso tune),[101] Leeming's description of the Proudhammers as a "cohesive black family" hardly seems supported by the text. Leo's memories of growing up in Harlem are preoccupied by descriptions of separation and loss and the disintegration of family life. Near the end of book 1, Leo recalls "our last days as a family,"[102] days that precede Caleb's arrest. The father has been laid off from work, they are evicted from their apartment, and Caleb quits school. The mother, who holds the family together, brings home scraps from Miss Anne's kitchen, which her proud husband refuses to eat. A shoe-shine box and shopping bags become the "emblems of [Leo's] maturity" as he tries to help his family out of desperate poverty.[103] Leo's family can neither protect him nor provide models for his adult life: "I was very nearly lost because my elders, through no fault of their own, had betrayed me. Perhaps I loved my father, but I did not want to live his life. I did not want to become like him, he was the living example of defeat."[104]

Some of the most poignant passages in the novel involve the relationship between Leo and Caleb, which is developed through a series of painful separations, reunions, and a reversal of roles in which Leo becomes his older brother's protector and lover at one point. Leo loses Caleb three times: first when Caleb is arrested for a crime he didn't commit, second when he is drafted to serve in the World War II, and third when he converts to evangelical Christianity. The Leo Caleb relationship is symbolic of Baldwin's critique of American racism, especially its assault on black men. It is not accidental that Leo loses Caleb to the three institutions that most frequently shape the lives of young black men, institutions which Baldwin believed continually perpetuated racism and denied black masculinity: the justice system, the army, and the church. Shattered by his experience in prison, and by his later experience in the army where he is betrayed by a white "friend," Caleb becomes afraid of his own rage and capacity for revenge. Burned twice and afraid of the fire, Caleb turns to the church for safety. While John Grimes's conversion to the Temple of the Fire Baptized is portrayed ambiguously, Caleb's conversion is not. John's conversion provides psychological and emotional advantages by joining him to his community and requiring the reluctant respect of his hostile father. But Caleb's conversion, viewed through his brother's eyes, is a psychological defeat. The old Caleb that Leo loved—warm, spontaneous, adventuresome—is gone for good. The new Caleb, like Gabriel in *Go Tell,* preaches a narrow, moralistic doctrine and judges others harshly. While prison and the army separated the brothers, Caleb's conversion to Christianity brings about an irreparable break in their relationship. In a reversal of *Go Tell,* Caleb's conversion also disappoints the father.

Caleb and Leo are foils; their lives evolve, suggesting different responses to poverty and racism. Both are actors—one in the pulpit and one on the stage. While Leo's life is the anomaly, Caleb's is more representative. Caleb, who doesn't think much of artists or their chaotic lifestyles, who refuses to attend Leo's first major performance, eventually becomes a respectable family man. Ironically, as Leo notes at the close of the novel, Caleb's family's respectability is underwritten by Leo's fame: "As we say in America, nothing succeeds like success—so much for the black or white, the related respectability."[105] But if Leo has lost a brother, he seems to have become his father's favorite son. The now-old Mr. Proudhammer resists his elder son's attempt to convert him: "in spite of the way Caleb went on at him about his soul, he never relented."[106] Mr. Proudhammer's black pride, his dream of ancient kingdoms, is redeemed by Christopher, Leo's militant young lover. The young man and the old man "spend hours together, reconstructing the black empires of the past, and plotting the demolition of the white empires of the present."[107] Baldwin brings the novel full circle by substituting Christopher for Caleb in a passage that repeats an earlier description of Caleb and his father: "They both looked very much like each other on those days—both big, both black, both laughing."[108] In the last paragraph of the novel, Leo repeats this phrase; however, this time he is describing Christopher instead of Caleb: "Christopher and my father and I spent a day together, walking through Harlem. They looked very much like each other, both big, both black, both laughing."[109] By replacing Caleb, in Leo's affection and imagination, Christopher, as his Christian name implies, serves to restore Leo to a lost moment of familial harmony. Like Elisha in *Go Tell,* Christopher is a conduit for the protagonist's desire for a repaired relationship with the father and with an expressive black identity signified by the words, big, black, laughing.

The homoerotic subtext of John's attraction to Elisha in *Go Tell It on the Mountain* is made explicit in Leo's love for Caleb, and later for Christopher, in *Tell Me How Long the Train's Been Gone.* In *Train,* as in *Another Country,* homoerotic desire functions as a political intervention, occurring in contexts that demonstrate the ways in which American racial hierarchies have depended upon homophobic and misogynist discourses. In *Another Country,* Rufus's abuse of Leona is read as an effect of the pressures that a racist, sexist, and patriarchal culture have placed upon the black male body.[110] Rufus represses his homoerotic desires for fear of losing his already threatened manhood, but this repression causes him to reproduce the very cultural script of black masculinity that imprisons him.

*Train* makes explicit the sexual dynamics of racism on the black male body in the story of Caleb on the southern prison farm, an episode that reads like a neoslave narrative, an iconography of American black male subjugation. Throughout his imprisonment Caleb is under the constant threat of rape by a white prison guard, Martin Howell, who verbally assaults Caleb, saying, "Nigger, if my balls was on your chin, where would my prick be."[111] Caleb responds by picking up a pitchfork to defend himself. Although he successfully resists Howell's sexual aggression, he is punished by being sent to the kitchen to do women's work. Howell again pursues Caleb, touching him on the behind in the kitchen and saying "something about my mama and my daddy."[112] Once again Caleb fights back and this time is banished to the cellar, where he again resists Howell's attempts to get him alone.[113] Caleb's long battle against sexual humiliation is figured as a battle for masculinity. Howell tries to turn Caleb into a woman: "I ain't my grandmother, I'm a man."[114] A debased feminine identity becomes the sign of the black male's subjugation by the white male. Although Caleb resists rape, he is still sent to the kitchen. Caleb's long struggle with Howell has left him beaten and hardened, alienating him from his family and from the possibility of intimacy with a woman. Leo says, "He was good to look at, good to dance with, probably good to sleep with; but he was no longer good for love. And certainly Caleb felt this, for in his dealings with the girls there was a note of brutality which I had never felt in him before."[115] Through Caleb's story, Baldwin explicitly delineates the relationship between racial and sexual oppression, the white male's libidinal investment in the black male body, and the connection between the fear of homoerotic desire, the fear of a loss of masculinity, and the collapse of gender hierarchies.

While depictions of internalized homophobia and misogyny are not new to Baldwin's work, what is new and striking in *Tell Me How Long the Train's Been Gone* is Baldwin's willingness to posit intraracial, homoerotic love as a "solution" to the debasement of black masculinity and thereby directly challenge the homophobic discourse of black nationalism. Caleb's experience on a southern prison farm provides the historical ground for a black homophobia that identifies homosexuality as an act of white oppression and as a sign of black submission. When Caleb returns from prison, he is bitter, broken, and frightened. The once-admired older brother becomes, like the father, "an object lesson."[116] Leo, outraged at the way the white world has treated his brother, falls asleep dreaming of revenge and cursing an unjust God. But, less expectedly, Leo wakes struggling with sexual desire for his brother, and the dream of revenge dissolves into a passionate embrace as Leo and Caleb sexually consummate their brotherhood. The sexual episode between Leo and Caleb occurs in the very center of the text and marks Leo's transition to manhood; no longer the little brother, Leo wishes to care for Caleb. He remembers this experience as the first time he tried to give love and the first time he felt himself "to be present in the body of another person."[117] Leo, like other Baldwin protagonists, experiences self-recognition (or identity) as an intersubjective, loving act. When Leo comforts and then makes love to his brother, he is rescuing Caleb from the effects of racism. Caleb's masculinity and his family ties are restored (at least temporarily) through an act of brotherly intimacy. The restorative effects of this intimacy are revealed the following day in one of the rare happy family scenes and by the fact that Caleb tells his prison story later, as if his intimate relationship with Leo made it possible to confess his humiliation. By figuring an incestuous homosexual act as repairing the damage of white homosexual rape (or threatened rape), Baldwin is challenging the homophobia in the Black Nationalist movement that equated all homosexuality with signs of white oppression and internalized self-hatred.

By symbolizing Leo's transition to manhood with an incestuous and homosexual act, Baldwin challenges Freudian psychology (which dominated cultural understandings of homosexuality throughout the fifties and early sixties) that read homosexuality as evidence of an unresolved Oedipus complex, a sign of arrested development, and a failure of maturity.[118] Indeed, *Tell Me How Long the Train's Been Gone* makes a very bold intervention not only in the political discourses of its time, but in psychological and literary ones as well. Following the Freudian script, Leslie Fiedler reads the "boy" stories of classical American literature as homoerotic, which he interprets as an evasion of heterosexual love and a sign of cultural immaturity.[119] On the other hand, Baldwin suggests that the true sign of

American immaturity is not to be found in its homosexual stories (coded or otherwise), but in the denial or—worse—the debasement of homoerotic desire. Unlike Rufus, Leo returns home, and unlike Rufus, opens "the unusual door,"[120] risks love, embraces his bisexuality, and finds his maturity, his manhood, in a troubled world.

# 3 The Artist Transformed: *If Beale Street Could Talk*

I f Beale Street Could Talk (1974) was published six years after *Tell Me How Long the Train's Been Gone,* the year James Baldwin turned fifty. While some of the novel's thematic concerns are familiar to Baldwin readers, it represents, in several respects, a major departure from his previous novels. In contrast to the leisurely, detailed retrospective of *Tell Me How Long the Train's Been Gone, Beale Street* is a slim volume, fewer than 200 pages. The story takes place, for the most part, in the present and moves along with a speed and lyricism not characteristic of Baldwin's other novels. Not only does it appear to be the least autobiographical of Baldwin's fiction, but it is the only Baldwin novel in which neither homoerotic love nor interracial love are present as subject or theme. *Beale Street* is a heterosexual, blues love story, told in the first-person voice of nineteen-year-old Tish Rivers, a poor black girl raised in Harlem. The novel begins with the revelation of Tish's pregnancy and ends with the birth of her child. The focus of Tish's narrative is her love for Fonny, a young sculptor, and her struggle to free him from prison. Fonny is supported not only by Tish, but by the entire Rivers family, whose strong bond and social consciousness sustain them in their struggle to defend Fonny from the unjust charge of rape. As protagonists, the Rivers represent the black family as a site of personal and political resistance to racist values and actions. In addition to the society that has imprisoned the young black artist (the society as represented by the police, justice system, church, and school), the immediate antagonists are Fonny's mother and sisters, the Hunt women, who despise Tish for her unwed pregnancy and who have always expressed contempt for Fonny for looking and acting black. *Beale Street* is a story of warring family values and a story of love and resistance.

In a letter to his brother David, James Baldwin described *Beale Street* as "the strangest novel I've ever written."[1] Perhaps by "strange" Baldwin was referring to the experience of writing from a young woman's point of view and to the kind of story that point of view allowed him to tell. Baldwin's experiment in narrative gender crossing was not, however, entirely unprecedented. His 1960 story "Come out the Wilderness," although told in the third person, is from the perspective of a twenty-six-year-old black woman, Ruth, who is also in love with an artist and who, like Tish, is unmarried and living with her lover in the Village. The salient differences in the story line are that Ruth's lover, Paul, is white, and he deserts her. Ruth has been alienated from her poor southern family every since they labeled her as "black and dirty"[2]; now, whenever the unfaithful and opportunistic Paul touches her, she becomes "blacker and dirtier than ever."[3] Perhaps *Beale Street* seemed strange to Baldwin (as well as to many of his readers) not just because of the distance in age and sex between author and narrator, but in the clearly (re)visionary story this narrator tells. Tish Rivers allowed Baldwin to "re-vision" not merely the story of Ruth in "Come out the Wilderness," but his own autobiographical text.

Adrienne Rich used the term "re-vision" to describe a quality of feminist writing: "Re-vision—the act of looking back, of seeing with fresh eyes, of entering an old text from a new critical direction—is for women more than a chapter in cultural history; it is an act of survival."[4] *If Beale Street Could Talk* is a re-visionary act in the sense that Rich employs the term, an act of radical critique, of self-definition, and of survival. In Rich's terms *Beale Street* may be said to explore "how our language has trapped as well as liberated us . . . and how we can begin to see and name—and therefore live—afresh."[5] Baldwin clearly saw this novel as a testimony to the survival of the black family, but the novel is also testimony to Baldwin's personal survival. Tish is closely linked to her creator from her big eyes and small stature to her voice and sensibility. Through Tish, Baldwin develops a powerful voice of love and faith, a voice unlike any other Baldwin narrator. Describing the relationship between author and narrator, one reviewer claimed: "beneath the whisper and the hurry of the story you can feel Baldwin and Tish in a subtextual dialogue. Tish engages, even astonishes Baldwin as no other character he has ever written about. . . . He's exactly the right distance from her. I've never encountered anyone quite like Tish in American fiction. But America's streets are full of her. We all know Tish."[6] *Beale Street* operates as a re-visionary text on several fronts both within the context of Baldwin's own oeuvre and in the larger social, political, and literary discourses of the times. Through the voice of Tish Rivers, Baldwin undertakes a complete overhaul of his father's biblical texts, bringing the sacred and secular discourses of black culture into a new alignment; he rewrites the story of "illegitimacy" and "salvation" in *Go Tell It on the Mountain;* he challenges sociological constructions of the black family; and finally, he reimagines the protest novel, revising what he viewed as its limited moral vision structured by violence, self-righteousness, and theological terror.

As re-visionary text *If Beale Street Could Talk* is a parable of how Baldwin came to understand his role as an African American "artist," which was to resist political and psychological oppression and to pass on the cultural resources of African American survival to others. This interpretation is evident toward the end of the novel as Tish describes Fonny's transformation in prison: his eyes burn, "like the eyes of a prophet." He comes to understand his vocation as useful to others: "'Now. I'm an artisan,' he said. 'Like a cat who makes tables. I don't like the word artist. Maybe I never did.'" With this new self-knowledge, Fonny plans to "build us a table and a whole lot of folks going to be eating off it for a long, long time to come."[7] The proverbial "welcome table" is an image that recurs frequently in Baldwin's writing and in this instance specifically contrasts with the San Francisco restaurant scene in the closing pages of *Tell Me How Long the Train's Been Gone,* when Leo Proudhammer perceives that the safety of the opulent restaurant, where he shares a meal with his closest friends, is an illusion. It is not the "welcome table" of which his mother spoke. The repetition of the image of the welcome table near the end of each novel emphasizes the different positions and roles of Leo Proudhammer and Fonny Hunt as African American artists-artisans vis-à-vis their communities. Fonny's commitment to build a "welcome table" suggests the possibility of a new and sustaining relationship between the artist and the community. Before he goes to prison, Fonny Hunt knows he is "a real artist. And [he is] going to be a very good artist—maybe, even, a great one."[8] His drive to sculpt wood and stone seem intensely personal until the end when his prison experience and the love that has sustained him through it transform his private artistic impulse into a vision of social consequence. The "real artist" becomes the committed "artisan," making something of use, something to sustain the people who love and protect him. As Houston A. Baker Jr. has argued, Fonny represents a black renaissance in which "the embattled craftsman is supported by the will of the family and the love of the black madonna."[9] The change in Fonny's self-conception represents Baldwin's own wish to distance himself from the label of "artist." *If Beale Street Could Talk* is written by Baldwin, the artisan-writer who wishes to depict the struggle of common people in a way that passes on the values of a sustaining black, blues culture in the United States.

## I.

David Leeming describes *If Beale Street Could Talk* as Baldwin's "prison parable, a fictionalization of his prison concerns during the 1968–73 period, and the natural illustration and culmination of his long meditation on psychological, emotional, and intellectual imprisonment."[10] Baldwin's concern for the fate and condition of black prisoners in America was not new. Experience with the racism of the legal system, especially the ill treatment of black youth by white police, was part of Baldwin's early experience in Harlem and in the Village, and it is a theme treated consistently in his fiction, beginning with Richard's false arrest and humiliation in *Go Tell It on the Mountain*. The events of the late sixties and early seventies, the arrests of black activists, the police assassinations of several Panthers, including the infamous attack in Chicago in which Fred Hampton and Mark Clark were killed in their beds by police, brought this longtime issue to the forefront of Baldwin's work in the early seventies.

In addition to these high-profile cases, however, was the case of Tony Maynard, Baldwin's former bodyguard, chauffeur, and friend.[11] Maynard's defense occupied Baldwin throughout the period he was working on *Beale Street*. He writes about the case in *No Name in the Street*, which ends with Maynard in Attica prison at the time of the infamous 1971 riot.[12] Initially, Maynard was taken into custody in Hamburg, Germany, in October 1967 when the United States charged him with the murder of a Marine in New York. The indictment was made after Maynard jumped bail on a phony car theft charge (which was later dropped) and left the country.[13] Maynard, a street hustler with a record for drug possession, was not popular with the police, but he swore to Baldwin that he was not guilty of murder, and the evidence against him was flimsy. He was beaten in prison in Germany, and his situation would certainly have been worse if Baldwin had not immediately flown to Germany, made sure Maynard had legal representation, and pleaded his case with politicians and the police. Tony Maynard was in prison for over five years; the first trial resulted in a hung jury, the second in a conviction. Eventually, the conviction was overturned and Maynard was released the same year *Beale Street* was published. Baldwin drew on the Maynard case when depicting both Daniel Carty's and Fonny Hunt's problems with the police and justice system. Like Maynard, Daniel is arrested on a phony car theft charge. There are some obvious parallels between Maynard's situation and Fonny's plight as well, including the prosecution's weak case based on a critical witness who disappears (in the novel it is the victim who disappears), racist police who target unsubmissive black males, the struggle to maintain body and soul in a brutal prison environment, the high cost of getting a fair trial, and the long wait for justice.

Although *Beale Street* was the first novel Baldwin published in six years, the intervening years were not an unproductive period for Baldwin the writer as well as for Baldwin the activist. Between the publication of *Train* in 1968 and *Beale Street* in 1974, he published four books, several short essays, and numerous inteviews.[14] The books are *A Rap on Race* (1971), an extended conversation with Margaret Mead; *No Name in the Street* (1972), an autobiographical essay on Baldwin's involvement with the Civil Rights movement; *One Day When I Was Lost: A Scenario Based on Alex Haley's " The Autobiography of Malcolm X"* (1972); and *A Dialogue* (1973), Baldwin's conversation with Nikki Giovanni. Baldwin was involved in other creative projects during this period as well. He directed John Herbert's play *Fortune and Men's Eyes* in Istanbul. He also wrote a screenplay, *The Inheritance,* which develops a parallel between Nazi Germany in the early 1930s and racist America in the early 1970s. The film was never made. The comparison between German Nazism and American racism underlying this screenplay is to be found in many Baldwin essays and interviews during this period, especially in his Jeremiah-like warnings of a coming American "holocaust." As in *Beale Street,* the central character in *The Inheritance* is a young African American woman.[15] During the early seventies, Baldwin also began collaboration on a children's story with his friend and illustrator Yoran Carzac. *Little Man, Little Man: A Story of Childhood,* written in Black English, is about two boys growing up in Harlem and was published a couple of years after *Beale Street*. All of this work provides a record of Baldwin's response to the changing political and social conditions in America and to his evolving understanding of the role of the black artist.

Three major themes emerge from Baldwin's work during this period: disillusionment, hope, and responsibility. Following the assassination of Martin Luther King, Baldwin frequently expressed his very deep disillusionment with liberalism and with the will of the American nation to bring about the major changes required to include blacks as full citizens and equal partners. However, he also found hope in the revolution in black consciousness led by the young, which he believed contained the seeds of social transformation that must be nurtured by elders like himself. Specifically, he thought it was the responsibility of the family and the artist to pass on the hidden history of struggle and survival and, most of all, to keep faith with the young. While all three themes appear more or less simultaneously in *No Name in the Street* and other essays and interviews, from 1969 to 1972, the theme of disillusionment with liberalism is pervasive.[16] Baldwin emphasizes the huge price that civil rights activists paid, the tragic loss of black leadership by assassination, and the betrayal of the movement by liberals whose "status in their own eyes is much more important than any real change."[17] Baldwin came to the conclusion that "it was a dream to suppose that the people of any nation had a conscience," although "some individuals within the nation might,"[18] and that, "White America remains unable to believe that black America's grievances are real."[19] The election of Republicans on "law and order" platforms was an ominous sign for America's underprivileged and underrepresented minorities: "Everyone overlooks the impact on the black population of our country of the present administration, and that is very sinister."[20] With the election of Nixon as president and Reagan as governor of California, the increased repression at home, and the ongoing war in Vietnam, Baldwin concludes that the "Western world . . . is coalescing according to the principle under which it was organized, and that principle is white supremacy."[21]

Martin Luther King's assassination becomes particularly symbolic for Baldwin, not only of the death of the Civil Rights movement, but of the end of "a certain kind of dialogue in America." Nonviolent demonstrations, petitions, and appeals to the American conscience were simply no longer effective avenues to pursue change. No one was listening. There was no one to appeal to. At the beginning and at the end of his two-day discussion with Margaret Mead, Baldwin refers to King's death as the end of his American dream:

I know my situation is not the same situation I was in when Martin Luther King was alive and when we were trying, when we hoped to bring about some kind of revolution in the American conscience, which is, after all, where everything in some sense has to begin. Of course, that's gone now. It's gone because the Republic never had the courage or the ability or whatever it was that was needed to apprehend the nature of Martin's dream.[22]

There was a time in my life not so very long ago that I believed, hoped—and I suppose hope falls with believed—that this country would become what it has always presented as what it wanted to become. I am sorry, no matter how this may sound: when Martin was murdered for me that hope ended.[23]

Coupled with strong statements of disillusionment are dire predictions for the future of the country and Baldwin's sense that the nation, and the world, are on the verge of enormous and as yet unknown changes. In his interviews and writing during this period, Baldwin insists on a parallel between German Nazism and American racism. Predictions of a coming "holocaust" appear in almost all of his published pieces at the turn of the decade. For example, he concludes the Auchincloss interview: "I'm not frightened of another war really. I'm just frightened of chaos, apathy, indifference—which is the road people took to Auschwitz."[24] In another 1970 interview, he tells David Frost: "for the first time the people legally white and the people legally black are beginning to understand that if they do not come together they're going to end up in the same gas oven."[25] When Frost refuses the comparison and charges Baldwin with "overstating the point," Baldwin insists that "if you were born in Harlem" there is a parallel. In his 1971 dialogue with Nikki Giovanni, he speaks of being responsible as a poet, so "when the holocaust comes . . . when I'm needed I'll be there."[26] In a 1972 interview for the *Intellectual Digest,* Baldwin tells Herbert Lottman that the subject of his new book (*No Name in the Street*) is the coming holocaust.[27] In another 1972 interview for *Muhammad Speaks* Baldwin says: "The world is heading for a certain kind of decentralization which I think is its only hope. But the powers that still rule the world don't see it that way or envision it that way. If I'm right, it will have to come about through one form or another of a holocaust. In a sense we wouldn't know where we are going until this present tension has been one way or another resolved."[28] However, when the interviewer asks if the United States will go through a "fascist stage," Baldwin says he doubts that America "will really become the concentration camp which so many people would like it to become. I don't know but I think a lot of the white citizens of this country have undergone a kind of awakening—through the war more than anything else."[29] (It is worth noting that Baldwin's tone varies to some degree with his audience. He is most harsh about the failures of liberals when speaking with white liberals themselves and more likely to talk of the possibility of black-white reconciliation with black militants, as if he is giving each audience the message he believes it needs—rather than wants—to hear.)

The tone of extreme disillusionment clearly upset several of Baldwin's white interviewers and dialogue partners. By the end of their conversation, Margaret Mead is so frustrated with Baldwin's doomsday approach, his conviction that America "will not change," that she accuses him of "[contributing] to its not changing."[30] She then asks a telling question: "Do you think if you tell them they won't change, they will? Are you just trying to provoke them into better behavior?"[31] Baldwin replies to Mead: "Allen Ginsberg said, 'Don't call the cop a pig, call him a friend. If you call him a friend, he'll act like a friend.' I know more about cops than that."[32] Although Baldwin's response implies that denying "reality" does not work, Mead is correct in suggesting that Baldwin's rhetoric is a strategy, and it is not a new strategy. Since the early sixties, most notably in *The Fire Next Time* (1963), Baldwin made classic use of the jeremiad to urge Americans to live up to their promises before it is too late. Yet the jeremiad becomes an increasingly problematic rhetorical strategy for Baldwin as his conversation with Mead demonstrates, not because he does not believe what he is saying, but because he does. If America has lost the ability of self-confrontation, recounting its sins will do little good. While Mead wants to find a point of agreement that establishes the possibility, at least, of a united front of progressive blacks and whites working together for social change, Baldwin cannot afford to trust it, because, as he says to Mead, "you, historically, generically, have betrayed me."[33]

*A Rap on Race* is the end point of Baldwin's jeremiad directed at the white liberal community, but it is not the end of his prophetic message. His references to a coming "holocaust" function like the Christian idea of an apocalypse. For Baldwin the holocaust not only signifies human disaster, but the inevitability of a new and better world to follow. While this idea is hinted at in his interview with *Muhammad Speaks,* the most dramatic presentation of it occurs at the conclusion of a 1973 interview with the *Black Scholar* in which Baldwin expresses this vision of a secular apocalypse:

> There have been civilizations which have lasted for thousands of years without policemen, without torture, without rape, where gold was an ornament, not the summit of human desire. It has happened before and it can happen again. I really begin to look on the 2,000 year reign of the theology of this system, which is coming to its end, as a long aberration in the history of mankind, which will leave very little behind it except those people who have created an opposition to it, if that makes sense. What it can give it has given. In America, what it gave was us and the music which comes to the same thing. Now, it's not even worth translating. It has translated itself. It was doomed. But those three little boys who are living in California, my godchildren, will not be doomed. We must take our children out of that civilization's hands. That will be easier than we think it is because this civilization is on its death bed.
>
> There are new metaphors, there are new sounds, there are new relations. Men and women will be different. Children will be different. They will have to make money obsolete; make a man's life worth more than that. Restore the idea of work, which is joy and not drudgery. People don't work for money, you know. You can't work for money. When you work for money, something awful happens to you. But we can work, and understand. The world begins here, entrusted in your head and in your heart, your belly and your balls. If you can trust that, you can change the world, and we have to.[34]

The difference between this vision and Baldwin's former jeremiad is that he no longer suggests that a coalition of progressive blacks and whites will be the agency of change, but focuses on the inevitable decay of a corrupt civilization and the salvation of those who have opposed it. The vanguard of change will not be an elite group of conscious intellectuals, but everyday, working class people like the Rivers family and artisans like Fonny Hunt whose talent is shaped and supported by a resistant community. The vision and characters of *If Beale Street Could Talk* come out of this reconstructed prophetic message. W. J. Weatherby rightly describes the novel as Baldwin's "witness to a new generation and to his own changed viewpoint."[35]

Within the structure of Baldwin's apocalyptic vision, one can see disillusionment segue into hope. For Baldwin hope comes, primarily, in the form of the younger generation of African Americans to whom he attributes an "enormous revolution in black consciousness." It is a generation whose members have "assessed their history" and freed themselves from it, a generation "who will never be victims again."[36] When Nikki Giovanni asks Baldwin what he thinks of the younger black writers, he replies: "You know, it can be misunderstood, but you have no idea, and I can never express to you, to what extent I depend on you. I mean you, Nikki Giovanni, and I also mean your generation."[37] Comparing his generation to Giovanni's, Baldwin finds a change in black people's attitude toward themselves. While cautioning against "romanticism," he clearly celebrates this change as a step in the right direction, a step away from the self-loathing that comes with internalizing white standards and collaborating in one's own oppression. Describing this change at greater length in the 1973 *Black Scholar* interview, Baldwin states that for children like himself born in the North following the great black migration in the early twentieth century, "there was no articulation of what it meant to be black."[38] As a result, part of the danger that menaced the family was its relationship to blackness, which was "very painful . . . a matter of humiliation." Baldwin argues that by 1955 something had begun to change; blacks began relating to one another "more coherently," and the value blacks attributed to white people's judgment began to diminish: "By 1973, a whole new generation has grown up without these crippling handicaps of my generation; with certainly different illusions and certainly different dangers, but with a freedom which barely could have been imagined 49 years ago."[39]

Several commentators have been quick to note that the admiration Baldwin expressed for the younger generation was not always mutual. Baldwin suffered cruel public attacks from militants who despised his homosexuality. The most notable attack came from Eldridge Cleaver, although there were others.[40] When *No Name in the Street* was published, liberals were dismayed by its strident tone, while militants assumed he was playing up to them so as to be "welcomed home." Leeming writes that Baldwin was hurt by some of the reviews and wrote his brother David: "'Have you ever known me to kiss ass?' He was trapped, he said, between the white fantasy and the black fantasy."[41] Henry Louis Gates Jr. has argued that the "Baldwin bashing" by Cleaver and others was responsible for Baldwin's decline as an artist, charging Baldwin with "chasing with unseemly alacrity, after a new vanguard, one that esteemed rage, not compassion, as our noblest emotion."[42] Gates continued:

> As I say, by 1973 the times had changed; and they have stayed changed. That I suppose, is our problem. But Baldwin wanted to change with them. That was his problem. And so we lost his skepticism, his critical independence.
>
> Desperate to be "one of us," to be loved by his own, Baldwin allowed himself to mouth a script that was not his own. The connoisseur of complexity tried his hand at being an ideologue. . . . He cared too much about what others wanted from him.[43]

There are, however, several problems with Gates's analysis of Baldwin's work in the seventies. First, it does not acknowledge the social conditions that produced the tone of anger and disillusionment in No Name and other pieces. Second, it misrepresents Baldwin's writing by calling it "ideological" when there is no evidence in No Name or other work that Baldwin adopted any systematic political philosophy, or "party line" (be it that of the Black Panthers or the Communist Party) that could be described as an "ideology," much less a "script." Third, the image of Baldwin as "desperate" to be "loved by his own" drastically oversimplifies his relationship to the younger generation. The idea that Baldwin became so desperate to be accepted that he lost his ability to speak with an authentic voice does not appear to be supported by his biographers and amounts to an emotional (and insulting) dismissal of Baldwin's later work. To the extent that Baldwin's tone became increasingly blunt and confrontational in the early seventies, one can take him at face value and locate the cause in his distress over what he believed was an American betrayal of the Civil Rights movement (as evidenced by the multiple assassinations of leaders he had met and worked with, by the political turn to the right, and by the worsening of conditions in the country's ghettos, where the majority of blacks continued to live), rather than in feelings of personal betrayal by Cleaver and others. It's also important to note that while Baldwin celebrates the revolution in black consciousness, he's neither naive about nor uncritical of some of its forms. "To come back to the question of white and black, I'm terrified of cultural commissars on either side of the line," Baldwin tells Nikki Giovanni.[44] The following passage, as well, demonstrates his willingness to distance himself from popular slogans, even at the height of the black power period, and indicates he was far from being an ideologue. In this section Baldwin and Giovanni are discussing the education of young children. The passage begins with a reference to an earlier point in the conversation where they discuss the interrelationship between morality and power:

Baldwin: But, my dear, that's all we've been talking about. You call it power, and as you say I do, I call it morals. But it's the same thing; it's exactly the same thing. What one is trying to do is to teach those children something which they will need much later, because they can become fascist very easily, especially if they really believe all the legends which are now being fed to them, such as "black is beautiful." Black is beautiful, and since it's beautiful you haven't got to say so. And it's very important to realize that.

Giovanni: The ego is the most important thing about exemplifying that beauty.

Baldwin: It's a very dangerous slogan. I'm glad it came along, and it had to come along, but I don't love all black people, you know.

Giovanni: True.

Baldwin: I know deacons, preachers, congressmen, judges, teachers and lawyers who are black, but not like me. And you're trying to tell the child something which transcends all those categories so he won't become what you see all around you every day.[45]

The theme of responsibility in Baldwin's later work develops from his sympathy with the revolutionary consciousness of the younger generation of blacks and is linked to his desire to revise representations of race in American culture, and to his exploration of the relationship between the artist and the community in the struggle for liberation. Baldwin's interviews at the turn of the decade reveal a shift in his conception of his role as a writer. In 1969 he says to Eve Auchincloss, "And let's face it I am a Negro writer,"[46] a comment which explicitly alludes to his statement a decade earlier that he left America in order to "prevent [himself] from becoming merely a Negro; or, even merely a Negro writer."[47] In the *Black Scholar* interview he says, "I also realized that to try to be a writer (which involves, after all, disturbing the peace) was political, whether one liked it or not."[48] In the same interview he disassociates himself from the term "artist" and calls himself a "poet." It is the poet's work, like the revolutionary's, "to change the world." Although Baldwin continues to talk about the antithetical pressures of being a writer and being a public figure, one senses a much greater integration of these roles in his thought in the seventies.[49] In both roles he is motivated by his strong sense of responsibility to the next generation. It is the moral duty of both the poet and the revolutionary to combat the demoralization of the young by a corrupt society.

Responsibility is not a new theme for Baldwin, although it takes on new implications and directions in the seventies. Responsibility implies the possibility of individual agency and reflects on Baldwin's old quarrel with Stowe and Wright and the naturalistic school of "protest" fiction which, he argued, portrayed blacks as helpless victims or socially constructed monsters. Baldwin believed that Rufus Scott in *Another Country* had "no antecedents" because he portrayed him as "partly responsible for his doom."[50] However Rufus, like David in *Giovanni's Room,* is a negative example. Both characters illustrate the consequences of the failure to be responsible to others as well as to themselves, because of internalized racism and homophobia, respectively. They are collaborators in their own demise and the demise of their loved ones, because they accept the world's standards. By the late sixties, Baldwin's disillusionment with appeals to the American conscience as an effective path of social change made the issue of black responsibility, especially black self-reliance, all the more urgent. In the *Black Scholar* interview he speaks of "the necessity to take care of each other because no one else is going to,"[51] and he comes to a similar conclusion in a 1974 interview in the *Washington Post,* when he says, "We know our freedom is in our hands."[52] In his "Open Letter" to Angela Davis he says, "We, blacks, the most rejected of the Western children, can expect very little help at their hands. . . . We cannot awaken this sleeper, and God knows we have tried. We must do what we can do and fortify and save each other."[53] With the revolution in black consciousness and the advent of the Black Arts movement, Baldwin began to explore the theme of responsibility from other angles. His focus changed from exposing the mechanisms of internalized oppression to exploring the possibility of health and survival within black history and the "hieroglyphics" of black culture.

Baldwin tells Nikki Giovanni, "you must begin to break out of the culture which has produced you and discover the culture which really produced you."[54] The first is based on "mercantile standards," while the second is based on modes of inspiration encoded in the music and religion of one's forebears:

> What it's all about is the attempt now to excavate something that has been buried. Something you contain and I contain and which your kid contains and we've got to carry. Something one has to hand down the line for the sake of your kid and for the sake of future generations, and even for the sake of white people, who have not the remotest idea what this means. We have an edge over the people who think of themselves as white. We have never been deluded into knowing, into believing, what they believe. And that sounds like a contradiction."[55]

The contradiction he refers to is that blacks have, in fact, been "deluded" by "white" standards, as Baldwin's characters, beginning with Gabriel, John, and Richard in *Go Tell,* demonstrate to varying degrees. What Baldwin suggests by this contradiction, however (and which is also suggested by the complexity of his fictional characterizations in *Go Tell* and later work), is that the black subject is not defined solely by the ways he or she has internalized the dominant culture. The experience of oppression and resistance have resulted in an excess of black subjectivity which can be employed for self-reflection, social critique, and survival.[56] As a young man Baldwin went to Europe to avoid being labeled a "mere negro" and to discover how the "specialness" of his experience could connect him to other people, both black and white. By middle age Baldwin was locating this "specialness" within a revised vision of black culture. *If Beale Street Could Talk* is Baldwin's attempt in fiction to "excavate," to "translate," and to pass on to American youth the resources of a resistant and enduring black culture inherent to black survival in America.

## II.

*If Beale Street Could Talk* received mixed reviews, but on balance they were more positive than those of *Tell Me How Long the Train's Been Gone*. As with *Train,* a number of critics found evidence of Baldwin's decline as an artist reading *Beale Street* as unrealistic "protest" fiction, but others saw evidence of Baldwin's social and political development and the emergence of a "freer," more hopeful sensibility.[57] The response to Tish's voice was sharply divided; some found it to be a remarkable achievement and others to be unconvincing and inauthentic. More remarkable than the disagreements over the novel's quality were the radically different readings of the novel's tone, message, and ending. *Beale Street* was variously characterized as sentimental, optimistic, bitter, and deeply pessimistic. Some reviewers believed that Fonny had gotten out of jail at the end, others thought he hadn't, and still others believed Baldwin was being intentionally ambiguous about the matter.[58] One reviewer read *Beale Street* as a statement that "blacks were happy with their lot" and another that blackness had become "a condition of helpless passivity."[59] Among those who had strikingly different responses were June Jordan and Joyce Carol Oates. Jordan regarded *Beale Street* as "sorry" and "unconvincing stuff," a sad contrast to Baldwin's achievement in *Go Tell It on the Mountain*. She objected to the thinness of the story, the "skeletal style," the "strained, tacky, conclusion," but most forcefully to what she perceived as sexism and a lack of political consciousness "such as most

Blackfolk have acquired since the '6os."[60] Jordan found little evidence of the contemporary black world. She described the family members as "weirdly isolated" and wondered why they don't reach out to their neighbors, the community, black lawyers, and the black media for support. "The individualistic method of the family's efforts says much more about Baldwin than it does about any contemporary 'us,'" claimed Jordan. Tish's voice sounds more like that of "a rather fatuous, articulate man who entertains himself with bizarre women-hating ideas at every turn," and her story is unlike that of "any pregnant and unmarried young Black woman I can conceivably imagine, let alone accept as real," she concluded.[61] Joyce Carol Oates, on the other hand, described *Beale Street* as a "traditional celebration of love" which affirms not only the love between a man and a woman, "but love of a type that is dealt with only rarely in contemporary fiction—that between members of a family, which may involve extremes of sacrifice."[62] She found the novel optimistic but not sentimental, and Baldwin's insistence on the primacy of emotions such as love, hate, or terror to be convincing and true to human psychology. Oates noted that the characters of *Beale Street* do not have the benefit of the Black Power movement to sustain them and responded quite differently from Jordan to the absence of a contemporary political ambiance. "Though their story should seem dated, it does not"; their political helplessness has strengthened the characters' emotional bonds, argued Oates. She described *Beale Street* as "so obviously based upon reality, that it strikes us as timeless—an art that has not the slightest need of esthetic tricks, and even less need of fashionable apocalyptic excesses."[63] For Oates the novel was not "thin" or "skeletal," but "economically, almost poetically constructed . . . a kind of allegory, which refuses conventional outbursts of violence, preferring to stress the provisional, tentative nature of our lives."[64] Oates found Tish's voice to be "absolutely natural," and her speculations on male and female, and black and white, relationships, as well as her descriptions of pregnancy to be "convincing."

Jordan and Oates notwithstanding, *Beale Street* received somewhat more positive reviews from the black press and from African American reviewers. The most perceptive review was written by John McCluskey in *Black World*. McCluskey explored the novel's relationship to the blues tradition and noted the revisionary relationship between the story of Tish and Fonny and the story of Elizabeth and Richard in *Go Tell It on the Mountain*. McCluskey described *Beale Street* as a "freer," "more tender," and "tougher" novel than Baldwin had previously written. He attributed the change to the simplicity and authenticity of Tish's blues voice, which he considered, despite "occasional lapses," to be the "primary achievement" of the novel.[65] He rightly notes, "If the story had been told with Fonny's voice, we might have witnessed the traditional demise of the apprentice-artist in the hostile labyrinth of the city. . . . It is Tish's sensibility which lifts the accounts of the dilemmas of the characters."[66] McCluskey continues:

> Until this novel, Baldwin has not often elaborated on the optimistic possibilities inherent in the blues tradition. . . . Blues-singers tell us that after the most horrendous catastrophes, including the loss of love, it is still the possibility of love (and therefore, life) which moves us. The Riverses are blues people-loving, demanding, enduring, not maudlin angels, or dreary victims or super-folk.[67]

Tish's voice is key to understanding the novel. It is also key to the novel's controversy. In addition to the issue of how well Baldwin is able to create a female voice are the political issues of what Tish does and doesn't represent. As a homosexual black male writer employing a black heterosexual female voice, Baldwin seemed able to express a level of optimism about both love and artistry that he was not able to express through his male narrators. (Given Baldwin's other fiction, McCluskey seems on target when he suggests that if the tale had been told by Fonny it would have had a very different tone.) Baldwin clearly enjoys speaking through Tish and finds within her a newly liberated, single-minded self, as compared to the double-minded Leo Proudhammer, torn between competing loyalties. An important issue, however, is whether Baldwin is simply exploiting a woman's voice in order to celebrate love for the black male and black manhood and in the process reifying traditional gender roles.

June Jordan's charge of sexism has been elaborated upon by Trudier Harris and Hortense Spillers. In her essay "The Eye as Weapon," Harris argues that Tish and Fonny create a new religion of human love, and by extension the family, tied to this new religion, is idealized as the ultimate unit of salvation. Both Trudier Harris and Hortense Spillers emphasize the connection between the text's symbolic currency (its Christian allusions) and its conservative and hierarchical construction of gender. Harris first brought attention to this issue when she analyzed Baldwin's use of the black spiritual "Steal Away" in the scene where Tish and Fonny first make love, as symbolically associating Fonny with the Lord and Tish with the converted: "Tish's state of virginity is a pure offering on the altar of her lord, a purity that enhances the sacredness of their religion."[68] Spillers extends and elaborates on the connection between the language of religious sentiment and the position of women in the novel, claiming that Baldwin's language "rehearses a rhetoric of received opinion."[69] As she puts it, Baldwin "has spliced together sacral impulse and secular practice into a swift concord of passion and purpose."[70] The "baggage of inherited belief" that is evident in the sacred and romantic quality of Tish and Fonny's love reinscribes the "Puritan equation between love, sex and duty" and reinforces the subordinate position of women. Spillers argues that the novel's situations are suspect "because the moral obligation of racial continuity devolves on the women," and that love in *Beale Street* is "predicated on the surrender of the female's imagination."[71] Tish is the waiting, patient female who lives for her man. Her role is to make a home for the black male artist and give birth to the next generation. While Sharon and Ernestine, Tish's mother and sister, certainly make important decisions and behave more confidently and assertively than previous Baldwin women, their motivation is to defend and protect men. As Spillers says, "female energy here is man-compelled, man-obsessed."[72]

In defense of Baldwin, one can point out that the dependency between men and women in *Beale Street* is mutual. Women are not only motivated to protect men, but men are also motivated to protect women. (Joseph acts to protect his wife and daughters, Fonny wants to protect Tish.) It is a woman who tells the man's story as well as her own, and women dominate the action of the story. The dominance of women within the narrative structure creates a dissonance with the ideology of gender difference, which is voiced by characters of both sexes. (In other words, it is ironic that so much female energy is spent defending and protecting men, when protecting and defending is supposed to be the male prerogative.) Yet it is not a dissonance that Baldwin seems interested in exploiting. Spillers's and Harris's arguments are persuasive and suggest that Baldwin sought separate though interdependent roles for men and women in the black family.

Baldwin does not interrogate the assumption of two separate sexes as he interrogates categories of race and sexual orientation. Throughout his writing Baldwin argues that differences of race and sexual orientation are socially constructed myths that serve power relationships. As he says in the conversation with Nikki Giovanni: "People invent categories in order to feel safe. White people invented black people to give white people identity. . . . Straight cats invent faggots so they can sleep with them without becoming faggots themselves."[73] Baldwin does view gender roles as socially constructed, linking the oppression of women to the same distortions of American masculinity that produce racism and homophobia.[74] However, as Cora Kaplan has argued, "Baldwin never argues that a projective paranoia quite leads men to invent women."[75] By arguing that categories of race and sexual orientation were invented in order to consolidate the power of white men to deny "manhood" to black males, Baldwin retains "manhood" as an essential category of reference in much of his writing until his late essay "There Be Dragons," where he posits androgyny as a universal human condition.[76]

Baldwin's formulation of sexual difference in the early seventies is bluntly stated in his conversation with Nikki Giovanni. Giovanni argues that the oppression of black men should not be made an excuse for domestic abuse and violence within the family. Baldwin responds:

A man is built as he's built, and there's nothing one can do about that. A man is not a woman. And whether he's wrong or right . . . Look, if we're living in the same house and you're my wife or my woman, I have to be responsible for that house. If I'm not allowed to be responsible for that house, I'm no longer in my own eyes—it doesn't make any difference what you may think of me— in my own eyes I'm not a man.[77]

In this formulation Baldwin constructs manhood as the ability to take on a traditional patriarchal role within the family. Baldwin traces the problem of domestic abuse in black families to the legacy of slavery and to the social and economic conditions that continue to prevent black men from becoming the primary provider and head of the family:

> You know, a black man is forbidden by definition, since he's black, to assume the roles, burdens, duties and joys of being a man. In the same way that my child produced from your body did not belong to me but to the master and could be sold at any moment. This erodes a man's sexuality, and when you erode a man's sexuality you destroy his ability to love anyone, despite the fact that sex and love are not the same thing. When a man's sexuality is gone his possibility, his hope of loving is also gone."[78]

What Baldwin doesn't mention is that the slave mother was also denied possession of her child. It is interesting that Baldwin associates the "joys of being a man" with the ability to claim and raise one's offspring rather than with more traditional definitions or symbols of worldly male success (one is reminded of the symbolic import of Bigger Thomas's desire to pilot an airplane). However, in defining the oppression of black men on domestic terrain, Baldwin, in this instance, seems to have supplanted and effaced the oppression of black women, who have become simply a contested part of male territory ("my child produced from your body did not belong to me but to the master"). If one acknowledges that black women slaves suffered similarly from the inability to claim, protect, and raise their children, where is the difference—the special case of black manhood that Baldwin insists upon—unless, of course, women are to be considered as children, who also must be claimed, supported, and protected? In this formulation, Baldwin's project of reinventing masculinity becomes a project to save black manhood through insisting on a patriarchal ideal.

However, gender roles and attitudes toward familial responsibility in *If Beale Street Could Talk* are in actuality more complex and less traditional than Baldwin's formulations on the subject suggest. The idealized bond between Tish and Fonny, the refiguration of the role of the artist, and the emphasis on familial solidarity work to undermine a hierarchy of gender. The interdependence of the Tish-Fonny dyad—the formulation of self as always contained in and by the other—closely resembles the idealized bond that Baldwin's male lovers strive for and, increasingly in the later fiction, manage to achieve, at least for a time. The characterization of Tish as the waiting, patient female who lives for her man belies her narrative role, one that allows her to speak of and for all the other characters, male and female, and to define herself in relationship to them. Although Tish begins her story with the observation "trouble means you're alone," her experience suggests otherwise. Because of her family's protection, Tish is able to visit Fonny daily: "they have set me free to be there. He is not alone; we are not alone."[79] The movement in Tish's narration from the fear of isolation to the experience of familial support and solidarity is important to Baldwin's parable of the interdependent relation between the artist and his (her) community. The artist can only survive with the support of others, and the community needs the artist to sustain itself. In later years Baldwin often compared the role of the artist to the role of the lover. With this in mind, it is reasonable to think of both Tish and Fonny as artist-lovers. Tish not only sustains Fonny, her artist-lover, but is, herself, an artist-lover. The analogy between artist and lover transverses the dichotomy between mind and body, or "intellectual" and "physical" modes of creativity. It also imagines art as an intimate process involving an intersubjective experience. Tish and Fonny both take part in this process, although their mediums are different. Fonny works with wood and stone, while the pregnant Tish works with words and flesh. Their goal is similar: to construct a "welcome table" that will feed, literally and spiritually, themselves and the next generation.

Tish's first-person point of view reflects the intersubjective process that is suggested by the image of the artist as lover. As a first-person narrator Tish positions herself in relationship to the events that she relates in a manner similar to Baldwin's other first-person narrators, especially to David in *Giovanni's Room,* to the older brother in "Sonny's Blues," and to Hall Montana in *Just Above My Head.* As narrators telling the stories of a much-loved "other" (the stories of Giovanni, Sonny, Arthur, and Fonny), none are at the absolute center of their stories, nor are they merely observers, although each story illuminates the narrator's development. Tish's story is as much about Fonny, her family, and her unborn child as it is about herself. In fact her "self" is a construction deeply connected to others. If this seems to be a particularly female construction of identity, it is worth remembering that Baldwin's male narrators are similarly constructed. Their "identities" emerge in the reflection of the quality of their relationship with a lover. What distinguishes Tish from Baldwin's male first-person narrators (as well as from Ruth in "Come out the Wilderness") is her lack of guilt, regret, or self-doubt. While David knows that he has betrayed Giovanni, and Sonny's brother and Hall Montana feel they have failed their brothers, Tish's love for Fonny is free of ambivalence. (Undoubtedly, the fact that Tish's love is sanctioned by her family—although not by Fonny's family—is instrumental in her free expression.)

The opening paragraphs of *If Beale Street Could Talk* are a meditation on identity that specifically invites a comparison between Tish Rivers and Baldwin's male narrators. Tish begins, "I look at myself in the mirror."[80] *Giovanni's Room* opens with David seeing his reflection in a windowpane and ends with a long passage in which David examines his body "trapped in [his] mirror."[81] At the beginning of "Sonny's Blues" the narrator stares at his reflection in a subway window, "trapped in the darkness which roared outside."[82] Early in *Go Tell* John Grimes stares at his face in a mirror as though it were "a stranger who held secrets that John could never know."[83] In the opening pages of *Just Above My Ahead*, Hall Montana describes his reaction to the news of his brother's death: "I was shaving someone else. I looked into my eyes: they were someone else's eyes."[84] Baldwin's characters confront the "other" in mirrors, windows, and other reflective surfaces. The mirror contains a part of the self that the character is not able to assimilate: John's "ugliness," David's "troubling sex," or Sonny's brother's "darkness." Mirrors are symbols of divided selves and the means of exploring a character's conflict with sexual, racial, or religious identity. Mirrors also suggest that subjectivity is always formed in relationship to the other people in an individual's life. David not only sees himself in the mirror, but the image of Giovanni's face as he goes to his execution appears in the mirror as well.[85] The face that John Grimes sees is the face his stepfather says is his, the face of Satan. And both Hall Montana and the unnamed protagonist of "Sonny's Blues" suddenly find themselves looking at their reflections because they have lost a brother. In Baldwin's work reflective imagery suggests the intersubjective nature of personal identity; the degree to which subjectivity is formed in mirrors held up by the "other." The story of Tish Rivers suggests that this mirror does not have to be a "trap."

When Tish looks into the mirror at the beginning of the novel, she does not describe an image of her face or body. Instead, she goes on to talk about her name and Fonny's name, making a distinction between their Christian names, Clementine and Alonzo, and the names that people call them, Tish and Fonny. Tish's opening discourse on names suggests that when she looks into the mirror, she knows who she is; her words reflect a degree of self-acceptance uncharacteristic of Baldwin's male protagonists. It also suggests the degree to which her sense of self has been formed by others who have raised and loved her. Tish is the affectionate name given to her by her family, and that is the name she uses. When Tish looks into the mirror she experiences her connections with others rather than separation, and it is this sense of belonging that allows Tish to resist the fatalism that almost overwhelms her:

> I look at myself in the mirror. I know that I was christened Clementine, and so it would make sense if people called me Clem, or even, come to think of it, Clementine, since that's my name: but they don't. People call me Tish. I guess that makes sense, too. I'm tired, and I'm beginning to think that maybe everything that happens makes sense. Like, if it didn't make sense, how could it happen? But that's really a terrible thought. It can only come out of trouble—trouble that doesn't make sense.[86]

If we think of both Tish and Fonny as "artist-lovers" then Tish, in her role as narrator, is as much a symbol of the renaissance of the black artist as Fonny is. Tish's point of view frustrated some critics who felt that her tendency to tell about events at which she wasn't present was a flaw in Baldwin's first-person technique. For example, Tish relates a private conversation between her father, Joseph, and Fonny's father, Frank, and describes her mother's solo trip to Puerto Rico in intimate detail, without providing any realistic rationale that would have made her privy to these events. Tish's ability to tell these events and others suggests that her narrative authority is not based on her actual presence, but on her relationship to the people she writes about. As a model of the intersubjective voice, Tish's narration demonstrates the bonds achieved between herself and others. That Tish can re-create her father's private conversation with Frank,[87] and that Tish can describe her mother's feelings when she is several thousand miles away, is testimony to the intimacy of the family relationship. Such a point of view goes against the polyphonic grain of much modernist fiction that equates mimesis with the juxtaposition of different, generally incompatible subject positions. By contrast Tish is the consummate insider, whose omniscient narrative abilities derive not from God, but from her role as "artist-lover." Tish's narration blends reality and dream, and it cannot be determined from what point or points in time she tells the story. Within the story she gives us a striking image of her paradoxical narrative position as "absent" and yet all-knowing.

At the opening of part 2, "Zion," Tish describes the anxiety of the artist who is immobilized before his work. The scene links art and freedom, indicating that the artist frees himself through his own creation, but it also suggests the possibility of "defilement," that instead of freeing himself, the artist could betray the lover and thus betray the self. As Fonny approaches the block of wood, the creative stakes are high:

> Fonny is working on the wood. It is soft, brown wood, it stands on his worktable. He has decided to do a bust of me. The wall is covered with sketches. I am not there.
>
> His tools are on the table. He walks around the wood, terrified. He does not want to touch it. He knows that he must. But he does not want to defile the wood. He stares and stares, almost weeping. He wishes that the wood would speak to him; he is waiting for the wood to speak. Until it speaks, he cannot move. I am imprisoned somewhere in the silence of that wood, and so is he.[88]

The struggle goes on for another half page until finally "the chisel begins to move. Fonny begins."[89] However, at the point the crisis is resolved and Fonny begins to work, he awakes to find himself in solitary confinement; the nightmare of his "real" prison supersedes the dream of a creative breakthrough. Tish has been narrating Fonny's dream as if it were an event in real time. The passage is complex and plays with the relationship between creativity, identity, and love, like a kaleidoscope breaking apart and reassembling a familiar image. The passage is an inside out version of the Pygmalion story. In contrast to Pygmalion, the misanthrope who falls in love with his own creation, Fonny's love for a flesh and blood woman implies an artistic responsibility that involves the transformation of both artist and subject. In a further twist, Fonny's story is told by his beloved, who imagines herself as an artistic conception not yet realized. By drawing attention to her absence—"I am not there. . . . I am imprisoned somewhere in the silence of that wood"—Tish not only identifies with Fonny's imprisonment (she will not be free until he is), but she allegorizes the paradox of her own omniscient narrative authority, which emanates from a dream of speech not yet articulated (a paradox suggested by the title itself: *If Beale Street Could Talk*). Through Tish's intersubjective voice and Fonny's struggle to carve but not "defile" the brown wood, Baldwin suggests his own creative challenge to represent a black community in both its actuality and its possibility.

Fonny's dream, in the opening passage of "Zion," cited above, is echoed in the last paragraph of the novel, thus creating an ambiguous ending. Just as critics have disagreed over the significance of John Grimes's conversion in the last part of *Go Tell It on the Mountain*, critics do not agree on the ending of *Beale Street*.[90] Those critics such as Pratt and Hakutani, who read the last paragraph as evidence that Fonny is released from jail, find the novel to be optimistic, while those critics such as Harris, who believe the novel ends with Fonny still in jail, or such as Gibson, who describe the ending as ambiguous, perceive the tone to be more nuanced. In fact, the text appears to be intentionally ambiguous about whether Fonny is released from jail. After Fonny awakes in solitary confinement, Tish quickly narrates a series of events in real time that lead up to the moment she goes into labor, including Sharon's return from Puerto Rico, the worsening jail conditions, Fonny's new determination, the trial's postponement, the promise that bail has been raised for Fonny's release, and the news of Frank's suicide. Shortly after Tish learns of Frank's suicide she goes into labor; she says, "and then I screamed, and my time had come."[91] The last paragraph of the novel follows, separated from the preceding sentence by a double space: "Fonny is working on the wood, on the stone, whistling, smiling. And, from far away, but coming nearer, the baby cries and cries and cries and cries and cries and cries and cries and cries, cries like it means to wake the dead."[92]

The repetition of the phrase "Fonny is working on the wood" suggests that the last paragraph of "Zion," like the first one, may refer to a dream rather than to a point in the future after Fonny's release from jail. In addition, the language of the paragraph is more poetic than mimetic. Is Fonny working on both wood and stone simultaneously? Where is he? If he is working in their loft apartment, how would the baby's cry start from far away and come closer? The image does not particularly imply a happy domestic reunion with Fonny back to work; it does imply, as suggested in the title "Zion," the messianic promise of a future ideal community. We really don't know whether Fonny gets out of jail, but we do know that Tish and Fonny's baby is a messenger of the new dispensation. Tish's narration sustains a delicate balance between grim realities and faith that a better tomorrow will come.

## III.

The language of *If Beale Street Could Talk* conflates sacred and secular discourses in order to elevate a blues story to high moral seriousness. Tish Rivers's first-person narrative is Baldwin's rendering of a female blues voice in fiction. Tish tells of love and loss in, for the most part, simple, straightforward language. Her narrative has moments of dark humor and demonstrates the blues as a style of resistance, a way of getting through, of transforming trouble into a spirit of resilience. Her narrative is also structured as a retelling of the Christ story, and she uses language from spirituals to describe the love that she and Fonny share. In *Beale Street*

Baldwin not only employs Christian songs and stories to moralize and to give symbolic significance to a Harlem love story, but his discourse works to revise Christian myth itself (as well as to remind audiences of the historically (re)visionary nature of African American Christianity, especially the coded language of the slave songs) and to revise the religious discourse of his own earlier work. The conflated sacred-secular discourse is immediately evident in Baldwin's title and subtitles, which cite both blues and spirituals. "If Beale Street Could Talk" comes from a line in "Beale Street Blues," composed by W. C. Handy in 1916.

> I've seen the lights of gay Broadway,
> Old Market Street down by the Frisco Bay,
> I've strolled the Prado, I've gambled the Bourse
> The seven wonders of the world I've seen
> And many are the places I have been.
> Take my advice folks and see Beale Street first.
> You'll see pretty Browns in beautiful gowns,
> You'll see tailor mades and hand me downs,
> You'll meet honest men and pick-pockets skilled,
> You'll find that business never closes till somebody gets killed.
> You'll see Hog Nose rest'rants and Chitlin Cafcs,
> You'll see Jugs that tell of bygone days,
> And places once palaces, now just a sham,
> You'll see Golden Balls enough to pave the New Jerusalem.
> If Beale Street could talk. If Beale Street could talk,
> Married men would have to take their beds and walk,
> Except one or two, who never drink booze,
> And the blindman on the corner who sings the Beale Street Blues.
> I'd rather be here than any place I know,
> I'd rather be here than any place I know,
> It's goin' to take the Sargent for to make me go,
> Goin to the river, maybe, bye and bye,
> Goin to the river, and there's a reason why,
> Because the river's wet, and Beale Street's done gone dry.[93]

Baldwin's title identifies the novel with the cultural project of W. C. Handy, to preserve the stories and songs of ordinary black people in their own language. When Handy wrote a blues song, "he sought to speak in the language of the folk singers—meaning not merely their words and turns of thought, but their musical language."[94] Yet as one can observe in a song like "Beale Street Blues," Handy was doing more than just recording a simple twelve-bar blues; he was elaborating and extending the form and message. While the last two verses are a basic "three-cornered blues," the introductory verses are not. They provide a frame that pays tribute to the place in Memphis, Tennessee, that was home and inspiration to many blues artists. In "Beale Street Blues" Handy extends the expression of the blues from an individual's story to the story of a place, a community which represents the blues' life.

As noted by historians McKee and Chisenhall, Beale Street in Memphis, Tennessee, was once referred to as the "Main Street of Negro America" and was long associated not only with the history of the blues but with the culture of ordinary black people in America: "Beale Street approaches more nearly an expression of the mass of American Negroes than any other place, including Harlem, for Beale is closer to the great bulk of the nation's colored population, and speaks more distinctly their traditional language of frustration, hope, struggle and slow advance."[95]

Beale Street became a black Mecca at the dawn of the twentieth century, thanks to Robert Reed Church Sr., the first black millionaire in the South. Accumulating property after most whites fled Memphis in a yellow fever epidemic, Church established a six-acre park and an auditorium that could seat 2,000 people in 1899. For many years it was the only place where black entertainers could perform for black audiences. The street also housed the offices of black business and professional people: doctors, dentists, lawyers, and undertakers. In the segregated South of the first half of the twentieth century,

Beale Street was not only the center for black entertainment, but for daily life. To the general public, the street was a tourist attraction and also infamous for its high murder rate, gambling and prostitution. The coming of integration in the late fifties and sixties made it possible for middle class blacks to move to other areas and for blacks to shop elsewhere. Integration was the beginning of the end of Beale Street, and by the '70s, as one long time resident put it, "Beale Street [was] as dead as a dodo . . . and hants walk[ed] the street like natural men."[96]

Beale Street is a complex symbol of black life in America. While it represented the escape, hope, and freedom described by the blues musicians and longtime black residents of the area, it represented vice, crime, and the fast life for the majority of whites and for upwardly mobile, middle-class blacks, many of whom wished to disassociate themselves from Beale. It also represented the loss of a distinctive black culture. By the time Baldwin wrote *If Beale Street Could Talk,* Beale Street, its buildings abandoned, its history neglected, was but a vestige of the past, a dream to be "excavated."

As a complex image of African American experience, Beale Street inspired the voices of many black creative artists, including Langston Hughes, who did more than any other poet of his time to transform the musical tradition of the blues into verse. Baldwin's title may also allude to Hughes's "Beale Street," one of Hughes's dream series poems.

> Beale Street
> The dream is vague
> And all confused
> With dice and women
> And jazz and booze.
> The dream is vague,
> Without a name,
> Yet warm and wavering
> And sharp as flame.
> The loss
> Of the dream
> Leaves nothing
> The same.[97]

In this poem Hughes makes Beale Street a symbol of African American dreams. The tone is characteristic of the blues, mixing hope and melancholy. Composed in the present tense, it conflates the past and present, suggesting that the dream Beale Street represents is both continuing and lost. The dream has been misunderstood and undefined, but at its center is an essential sustaining quality. On the most literal level the last stanza reflects the "death" of the once famous street, the loss to urban decay, the loss to "integration." But it is also a reminder to keep the flame lit, to preserve the stories and music of ordinary people.

Baldwin's title, *If Beale Street Could Talk,* recalls both place and spirit central to the blues as well as the lyrics of one of the most famous of the early blues musician-writers. The title's allusion to Handy, and possibly to Hughes as well, signals Baldwin's alliance with the cultural project of the blues musician and the poet. Rivers, the last name of Beale Street's central family, also alludes to a Hughes poem, "The Negro Speaks of Rivers," in which rivers (the Euphrates, the Congo, and the "muddy Mississippi") represent the continuity and strength of the black race from prehistory through the end of American slavery.[98] The Rivers family embodies the qualities that Hughes celebrates in his poem, and the name is certainly appropriate for a family whose father works on the docks, whose mother, Sharon, had been a blues singer, and whose daughter, Tish, tells a blues tale of separation, loss, and hope. Rivers, the Mississippi River in particular, were the lifeblood, the arteries along which the southern black blues culture formed. The name Rivers signifies the southern roots and culture of this Harlem family.

While the title of Baldwin's early collection of essays, *Notes of a Native Son,* placed his work in a signifying relationship to the novels of Richard Wright, the title of his fifth novel implies a new set of fathers. If Wright represents a "protest" tradition in African American literature, in which the emphasis is on interracial conflict and the destructive, psychosocial effects of racism, Handy and Hughes represent a black arts tradition, in which the emphasis is on intraracial relationships and the sustaining flame of a black blues culture. Like Handy and Hughes, Baldwin wanted to record, contextualize, and interpret the blues, to make them available to a larger audience, and to pass them on to the next generation. Unlike Handy and Hughes, however, Baldwin's language is deeply inflected by Christian image and metaphor, which results in a tone of high moral seriousness somewhat at odds with the blues.

While the title of *If Beale Street Could Talk* is from the secular blues tradition, the epigraph to the novel—"Mary, Mary, / What you going to name / That pretty little baby?"—and the subtitles—"Troubled about My Soul" and "Zion"—are from spirituals. The term "Zion" carries a complex meaning, not unlike "Beale Street": both reflect a lost "historical" place and community (a hill in Jerusalem, a street in Memphis), an image of occupied territory, and the dream of restoration. Both suggest the spirit of an ideal community (a heavenly city). The particular mix of secular and sacred black musical traditions evident in the subtitles and epigraph of *If Beale Street Could Talk* comprise Baldwin's unique signature and vision. Trudier Harris has described *Beale Street* as illustrative of Baldwin's progression away from the church, noting that his "vision has become paradoxically more secular even as it becomes more religious."[99] Baldwin's movement away from the church is reflected in the novel's title and in the depiction of the church-going Mrs. Hunt, whose religiosity is nothing more than self-righteous hypocrisy. Mrs. Hunt lacks the complexity of a Gabriel Grimes, and the church experience in *Beale Street* is stripped of any appeal. However, the novel clearly combines an antichurch sentiment with a powerful religious vision, which is implicit in the epigraph, the subtitles, and the language taken from black spirituals used to describe Tish and Fonny's lovemaking. Love promises not only personal salvation, but the communal and political salvation implied by "Zion." By sacralizing the experience of "ordinary" people, blues people, *Beale Street* becomes, as Trudier Harris points out, an effort to redefine the very concept of religion.

Redefining religion, Christianity in particular, is an important way in which Baldwin locates his work in a larger African American cultural tradition. As he tells Nikki Giovanni, "what we did with Jesus was not supposed to happen . . . we took that cat over and made him ours."[100] Certainly many of the nineteenth-century slave narrators, including Frederick Douglass, established an explicit contrast between the hypocrisy of the southern white church, whose leaders cited the Bible to justify slavery, and the religious convictions of black slaves, who read the promise of their own liberation in the same text. The African American religious tradition is an important part of the culture that Baldwin wishes to "translate" for the next generation. In responding to Kalamu ya Salaam's question about whether the church has been a "redemptive" force, Baldwin replies:

> This is something very complex. It depends. When I said the church, I was thinking about the overall, two thousand year history of the Christian church, one of the results of which was the enslavement of Black people. On the other hand, what happened here in America to Black people who were given the church and nothing else, who were given the bible and the cross under the shadow of the loaded gun, and who did something with it absolutely unprecedented which astounds Black people to this day. Finally, everything in Black history comes out of the church. . . . The essential religion of Black people comes out of something which is not Europe. When Black people talk about true religion, they're "speaking in tongues" practically. It would not be understood in Rome. . . . [The church] was how we forged our identity.[101]

The epigraph to *Beale Street*—"Mary, Mary, / What you going to name / That pretty little baby?"—not only sacralizes the experience of Tish Rivers, it also contains Baldwin's criticism of Christianity. The story of the virgin birth preoccupied Baldwin. This myth, he felt, was central to the worst elements of Christianity: the attribution of sinfulness to sexual desire and the label of "illegitimacy" to children born out of wedlock. In *No Name in the Street* Baldwin refers to the "dirty joke which has always been hidden at the heart of the legend of the Virgin birth."[102] In his conversation with Nikki Giovanni, Baldwin says,

> The whole heart of the Christian legend has always been in some sense and sometimes impresses me as being really obscene. . . . And when you attack it you're accused of being blasphemous. I think the legend itself is a blasphemy. What is wrong with a man and a woman sleeping together, making love to each other and having a baby like everybody else? Why does the son of God have to be born immaculately? Aren't we all the sons of God? That's the blasphemy.[103]

In *Go Tell It on the Mountain* "illegitimacy" is the central condition of John Grimes's life, as it was of Baldwin's own. Describing himself as a "bastard of the West," Baldwin employs his illegitimacy metaphorically to represent the situation of all blacks in America. David Leeming identifies "illegitimacy and an almost obsessive preoccupation with his stepfather" as constant themes in Baldwin's work: "If Baldwin ever knew who his real father was, he kept the knowledge to himself. He preferred to use the fact of his illegitimacy, as he did his minority status and his homosexuality, as supporting material for a mythical or representative persona indicated in such titles as *Nobody Knows My Name, No Name in the Street,* or 'Stranger in the Village.'"[104]

However, by the 1970s Baldwin is clearly distancing himself from the metaphor of "illegitimacy" or rewriting it in ways to reflect his themes of black self-reliance, family, and community. It should be noted that *No Name in the Street* (1972) reverses the direction of namelessness as a metaphor. Rather than associating namelessness with the condition of an oppressed minority, namelessness becomes the oppressors' punishment. The title is taken from Bildad's curse in the Book of Job:

> Yes, the light of the wicked shall be put
> out, and the spark of his fire shall not shine.
>
> \* \* \*
>
> His roots shall be dried up beneath, and
> above shall his branch be cut off.
> His remembrance shall perish from the
> earth, and he shall have no name in the street.[105]

*If Beale Street Could Talk* rewrites the "obscene" legend by associating Tish Rivers with the Virgin Mary. Tish and Fonny's offspring, a product of undivided carnal and spiritual love, is embraced by its family, suggesting a new "representative persona" for blacks in the new world. *Beale Street* follows thematically from the conclusion of *No Name,* which announces the death of the old world and the promise of a new one, "kicking in the belly of its mother."[106] Comparing the mother of George Jackson to the Mother of God, Baldwin ends the essay: "Now, it is the Virgin, the alabaster Mary, who must embrace the despised black mother whose children are also the issue of the Holy Ghost."[107] At its conclusion *Beale Street* symbolically brings that new world into being with the birth of Tish's messiahlike baby, who "cries like it means to wake the dead."[108] The "despised black mother" of *No Name* is Tish Rivers (unwed, teenage mother) of *Beale Street*. That the birth of her child signals the salvation of the worldly nation (in particular the American nation) is underlined by the date that Baldwin inscribes to indicate the novel's completion: "[Columbus Day] Oct. 12, 1973."[109]

Baldwin's use of sacred phrases, songs, and stories to shape his "secular" texts is characteristic of his work—fiction and nonfiction—from the beginning. His 1955 essay "Notes of a Native Son," initially titled "Me and My House," in reference to his father's favorite biblical text, provides an important clue to Baldwin's characteristic use of sacred language.[110] This early autobiographical essay centers on the death of Baldwin's stepfather and Baldwin's effort to come to terms with the legacy of this fanatically religious man. In a key passage Baldwin recalls the text his father often quoted:

> *And if it seem evil unto you to serve the Lord, choose you this day whom you will serve; whether the gods which your fathers served that were on the other side of the flood, or the gods of the Amorites, in whose land ye dwell: but as for me and my house, we, will serve the Lord.* I suspected in these familiar lines a meaning which had never been there for me before. All of my father's texts and songs, which I had decided were meaningless, were arranged before me at his death like empty bottles, waiting to hold the meaning which life would give them for me. This was his legacy: nothing is ever escaped."[111]

This particular passage is a useful touchstone to Baldwin's themes and method even twenty years later. The father has left a problematic textual legacy, of which the son must make sense, not by discarding the texts (since "nothing can be escaped"), but by giving old texts new meaning. The legacy of the text as an "empty bottle" is a striking image of Baldwin's relationship to the language of the black church and the Christian tradition, which he claimed as his own, exploiting its beauty, emotional power, and ethic of love, while simultaneously discarding much of its ideology. The resulting tension between form and content is at the heart of much of the critical disagreement surrounding *Go Tell It on the Mountain*. Some critics have viewed *Go Tell* as an indictment of Christianity; others have argued that it is an apology for or even a vindication of Christianity; still others claim that "the church idiom riddled [Baldwin's] message more than redeemed it."[112] Although Baldwin imagined that he would fill the empty bottles with "meaning" from his own life, he neglected to note that the bottles themselves, in providing shape to their contents, carry meanings of their own, as form and substance cannot be separated. Although the title "Notes of a Native Son" places Richard Wright in the position of the "father" to whom Baldwin is responding, the extent to which Baldwin's discourse would remain bound to his stepfather's is acknowledged by his initial title for the essay, "Me and My House."

The metaphor of the biblical song and text as an "empty bottle" is apropos of the function of religious image and language in *Beale Street*. Just as a bottle gives shape to that which fills it, so do the references to the Christ story (e.g., Fonny as "prophet," Tish as "Mary," Tish's father as "Joseph," and the baby as "messiah") shape the blues story of Tish Rivers. Unlike the characters in *Go Tell*, the sympathetic characters in *Beale Street* are not churchgoers or "religious" in a conventional manner. There is a complete separation between Baldwin's use of religious language and his depiction of religious institutions in the novel. In one sense the message of *Beale Street* seems less "riddled" than the message of *Go Tell*, because the criticism of the church is unambiguous in the later novel. Yet to the extent that *If Beale Street Could Talk* retells the Christ story, it imparts an apocalyptic view of human events and a vision of salvation.

"As for me and my house, we will serve the Lord." The passage is a Baldwin "urtext": the image of the righteous patriarch leading his house, the unambiguous division between good and evil, and the command to "choose you this day" between false gods and the true one. These are the terms that Gabriel bequeaths John in *Go Tell It on the Mountain*; this is John's conflict, whom to serve, the narrow religious world of his father or the broad way of danger, dreams, and worldly aspirations. It is also the conflict of *If Beale Street Could Talk* written large. Signifying ironically on his father's text, Baldwin builds the parable of *Beale Street* around two houses, one which "serves the Lord" and one which does not. The moral of this parable is evident in the juxtaposition of values associated with each family, the Rivers and the Hunts, and with the implied redefinition of "religious" service as the service human beings at their best provide to one another in their time of need.

Although not nominally the head of her family, Mrs. Hunt's destructive influence makes her its most powerful member. A "sanctified" woman who belongs to the Lord (rather than to her husband), Alice Hunt represents a complex of negative values that Baldwin associated with the church, values that alienated blacks from one another and made them vulnerable to despair.[113] Alice Hunt's religiosity is associated with her ability to love her family—especially her husband and her son—with only a shallow self-absorption, and with a narrow, judgmental moralism. Her denial of sexual desire, her association of sex with sin and lust, her concern with appearance and respectability, her class pretensions, and, most of all, her valuing of "whiteness" associate her with a dominant, middle-class morality at the heart of internalized racism. The values she represents are similar to those of Gabriel Grimes, but unlike Gabriel, she is drawn as a caricature. Rather than dominating the story as Gabriel does, she is last seen less than halfway through the novel, successfully banished from the lives of the Rivers family.

Alice Hunt's character is revealed in three striking passages that ridicule her religious pretensions. First, her mission to convert her husband is revealed to be a thin disguise for sexual desire. Fonny humorously describes his parents' sexual encounters as a parody of religious ritual:

> And she'd say, Oh, Frank, let me bring you to the Lord. And he'd say, Shit, woman, I'm going to bring the Lord to you, I'm the Lord. And she'd start to crying, and she'd moan, Lord, help me help this man. You give him to me. I can't do nothing about it. Oh, Lord, help me. And he'd say, The Lord's going to help you, sugar, just as soon as you get to be a little child again, naked, like a little child. Come on, come to the Lord. And she'd start to crying and calling on Jesus while he started taking all her clothes off.[114]

Second, Alice Hunt's church attendance is motivated by a desire to make an impressive public performance rather than by genuine religious feeling. Tish describes the unforgettable day she accompanied Fonny and his mother and sisters to church. Watching Mrs. Hunt and another woman crying "Holy" and waving their arms, Tish says, "It was like they were trying to outdo each other."[115] Tish perceives that the music and the dancing provide an emotional release, but do not provide the parishioners with true community or a loving connection. As in *Go Tell* the drama of the church service connects people to their own bitter memories, but not to each other: "No doubt, the congregation had their memories, too, and they went to pieces. The church began to rock. And rocked me and Fonny, too, though they didn't know it, and in a very different way. Now, we knew that nobody loved us: or, now, we knew who did. Whoever loved us was not here."[116]

Third, Mrs. Hunt's moral code is cruel and vindictive, as revealed in the final scene in which she appears. The Hunts have been summoned by the Riverses to learn of Tish's pregnancy, to learn that they will be grandparents. In contrast to the supportive, even celebrative, response Tish received from her own family, Mrs. Hunt is outraged:

> "I guess you call your lustful action love," she said. "I don't. I always knew that you would be the destruction of my son. You have a demon in you—I always knew it. My God caused me to know it many a year ago. The Holy Ghost will cause that child to shrivel in your womb. But my son will be forgiven. My prayers will save him."
>
> She was ridiculous and majestic; she was testifying.[117]

The scene ends in a knock-down-drag-out fight (Frank Hunt knocks Alice Hunt down), and Mrs. Hunt is banished from the Rivers home, with Ernestine's (Tish's sister) curses following her out.[118]

From the beginning, Mrs. Hunt's belief in her own superiority is connected to her skin color. Considered very beautiful in her youth, a fair-skinned woman from Atlanta with "that don't-you-touch-me look,"[119] Mrs. Hunt associates truth and beauty with whiteness.[120] Unable to truly love her son, Fonny, who has darker skin and nappy hair, she can only make periodic attempts to "save" him by trying to straighten his hair and drag him to church. Her daughters, Sheila and Adrienne, on the other hand, are fair like their mother, although not so beautiful. College students and raised to be proper virgins, they believe in their superiority to common blacks, including their brother. Their false sense of superiority has yielded them nothing but lovelessness and a premature old maid status. The house of Mrs. Hunt is doomed. Her daughters will not bring home any "bastards," as she puts it, but it is unlikely they will ever reproduce:

> They had been raised to be married but there wasn't anybody around them good enough for them. They were really just ordinary Harlem girls, even though they'd made it as far as City College. But absolutely nothing was happening for them at City College—nothing: the brothers with degrees didn't want them; those who wanted their women black wanted them black; and those who wanted their women white wanted them white.[121]

The values the Hunt women represent are part of the dying old world Baldwin ushered out at the end of *No Name in the Street*. The Hunts represent a black middle-class fantasy which Baldwin called "a copy of an illusion." The original illusion is the white middle-class fantasy, which Baldwin described in Thoreau-like terms as "an enormous group of people who live both subtly and desperately beyond their needs" and "who think money makes them safe."[122] Frank Hunt's suicide at the end of the novel was considered "unrealistic" by John McCluskey. However, if we consider his long marriage to Alice Hunt as the primary cause of his suicide, which occurs after he is caught stealing from his job in the garment industry, his death is more credible. His demise represents the demise of the house of Hunt. The future is with the Rivers family and with Fonny, their adopted son (-in-law). Mrs. Hunt has provided the foil against which we can view their virtues.

The Rivers family is characterized by their love and solidarity, their lack of either religious pretension or worldly ambition, and their understanding of the history of black struggle in America. The father, Joseph, originally from Boston, was a merchant seaman who now works on the docks in order to be close to his family. The mother, Sharon, originally from

Birmingham, set out to be a blues singer, but at twenty she "had come to realize that, though she had a voice, she wasn't a singer; that to endure and embrace the life of a singer demands a whole lot more than a voice."[123] Sharon meets Joseph at a bus stop in Albany. He is attracted to her ill-concealed vulnerability, which provokes in him a classic blues response: "She was trying to look tough and careless, but she just looked scared. He says he wanted to laugh, and, at the same time, something in her frightened eyes made him want to cry."[124] Within a week they are married. Ernestine, the eldest sister, is an activist who is busy saving children (of all races) by working in a settlement house. She has given up the vanity of her youth, is an avid reader, and chooses self-education over college. Tish, the youngest member of the family, works at the perfume counter of a department store and plans to marry her lover, Fonny. The family lives together in a housing project in Harlem. They are members of the Abyssinia Baptist Church, a mainstream denomination "more respectable, more civilized, than sanctified,"[125] but they seldom attend.[126]

The values of the Rivers family are revealed in their response to Tish and Fonny's trouble. Rather than responding with shame, accusation, and prayer to Fonny's incarceration and Tish's pregnancy, as the Hunt women do, the Rivers family responds with love and action. They work together, taking extraordinary measures to get Fonny out of jail and to protect Tish and her unborn child. Tish's mother tracks down Fonny's accuser, Mrs. Rogers, in Puerto Rico and tries (unsuccessfully) to get her to realize that she has misidentified her attacker; Tish's father steals from his job to raise Fonny's bail. They view the trouble that Tish and Fonny face as part of the historical oppression of blacks in America rather than the result of "sin" or personal failing. They never doubt Fonny's innocence, nor do they think of Tish's child as "illegitimate." Sharon's immediate reaction to the news of Tish's pregnancy sets the tone of the family's response:

> "Now, listen," she said, "you got enough on your mind without worrying about being a bad girl and all that jive-ass shit. I sure hope I raised you better than that. If you was a bad girl, you wouldn't be sitting on that bed, you'd long been turning tricks for the warden."

She came back to the bed and sat down. She seemed to be raking her mind for the right words.

"Tish," she said, "when we was first brought here, the white man he didn't give us no preachers to say words over us before we had our babies. And you and Fonny be together right now, married or not, wasn't for that same damn white man. So, let me tell you what you got to do. You got to think about that baby. You got to hold on to that baby, don't care what else happens or don't happen. You got to do that. Can't nobody else do that for you. And the rest of us, well, we going to hold on to you. And we going to get Fonny out. Don't you worry. I know it's hard—but don't you worry. And that baby be the best thing that ever happened to Fonny. He needs that baby. It going to give him a whole lot of courage."[127]

For Joseph and Sharon there is no question of rejecting their children: Fonny is as much their child as Tish. Tish and Fonny have "been together, from childhood on"[128] and Fonny thinks of the Riverses as "the only family I've ever had."[129] The bond between the young lovers is similar to that of Barbara and Leo in *Train* in that it conflates filial, romantic, and sexual love. However, unlike Barbara and Leo, Tish and Fonny are supported by Tish's parents, who view the unborn child as an affirmation and continuation of their family, and whose safe passage into this world must be protected by protecting both the father and the mother in their time of trouble.

Baldwin's creation of the Rivers family allowed him to rewrite the story of Elizabeth and Richard in *Go Tell* and to signify on the moral code of the "protest novel" in ways that reflect his project of "translating" a resistant black culture for a new generation. By rewriting Elizabeth and Richard's story, Baldwin rewrites the circumstances into which John Grimes is born and thereby rewrites the "fiction" of his own life. A number of details indicate strong points of similarity and difference between the two stories. Both Tish and Elizabeth share characteristics linking them to Baldwin. They are described as dark, small, and not physically attractive. Richard's affectionate nicknames for Elizabeth, including "frog-eyes,"[130] were names Baldwin associated with his own appearance. Both Tish and Elizabeth express strong, loving attachment to their fathers. Both Tish and

Elizabeth become pregnant at nineteen by men they love deeply and to whom they are not married. Their lovers, Fonny and Richard, are poor black men in their early twenties with little formal education who are intelligent and proud. Richard, "a wild, unhappy boy," self-educated far beyond his station in life, is particularly fascinated by the African statuettes and totem poles in the Metropolitan Museum of Art.[131] Fonny, who is able to actualize his artistic impulses as a sculptor, appears to be Richard in more fortunate circumstances. Both Fonny and Richard are arrested for crimes they didn't commit by racist police, both cases of "mistaken" identity, although Fonny is intentionally set up by Officer Bell, while Richard's arrest is a matter of guilt by association. Both are held in New York City's Tombs, both are beaten, Richard because he refuses to sign a confession, Fonny because he refuses to be raped. Tish's encounter with Officer Bell echoes Elizabeth's encounter with the white policeman who tells her of Richard's arrest. The policeman gives Elizabeth a "lascivious smile" and says she "look[s] like a girl a man could rob a store for."[132] Like Tish, Elizabeth contains her fear and hatred. While Tish imagines transforming Officer Bell in a violent confrontation, Elizabeth fantasizes killing the policeman with his own weapons.[133]

Baldwin's revision of Elizabeth's story is evident in the opening scene of *If Beale Street Could Talk* when Tish tells Fonny that she is pregnant. It is this crucial decision that marks the central difference between the two stories. Elizabeth keeps her pregnancy secret from Richard, because she is afraid of adding to his burdens. Although Richard is released from jail, the humiliation of the experience is so deep that he commits suicide, never knowing that he will be a father. Because of the shame associated with an "illegitimate" child, Elizabeth, a virtual orphan, hides the truth from her aunt and her father, raising John in isolation until she meets Gabriel, who vows to protect her and her child. Gabriel, however, never lets Elizabeth forget her "transgression" and never loves John as his own child. John, on the other hand, is never told the truth of his origins, nor does he learn this truth by the end of the novel. As much as the novel centers on Gabriel and John's conflicted father-son relationship, it is also about the loss of fathers. Not only does John never know the father who might have loved him, but

Elizabeth is taken away from her father by an unloving aunt who, motivated by Christian duty, decides that Elizabeth's father is morally unfit to raise her. When Elizabeth looks at John, he reminds her of her father and the lost familial connection:

> . . . she thought how he would have loved his grandson, who was like him in so many ways. . . . At moments she thought she heard in John echoes, curiously distant and distorted of her father's gentleness, and the trick of his laugh—how he threw his head back and the years that marked his face fled away, and the soft eyes softened and the mouth turned upward at the corners like a little boy's mouth—and that deadly pride of her father's behind which he retired when confronted by the nastiness of other people."[134]

John's life is marked by the absence of a father and a grandfather. As John struggles to find his place in his family and in his church, the question of his identity remains hidden in the face of an unknown father and grandfather, an unknown history.

Elizabeth's story illustrates the destructiveness of a narrow Christian moralism. She is caught between the values of the church, represented by her aunt and by Gabriel, and by her own loving feelings for Richard and for her son. At the opening of "Elizabeth's Prayer" in *Go Tell*, Elizabeth wonders if she is being punished by God, because she does not truly repent her intimacy with Richard and the birth of her illegitimate child. What Elizabeth does repent is not telling Richard she was pregnant, not demanding his strength, and not trusting in their love: "She had made her great mistake with Richard in not telling him that she was going to have a child. Perhaps, she thought now, if she had told him everything might have been very different, and he would be living yet."[135] By creating Tish Rivers, Baldwin gives Elizabeth a chance to do it differently, but in order to do it differently Tish needs a family that is not brainwashed by a moral code that regards sexuality as sinful and separates "legitimate" from "illegitimate" children, a family that will support her rather than condemn her. Like Elizabeth, Tish does not want to add to her lover's burdens, but Tish has the wisdom that Elizabeth gains only in hindsight:

[Fonny] worries too much already, I don't want him to worry about me. In fact, I didn't want to say what I had to say. But I knew I had to say it. He had to know.

And I thought, too, that when he got over being worried, when he was lying by himself at night, when he was all by himself, in the very deepest part of himself, maybe, when he thought about it, he'd be glad. And that might help him.

I said, "Alonzo, we're going to have a baby."[136]

By rewriting Elizabeth's story, Baldwin rewrites the possibilities of John Grimes's life. John, born again on the threshing floor of the Fire Baptized, where "the light and the darkness had kissed each other,"[137] emerges with "the new voice God had given him."[138] Within the context of a Christian tradition that has caused so much guilt and personal suffering and has blinded John to the truth of his origins, his "new" prophetic voice is severely compromised. On the other hand, Tish's baby will know its father and its grandfather; its mother will not suffer guilt and uncertainty. Not burdened by the stigma of illegitimacy, this child will know its name, its history, and it will not need to be "born again" to speak with authority. Grandchild of Joseph and Sharon Rivers, child of Tish and the artisan-prophet, Fonny, this child heralds a new dispensation.

The Rivers family is Baldwin's dream of the American black family as a site of resistance, a model for oppressed people, a vanguard for a revolution which "begins first of all in the most private chamber of somebody's heart, in your consciousness."[139] The Rivers family is the fictional realization of the idea of the black family that Baldwin articulated in his 1973 interview with the *Black Scholar*:

The importance of the black family at this hour in the world's history is to be an example to all those other dispersed all over the world because in a sense, the American Negro has become a model. In a very funny way the vanguard of a revolution which is now global, and it does begin with what you call the black family. My brother in jail, my sister on the street and my uncle the junkie, but it's my brother and my sister and my uncle. So it's not a question of denying them, it's a question of saving them.[140]

In the world of *Beale Street* the family is the only "institution" that the individual can turn to in time of trouble; if the family fails, as in the case of the Hunts, there is nowhere else to go. The educational system in *Beale Street* is an instrument of socialization where "they are really teaching the kids to be slaves";[141] the legal system perpetuates the suffering of blacks through racist police and district attorneys; and the church prays to Jesus while the young men die of drugs and the young women turn to prostitution.[142] Although *Beale Street* is replete with helpful individuals (interestingly, they are all ethnic whites), a landlord, a lawyer, a grocer, and a restaurant owner, it is the black family upon whose shoulders rests the salvation of the black artist and of the race itself.

By placing the family at the center of black survival in America, Baldwin enters a national discourse on the black family initiated by the controversial *Moynihan Report* almost a decade earlier. Daniel Patrick Moynihan, then assistant secretary of labor, completed "The Negro Family: The Case for National Action" in March 1965. The report was the basis for a speech President Lyndon Johnson gave at Harvard's commencement that year which announced that the "next and most profound stage" of the civil rights struggle must go beyond the guarantee of legal justice for Negroes and address social and economic factors (jobs, housing, and family life) that continued to prevent Negroes from sharing an equal life in America.[143] Although Johnson's speech was considered a positive step by civil rights leaders, Moynihan's confidential sociological study on which it was based, and which was released later in 1965, became the center of controversy. The report focused on the intertwining effects of socioeconomic deprivation and family organization, arguing that "at the heart of the deterioration of the fabric of Negro society is the deterioration of the Negro family."[144] Deterioration was evident in that one-fourth of Negro marriages were dissolved, one-fourth of births were illegitimate, and one-fourth of households were led by women, argued Moynihan. He attributed the "failure of youth"—the disproportionate school failure and dropout rates, the higher rates of crime and drug addiction, and the alienation of Negro men from the family—to the "tangle of pathology" evident in the "matriarchy" of the Negro family. As a result, he claimed, many Negroes were not in the position to take advantage of the new opportunities now open to them following legal gains in civil rights. Moynihan believed the roots of the problem went back to slavery and to the position of the Negro male in urban society, to unemployment, and to poverty. The basic premises of the report were not new. Moynihan drew ideas from the 1930s work of the black sociologist E. Franklin Frazier, and the phrase "tangle of pathology" to describe a part of the urban Negro community came from the black psychologist Kenneth Clark.[145]

Although the ideas were not particularly new, they became controversial at this time in part because of distortions in the press coverage, problems with Moynihan's statistics, and, especially, concerns over the report's political application. Moynihan's main goal was to define the problem rather than propose solutions, and there was understandable concern among civil rights leaders and advocates that this report, with its emphasis on the black family as an obstacle to the improvement of conditions for black Americans, would lead to a politics of blaming the victim and justifying the status quo. Responding to the report, Whitney Young Jr. wrote that "the problems the Negro family faces today are caused by its economic disadvantages, which are in turn mainly the result of the discrimination and unequal treatment of today—not chiefly the result of slavery, as the report argues."[146] The description of the black family as pathological was also deeply insulting. The family structures that appeared "pathological" when compared to the norm of American society could also be understood as adaptations to the extreme conditions many blacks continued to face in America and a testament to African American resilience.[147] In an address in New York in 1965, Dr. Martin Luther King described the history of the Negro family's struggle to survive:

> The Negro family is scarred, it is submerged, but it struggles to survive. It is working against greater odds than perhaps any other family experienced in all civilized history. But it is winning. Step by step in agony it moves forward. Superficial people may superciliously expect it to function with all the graces and facility of more advantaged families. Their unfeeling criticism may hurt, but it will not halt progress.[148]

*If Beale Street Could Talk* responds to key elements of the *Moynihan Report* and the ensuing controversy. First, it repeats the fundamental assumption that the family is the defining social institution. *Beale Street* demonstrates the sentiment expressed by Martin Luther King that "the institution of the family is decisive in determining not only if a person has the capacity to love another individual but in the larger social sense whether he is capable of loving his fellow men collectively. The whole of society rests on this foundation for stability, understanding and social peace."[149] By making the Rivers family an agent of resistance rather than a microcosm of destructive social forces, the novel seems to reinforce the idea that families make society rather than vice versa. The centrality of the family in sustaining the individual is reinforced by the absence of organizations (such as the church, political groups, neighborhood groups, or social services) involved in Fonny's defense and the family's support. Second, *Beale Street* not only reflects the *Report*'s focus on the family as the defining institution of black life, but the idealized Rivers family reflects the image of the family headed by an employed adult male, a nuclear, patriarchal family, as the desired formation or norm. The importance of fatherhood as a central theme is demonstrated through the character of Joseph, who lives up to both his Old Testament and New Testament forebears as the good father who successfully raises a family in "Egypt" and who "fathers," in this case grandfathers, a savior. Also, it is his impending fatherhood that gives Fonny his will to survive the horror of imprisonment. Fonny tells Tish, "I've got to hold our baby in my arms. It's got to be. You keep the faith."[150]

While *Beale Street* seems to reinforce the *Moynihan Report*'s emphasis on the family as key to African American survival and progress, it clearly revises the association of "pathology" with the black family by placing the responsibility for Tish and Fonny's troubles on the pathology of racism. As the title of the novel suggests, Tish will give us an insider's view of her situation, one which challenges the view of the dominant discourse on the black family. Through the lens of Moynihan's sociology, Fonny's imprisonment and Tish's pregnancy are two examples of the statistics pointing to the "failure of youth" resulting from the "tangle of pathology" in poor, urban black families. Tish is aware of this vision of her troubles, a vision which makes her at best an object of pity and at worst a despised and rejected "other." Returning home after visiting Fonny in prison in the novel's opening scene, she thinks:

> I can't say to anybody in this bus, Look, Fonny is in trouble, he's in jail—can you imagine what anybody on this bus would say to me if they knew, from my mouth, that I love somebody in jail?—and I know he's never committed any crime and he's a beautiful person, please help me get him out. Can you imagine what anybody on this bus would say? What would you say? I can't say, I'm going to have this baby and I'm scared, too, and I don't want anything to happen to my baby's father, don't let him die in prison, please, oh, please! You can't say that. That means you can't really say anything. Trouble means you're alone.[151]

Tish describes her narrative challenge as the struggle to overcome the silence and isolation imposed on her by an unsympathetic audience. In her direct query, "What would you say?" she identifies her readers with the strangers on the bus, challenging them to acknowledge preconceived assumptions that her situation evokes. Later in the novel Fonny's sister, Adrienne, speaks in the voice of this assumed audience when she demands in contempt: "Who's going to raise this baby? And who is? Tish ain't got no education and God knows she ain't got nothing else and Fonny ain't never been worth a damn."[152] By this point the reader, however, knows enough of Tish's story to reject Adrienne's assessment of Tish and Fonny out of hand. The irony in Adrienne's harsh tone, the putative concern for the child combined with the contempt for the parents, exposes the mentality of blame underlying Adrienne's perspective, a perspective reflecting the dominant discourse on the troubles of poor black families.

Told from Tish's point of view, Fonny's imprisonment (and thereby his failure to marry Tish) is the direct result of a pathological white racism. The idea of pathology is squarely located in the character of Officer Bell, whose disturbed, predatory sexuality represents an American history and mythology that Baldwin found to be at the root of racism. Bell's character has antecedents in Baldwin's work in the characters of Lyle Britten in *Blues* for *Mister Charlie* and Jesse in "Going to Meet the Man," southern white males for whom violence against blacks is a means of sexual pleasure. In *Beale Street* Baldwin associates this perverse psyche with mainstream American heroes. Bell walks like John Wayne and his "eyes [are] as blank as George Washington's."[153] At the center of the "unblinking blue eye" is a "bottomless cruelty. . . . In that eye, you do not exist: if you are lucky."[154] If the eye sees you, you can become trapped in its gaze: "These eyes look only into the eyes of the conquered victim. They cannot look into any other eyes."[155] The final, climactic scene of part 1, "Troubled about My Soul," is a confrontation of gazes between Officer Bell and Tish:

> I looked into his eyes again. This may have been the very first time I ever really looked into a white man's eyes. It stopped me, I stood still. It was not like looking into a man's eyes. It was like nothing I knew, and—therefore—it was very powerful. It was seduction which contained the promise of rape. It was rape which promised debasement and revenge: on both sides. I wanted to get close to him, to enter into him, to open up that face and change it and destroy it, descend into the slime with him. Then, we would both be free: I could almost hear the singing.[156]

The encounter ends in a stalemate. Although Tish is not "seduced" by Bell, the scene suggests her powerlessness to change the conquering gaze except in her imagination; as Bell continues to stare at her she feels a "desolation" that she "had never felt before."[157] Bell's dehumanizing gaze represents the "pathology" of American racism that imprisons both victim and victimizer and threatens the integrity of the black family's intimate relationships. In order to set things right Tish would have to "descend into the slime." In *If Beale Street Could Talk* Baldwin reverses a discourse that blamed the "failure" of black youth on "pathology" in the family. Tish is able to resist Bell's seduction and survive the "desolation" of his dehumanizing gaze because of her family and her love for Fonny.

*Beale Street*'s emphasis on the role of the black family as the primary site of resistance to oppression raises a number of issues in relationship to what some critics described as an "evolution" in Baldwin's political thinking and to *Beale Street*'s relationship to the "protest novel." Craig Werner has argued that *Beale Street* "represents a major advance in [Baldwin's] analysis of the relationship between the system and the individual" because the "approved" characters have disassociated themselves from the system oppressing them by rejecting an "economic perception of value."[158] Donald B. Gibson was somewhat more cautious in noting Baldwin's "progress" from what he saw to be the "roundly conservative outlook" of *Go Tell It on the Mountain*. In *Beale Street* Baldwin explores racial oppression "from a broader social perspective than [in] any of the preceding novels"; however, Baldwin continues to be primarily a "moralist" and continues to see the source of oppression as "emanat[ing] from the human heart," argues Gibson.[159] It would seem that what changes in *Beale Street* is not so much Baldwin's analysis of the causes of racial oppression (or for that matter an analysis of its effects), which seem rather consistent throughout his work, but his response to it—his interest in representing how blacks can and must resist internalizing the racial gaze, act in solidarity, and confront what he called in "Everybody's Protest Novel" "that cage of reality bequeathed us at our birth."[160] The emphasis on resistance gives the novel a didactic quality that is mostly absent from his earlier fiction and places *Beale Street* in a signifying relationship to what Baldwin had pejoratively described back in 1948 to be the "protest novel." A number of early reviewers condemned the novel for its didactic qualities, which are evident in Baldwin's use of character types to represent opposing forces of good and evil. They claimed that Baldwin had lost his vision or commitment to present human beings in all their complexity. For the most part, however, those critics who condemned *Beale Street* as protest fiction, and thereby thought they were hoisting Baldwin on his own petard, did not have a clear understanding of his criticism of the genre.

The opening paragraphs of "Everybody's Protest Novel" frame Baldwin's criticism on moral grounds. Baldwin's complaint about the aesthetic quality of protest novels is introduced later as a logical corollary of their bankrupt morality. Using *Uncle Tom's Cabin* as the progenitor of American protest fiction, Baldwin critiques Stowe's novel for its "medieval morality," its "theological terror," which is achieved through a "catalogue of violence" that underscores Miss Ophelia's exclamation that slavery is "perfectly horrible." Baldwin argues that Stowe wishes to prove that slavery is wrong, but not to examine what moved her people to such deeds. Her motivation for condemning slavery has less to do with improving people's lives and relationships, and more to do with saving her own soul and her fear of the darkness. Stowe's "virtuous rage" has its origins in "a panic of being hurled into the flames, of being caught in traffic with the devil."[161] Furthermore, Stowe (and Miss Ophelia as her spokesperson) "could not embrace [blacks]. . . without purifying them."[162] Her medieval morality is basically antiblack and antiflesh, and like "those alabaster missionaries to Africa," she "cover[s] the nakedness of the natives, to hurry them into the pallid arms of Jesus."[163] It is this "medieval morality" which is most clearly the target of *Beale Street,* and Baldwin in a signifying move represents the "hot, self-righteous, fearful" spirit of *Uncle Tom's Cabin* in blackface, in the character of Mrs. Hunt. In Mrs. Hunt's self-dramatizing and darkly humorous scenes we see the "ostentatious parading of excessive and spurious emotion [which] is the mark of dishonesty, the inability to feel . . . [the] fear of life . . . the signal of secret and violent inhumanity, the mask of cruelty" that Baldwin roundly condemned in "Everybody's Protest Novel."[164] As Stowe makes Uncle Tom pay the price of darkness by robbing him of his humanity and divesting him of his sex,[165] Mrs. Hunt tries to "save" Frank and Fonny from their "blackness" while, in fact, condemning them.

*Beale Street* also signifies on what Baldwin called *Uncle Tom*'s "hard boiled descendants," especially Richard Wright's *Native Son.* One early reviewer clearly wanted the novel to be more like *Native Son* when he argued that *Beale Street* would have been more believable if the rape victim were white and of "good character," if Fonny weren't so good, if the families were poorer and the laws not so consciously malevolent.[166] Such response calls into question the success of Baldwin's signifying move—at least with some contemporary audiences—and reinforced the continuing power of *Native Son* to define what was "believable" protest. Mary Fair Burks notes similarities between *Beale Street* and *Native Son* but also misses the signifying import of Baldwin's novel. A good example is her claim that the white defense attorney, Hayward, is a stereotype, "lifted outright from Wright's *Native Son*." [167] In fact, if we compare Hayward to Wright's Max we can see that Baldwin has significantly reconfigured the character of Max and the lawyer-client relationship. In Wright's novel Max is the prototypical voice of left liberal authority who analyzes and interprets not only Bigger Thomas's actions, but Bigger's personality, as symptomatic of the larger social malignancy of racism. At the end of Wright's novel, when Bigger achieves a sense of individual identity by claiming responsibility for Mary Dalton's murder, Max can only recoil in fear. In contrast Baldwin's attorney, Hayward, does not carry the interpretive authority of Max; Hayward is the one who becomes educated in the process of defending Fonny. Hayward is also put at risk professionally as he attempts to counter the injustice of the legal system, and because of this process, he is brought into a relation of increased empathy and understanding with his client's family. Throughout *Beale Street* when Baldwin appears to be "repeating" certain characters or stories from his own or other works of fiction, he does so with a difference. It is this difference that many of the negative reviews, in particular, failed to perceive. The most important ways that *Beale Street* signifies on *Native Son* are the active involvement of the family in Fonny's defense, the missing "catalogue of violence" characteristic of the protest novel, and the reconstructed moral landscape as represented by the Rivers family through which Baldwin attempts to provide an alternate vision of socially engaged fiction.

Like the "protest novel," *Beale Street* does give a relentless picture of social injustice, and its characters represent types in a larger moral conflict. Yet the "protest" in *Beale Street* is radically redirected from the tradition associated with Wright and the earlier African American slave narrators, which set out to expose the horrors of slavery and segregation to a naive audience and argue for black humanity. *Beale Street* presents injustice as a given, a constant condition against which the characters must respond. Racism in the school, the workplace, and the justice system is assumed but not graphically demonstrated. For example, the reader never directly witnesses Fonny's or Daniel's arrests or their brutal treatment. The only incidents of racial conflict actually dramatized in Tish's narration are largely symbolic, the exchanges of gazes between Fonny and Bell and later between Tish and Bell. As a result, *Beale Street* assumes the conditions that earlier "protest" fiction explicates. On the other hand, the novel dramatizes a variety of responses to oppression through the conflict between the Rivers and the Hunt families over values, through Sharon's trip to Puerto Rico (which suggests that the poor need to make alliances across boundaries of race, ethnicity, and nation), through Fonny's sculpture, and through the personal commitment and faith represented by Tish and Fonny's relationship and by Tish's pregnancy. As a result, the novel moves beyond Miss Ophelia's proclamation that slavery is "perfectly horrible" and argues for a form of resistance that dramatically conflicts with the moral framework of the "protest novel."

*Beale Street* differs from much of the American and African American protest tradition in the way its "good" characters define their own ethics rather than appeal to those of a presumed middle-class or white reader. An important way that protest literature dramatizes social injustice is through depicting characters who become morally compromised because of overwhelming social forces that act upon them. Slavery, racism, and economic injustice may leave the protagonist very little choice but to violate sexual, social, or legal codes if the protagonist is to survive. In more traditional protest literature, when such violations occur (for example, the acts of theft that allow Wright to go North in *Black Boy*) they are accompanied by explanations of the extenuating circumstances and often by the protagonist's insistence on the psychic cost of the choice he had to make.[168] By contrast the discourse around sexuality and theft in *Beale Street* unapologetically confronts or as some, such as William Edward Farrison and Carolyn Wedin Sylvander, felt *affronts* conventional morality.[169] No shame is attached to Tish's unwed pregnancy or to stealing, except by those characters whose voices we are meant to discount as unloving and hypocritical. Sharon tells Tish, "you got enough on your mind without worrying about being a bad girl and all that jive-ass shit. I sure hope I raised you better than that."[170] When Frank Hunt despairs about where the money for Fonny's defense will come from, Joseph reveals that stealing is not new for him:

If we start to worrying about money now, man, we going to be fucked and we going to lose our children. That white man, baby, and may his balls shrivel and his ass-hole rot, he want you to be worried about the money. That's his whole game. But if we got to where we are without money, we can get further. I ain't worried about they money—they ain't got no right to it anyhow, they stole it from us—they ain't never met nobody they didn't lie to and steal from. Well, I can steal, too. And rob. How you think I raised my daughters? Shit.[171]

Small-scale theft is a way of life for Fonny and Tish as well as for Joseph. Fonny steals art supplies from his former vocational school, and Tish steals from Jewish shop keepers.[172] Given the description of the school as an institution of social control where kids are told they're dumb and required to make useless objects that no one wants, Fonny's appropriation of the school's supplies for his own artistic purpose suggests a political act of theft in which the master's tools are used to tear down the master's house. While theft is a useful (and necessary) tool of resistance for the Rivers, it is also risky and, in the case of Frank Hunt, indirectly results in death. Caught stealing from his job (in an effort to raise bail money for his son), Frank is fired and subsequently commits suicide. Given the novel's construction of the ethics of theft, one must conclude that Frank's suicide is the result of his being figuratively, as well as literally, wedded to the moralistic Alice Hunt.

In portraying the Rivers family as "heroic," Baldwin not only refuses to appeal to conventionally held moral values, but unsettles the image of the moral hero or antihero Uncle Tom/Bigger Thomas (whom he described as two sides of the same coin). The members of the Rivers family express their ethical commitments through their family loyalty and through their identification with the poor and the oppressed, not through a devotion to abstract national ideals, institutions, or traditional moral or legal codes. The familial values of *Beale Street* are at odds with the social order and the moral judgments which help sustain it. To this extent the novel does not follow the pattern or argument of a "protest novel." *Beale Street* affirms the possibilities of love and loyalty under conditions of oppression that have changed little over three hundred years. When Tish is reminded of the slave ships while riding the New York subway, she is historicizing the present to suggest the continuity of oppression in black life. While a standard argument of the protest novel is that racism and injustice are reprehensible because they contribute to the demoralization of individuals, Baldwin turns this argument on its head. Resisting racial and economic injustice involves resisting the moralizing discourses that implicate subjects in their own victimization.

If Baldwin's re-vision of the moral code of the protest novel makes *Beale Street* a radical departure from its predecessors in the protest tradition, its idealization of the family as a potential site of resistance makes the novel much less radical from a feminist point of view. *Beale Street* reinforces a heterosexist view of the world that seems at odds with Baldwin's earlier novels as well as with his last novel, *Just Above My Head*. The heterosexism of Baldwin's fourth novel was celebrated by some. Louis H. Pratt's analysis of *Beale Street*—as the first Baldwin novel where love is finally "fulfilled"—links the loving family with a norm of heterosexuality (and patriarchy). According to Pratt, the failure to identify with fathers in Baldwin's work results in the homosexual and bisexual tendencies of earlier Baldwin protagonists, including John Grimes (*Go Tell*), David (*Giovanni's Room*), Rufus, Vivaldo, and Eric (*Another Country*), and Leo (*Train*). Fonny's heterosexuality is, according to Pratt, the result of loving family relationships:

> But in contrast to these earlier novels, not only does the family unit in *If Beale Street* function as a protective shield for Fonny, but it also exerts a dominant influence on his sexuality. From the very beginning of the novel we are aware that Fonny idealizes Frank, and he is quick to understand that the elder Hunt has gained the strength to endure the unbearable life with Fonny's mother solely through the father's immeasurable love for his son. And, unlike the gamut of male characters that dominate Baldwin's previous novels, Fonny enjoys a mutual and abiding love for his "protective" family. Because of the peace and security which this family affords him, Fonny is able to ward off the homosexual advances made toward him during his penal confinement. He cherishes the memories of his intimacies with Tish, and he yearns to return to his heterosexual role as husband and lover. Consistent with this point of view,

Baldwin's depiction of the heterosexual relationship suggests a reversal of the earlier portrayals in *Go Tell*. . . . The act of copulation becomes a movement toward life; it becomes a creative act which ultimately celebrates the continuity of the human race.[173]

Pratt's analysis of *Beale Street* was written before Baldwin's last novel, which combines the loving family, the "good" father, and the homosexual son. *Just Above My Head* suggests that Pratt has misread the trajectory of Baldwin's understanding of homosexuality and the family. All the same, Pratt's reading of *Beale Street* is understandable, considering the strictly negative depictions of homosexuality in this novel and the unironic and unproblematic use of terms such as "faggot" in Tish's narration.

The heterosexism of *Beale Street*, however, is somewhat deceptive. Within this world of heterosexual love, Baldwin appropriates the female voice and body to explore his true desires, which ultimately have very little to do with women or heterosexuality, but are connected with a community where men love and respect one another. While I would agree with those critics who felt that Tish's voice was generally believable, there are times when the mask slips. Tish, whose lack of beauty, breasts, and hips makes her the least feminine of the female characters, voices not only her love for Fonny, but Baldwin's love for men. An example is the set piece that follows Fonny and Tish's evening in the Spanish restaurant where Tish observes Fonny with other men and claims that she had "never [before] seen the love and respect that men can have for each other."[174] The long (and fairly incoherent) meditation on gender relationships which follows this statement indicates the problems Baldwin had thinking through gender issues from a female perspective. The passage sounds neither like the nineteen-year-old Tish nor like Baldwin at his best, although it is recognizable as the author speaking directly to the reader. Tish-Baldwin tries to explain why most women feel threatened by the "warmth and energy" of the male bond in "this fucked up time and place."[175] Yet over the course of the paragraph it is impossible to determine what "place and time" have to do with the supposedly illusory threat that most women are said to feel when observing scenes of male "love and respect." The narrator proceeds to posit a series of binary relationships, such as men are noisy, outward, and open, while women are secretive and silent. Baldwin-Tish claims that it's harder for men to grow up, and it takes longer for men to grow up than for women to grow up. Women "must watch and guide" while men "must lead."[176] Nowhere in the passage is there a recognition that women also have relationships with each other outside the family, that there is also a society of women who "love and respect" each other and who have "a language which men cannot decipher." At one point the narrator appears to posit women's resentment of men's society as a response to patriarchy: "I suppose that the root of the resentment—a resentment which hides a bottomless terror—has to do with the fact that a woman is tremendously controlled by what the man's imagination makes of her—literally, hour by hour, day by day; so she becomes a woman. But a man exists in his own imagination, and can never be at the mercy of a woman's."[177] At this point Baldwin comes close to making the same assertion about the formation of gender hierarchies that he had long made about race and sexual orientation—whites invented blacks, heterosexuals invented homosexuals, and now, perhaps, men invented women. Yet the narrator does not seem to be interested in deconstructing the false difference between men and women for the purpose of exposing male dominance and of liberating women (which would be comparable to his use of this strategy to analyze race and sexual orientation). Instead he reappropriates the value of "imagination" from its "false" association with the feminine and suggests that imagination is rightfully a "male" quality. Tish-Baldwin continues:

> Anyway, in this fucked up time and place, the whole thing becomes ridiculous when you realize that women are supposed to be more imaginative than men. This is an idea dreamed up by men, and it proves exactly the contrary. The truth is that dealing with the reality of men leaves a woman very little time, or need, for imagination. And you can get very fucked up, here, once you take seriously the notion that a man who is not afraid to trust his imagination (which is all that men have ever trusted) is effeminate. It says a lot about this country, because, of course if all you want to do is make money, the very last thing you need is imagination. Or women, for that matter: or men.[178]

In *Beale Street* Baldwin appropriates the female voice (and body) to celebrate the family and to bear the black child who heralds a new dispensation where male love and respect will flourish and where females will be both the vehicles and (supposedly) the beneficiaries of this new order of men.

The black men of *Beale Street* are victims or survivors, or both. They are relatively weak, like Frank and Daniel who perish, or relatively strong, like Joseph and Fonny who survive. The black women, on the other hand, are good and evil, and it is precisely their relationship to men that define their position in *Beale Street*'s moral spectrum. To the extent that *Beale Street* employs the feminine to represent a corrupt society and distorted moral values, the novel repeats the moral dynamics of much of the tradition of classic male American literature. Mrs. Hunt and her "two camellias," otherwise referred to as the "three hags," represent the feminine and as such also represent social conformity, religious hypocrisy, and white supremacy. Their predecessors include characters such as Mark Twain's Miss Watson or Aunt Polly, who represent the antithesis of male freedom and imagination. In contrast to the "feminine" Mrs. Hunt and her two daughters (women who have wardrobes and good looks) are Mrs. Rivers, whom Tish describes as a "kind of strange woman,"[179] and her two daughters, Ernestine, who has rejected the "vanity" of her youth, and small, dark, frog-eyed Tish (the author in drag). In order to celebrate the family of man, Baldwin must banish the debased "feminine" and create a family of "strange women," antifeminine women whose power is employed, as Hortense Spillers argued, in the service of men.

# 4 The Singer's Legacy: *Just Above My Head*

Every writer has only one tale to tell, and he has to find a way of telling it until the meaning becomes clearer and clearer, until the story becomes at once more narrow and larger, more and more precise and more and more reverberating.

—"An Interview with James Baldwin," David C. Estes, 1986

Just Above My Head (JAMH), published in 1979, five years after *If Beale Street Could Talk,* is Baldwin's last novel. It is also his longest and most ambitious work, 597 pages in the Dial Press edition. *JAMH* spans a time period of about thirty years, from the mid-forties to the mid-to-late seventies, and follows the lives of four main characters and three generations of the Montana family. The central foci are the life of Arthur Montana, who begins his career as a gospel singer, then gains worldwide fame as the Soul Emperor, and the life of his brother, Hall, who tells the story two years after Arthur's death. The other main characters, Julia and Jimmy Miller (family friends and later lovers of Hall and Arthur, respectively), figure prominently in the events and help Hall tell the story. The complexity of the novel is not simply a matter of the number of characters and stories or the time and space it traverses (locations include Harlem, various points in the American South, San Francisco, Paris, London, and Abidjan), but also its range of thematic and artistic concerns.

*Just Above My Head* continues to explore the relationship between the black artist and the family and the artist's role in the struggle to resist oppression. In *Just Above My Head,* however, Baldwin revises the "price of success" theme as developed in *Tell Me How Long the Train's Been Gone.* While *Train* explores the effects of "success" on an individual black actor, who has made it on "the great white way," *JAMH* explores the effects of success on a black vocal artist whose medium is a specifically black cultural form. Thus, the meditation on success in *JAMH* takes on implications beyond the life of the individual artist. Arthur Montana rises to international fame singing and signifying on the musical inheritance of his ancestors; yet somewhere along the way he loses the intimate sustaining relationship with his audience and thus loses his "song" and, ultimately, his life. Among other things, Arthur's career demonstrates the way the commercial success of black music alters the dynamic relationship between performer and community, which is at the heart of the gospel impulse.

In addition, *Just Above My Head* continues Baldwin's project of passing on the resources of a resistant and enduring black culture to the next generation. As Hall says about his brother's life: "I am their only key to their uncle, the vessel which contains, for them, his legacy. Only I can read this document for them."[1] *JAMH* combines a celebration of black cultural forms with a cautionary tale, making the novel a more nuanced treatment of the individual's relationship to his or her cultural legacy than Baldwin developed in *Beale Street.* As Baldwin said in an interview, Arthur's legacy is "an enormous question. The question is: What is history, what has it made of us, and where is a witness to this journey?"[2] By reintroducing the figure of the homosexual black artist as the medium through which the legacy is transmitted, Baldwin complicates the cultural project he formulated in *Beale Street* and reflects on his own challenge as a black artist, identified as homosexual, attempting to write himself into the American and African American literary traditions. *Just Above My Head* is an extraordinarily self-reflective and self-reflexive novel, which not only revisits Baldwin's earlier fiction and nonfiction, but also represents Baldwin's effort to shape his own personal legacy as well as to challenge historical legacies.

As with all of James Baldwin's work from the mid-sixties onward, *Just Above My Head* received mixed reviews. A few were notably enthusiastic. Edmund White judged *JAMH* as "the work of a born storyteller at the height of his powers."[3] Others, however, described the novel pejoratively as "swollen," as "curiously static," even "stillborn," and its language as "pretentious" or "polemical."[4] Although a number of reviews portrayed the novel as flawed, the more negative ones still gave *JAMH* credit for containing memorable scenes and powerful writing.[5] Homophobia continued to be an important factor in Baldwin's reception as the tone of antipathy in some of the reviews that focused on the novel's homosexual scenes and themes revealed.[6] Yet the novel also received mixed reviews in the gay press and among critics who were sympathetic to gay concerns.[7] There was recognition that *JAMH* was Baldwin's most ambitious portrayal of black family and communal life since *Go Tell It on the Mountain,* but disagreement on the strengths and weaknesses of this portrayal.[8] Some reviewers, as well as later critics, have argued that the narrative point of view is a major flaw of the novel, that Hall is not an effective vehicle to tell his brother's story, and as a result Arthur's character is underdeveloped and the causes of his demise are insufficiently explained.[9]

Among the early reviewers only James Campbell and Eleanor Traylor made reference to the importance of music in the novel. Campbell claimed that music provides a "second voice," one that supplements Hall's imperfect memory and provides access to the inner life of a people: "Jazz, blues, gospel constitute the vocabulary in which black history is written. It is a form of memory which outwits the white 'nightmare called history.'"[10] Thus, in Campbell's analysis, the magnificence of the novel's conception is its effort to reimagine "history" through black oral tradition and thereby reinvent a literary genre.[11] Eleanor Traylor provided insight into *JAMH*'s relationship to Baldwin's work as a whole, stressing the continuity of narrative voice and character in his work. She described Hall as the most recent "Baldwin narrator-witness" and Arthur as the most fully developed of Baldwin's "blues boys" who struggle to become "blues men." Her description of the narrative voice is particularly acute. Hall's imagination, while blind "to manifest ambiguities within himself," is "embracive" and "epic" in scope and "musical in its presentation." Hall "hears his brother's life as one melodic theme off which he riffs the personal history of those whose rhythms lend that theme both assonance and dissonance. Off the melody of Arthur's life, he also riffs the history of an era as the details of that history affect the interiority of a cultural community."[12] Hall becomes a blues hero in his own right, because through a feat of will he narrates his story from the "abyss" while "encouraging us in celebration of our possibilities."[13] Placing *JAMH* at the center of an African American storytelling tradition, Traylor's essay ends with a "vision" of Baldwin in the center of a "House of Tales," where he dwells with Wright, Ellison, and the ancestors. Traylor's sense of *JAMH* as a storyteller's novel told in a musical mode is a particularly useful approach that I wish to expand upon later in this chapter.

## I.

In various interviews Baldwin spoke of *Just Above My Head* in both autobiographical and autotherapeutic terms. It is a novel derived from Baldwin's memories of personal and cultural experience and from his earlier representations of those experiences in his writing. In many respects *Just Above My Head* is the culmination of a long autobiographical quest. Baldwin described it as a novel that had been with him a long time.[14] He noted its relationship to *Go Tell It on the Mountain,* "Sonny's Blues," and *Tell Me How Long the Train's Been Gone,* all of which, in retrospect, could be seen as rehearsals for this novel. Two years before *JAMH* was published, he predicted that the novel would be the end of a "long apprenticeship."[15] In a later interview at the time *JAMH* was released in the U.S. he said, "I've finally come full circle. From *Go Tell It on the Mountain* to *Just Above My Head* sums up something of my experience—it's difficult to articulate—that sets me free to go someplace else."[16] When *JAMH* was released in Europe, Baldwin again spoke at some length about it, expressing the importance of music as embodying his personal journey and the journey of a people. Once again he referred to *JAMH* as "coming full circle" from *Go Tell:*

I grew up with music, you know, much more than with any other language. In a way the music I grew up with saved my life. Later in my life I met musicians, and it was a milieu I moved in much more than the literary milieu, because when I was young there wasn't any. So that I watched and learned from various musicians in the streets.

When I was under age I was listening to the very beginning of what was not yet known as bebop. And I was involved in the church, because I was a preacher and the son of a preacher. And all of that has something to do with *Just Above My Head,* with an affirmation which is in that life and is expressed by that music, which I have not found in that intensity anywhere else. The book has something to do with the journey of a people from one place to another, a kind of diaspora which was unrecognized as yet, and in that journey what has happened to them and what has happened to the world as a result of their journey and is still happening to the world. They brought themselves a long way out of bondage by means of the music which *Just Above My Head* is at bottom about. So in a sense the novel is a kind of return to my own beginnings, which are not only mine, and a way of using that beginning to start again. In my own mind I come full circle from *Go Tell It on the Mountain* to *Just Above My Head,* which is a question of a quarter of a century really. And something else now begins. I don't know where I go from here yet.[17]

For Baldwin the potentially autotherapeutic relationship between a musician and his song parallels that between a writer and his book. When Baldwin speaks of the relationship between his life and his work and the ways in which the two interact and transform each other, one is reminded of his musician characters for whom musical expression is a difficult but necessary lifeline of love and self-expression that connects the self to others. In a 1986 interview David Estes asked Baldwin about his use of autobiographical material in his writing. Baldwin described his writing as a process of self-discovery that changed his relationship to the past and thus changed his relationship to the self and to the future. Writing was both "terrifying" and liberating; it had taught him more about the "frightened child" he was, and thereby liberated him from his "self-image" and allowed him to move into a "larger space."

> When I was writing *Just Above My Head,* I'd never been more frightened in my life either as a man or as a writer. Yet I knew it had to be done. That book is not directly autobiographical at all, but it is autobiographical on a much deeper level. There are elements which you can place in my life. . . . Yet there are no direct, one-on-one relationships between my life and the lives of the people in that book. It truly is a composite. A novel or anything I write begins with an incoherent disturbance, and you can't run away from it. You have to sit and wait and see what it is. It may be the things I've forgotten or think I've forgotten that suddenly begin to stir.[18]

Baldwin's reflections on *Just Above My Head* lead one to ponder the precise nature of its relationship to *Go Tell It on the Mountain.* What does it mean to "come full circle"? His comments also lead one to ponder his uses of autobiographical material. How is a "composite" of an author's experience autobiographical on a "much deeper level" than a book whose characters represent a more direct correlation to the life of the author? In what way does an autotherapeutic approach to writing imply a continual revision in the representation of an autobiographical self?

To "come full circle" suggests completion rather than simple repetition. *JAMH* returns to the world of *Go Tell,* to Harlem, to the church and black religious experience, but with important differences in perspective and scope. In one sense *JAMH* fulfills the promise that the autobiographical character, John Grimes, makes at the end of *Go Tell.* The last words of the novel are "'I'm ready,' John said, 'I'm coming. I'm on my way.'"[19] John's words imply that his apparent religious conversion, somewhat paradoxically, allows him to move outward into the larger world of experience. Through an intense immersion into a religious-cultural experience, represented by his fall to the threshing floor, John Grimes locates something which sustains him in the black life he had despised and from which he wished to escape. John's words suggest that he has learned to use the contradictions of his experience to bridge the gap between the world of his father's house and the larger world he wishes to enter. John's fictional experience parallels that of James Baldwin the writer who saw *Go Tell It on the Mountain* as a novel which had to be written before he could go on to other things. In Baldwin's subsequent work, although he returns many times to the subject of the church and black religious experience (*Amen Corner, Blues for Mister Charlie, The Fire Next Time, Tell Me How Long the Train's Been Gone,* and *If Beale Street Could Talk*), he does so, for the most part, only to critique its limitations. It is not until *Just Above My Head* that Baldwin again treats black religious experience with the complexity of *Go Tell.*[20] If John Grimes finds a way to use his religious experience to empower the self, in *JAMH* Baldwin expands upon John's personal vision to find a way to show how black religious experience has helped to sustain a people. By focusing on the life of a famous gospel singer, and the connection between music, preaching, and political action that informed the Civil Rights movement, Baldwin is able to examine black religious experience from a broader context than the storefront church of his youth. In *JAMH* the "church" is wherever Arthur is singing. The church comes to embody the world and to represent both the success and failure of human love.

*Just Above My Head* is not just a return to the world of the black church and Harlem expressed in *Go Tell* and other works; it is part of Baldwin's ongoing effort to create a form of self-representation that does justice to the complexity of African American subjectivity. Baldwin continually sought ways to fashion autobiographical material into forms that would be representative of the larger African American cultural experience. In *Go Tell* Baldwin sought to achieve this goal by embedding the story of John Grimes in the stories of his father, mother, and aunt. In *Tell Me How Long the Train's Been Gone* Baldwin sought to achieve this goal by revising the structure of ascent and descent in African American autobiography (see chapter 2). However, in both *Go Tell* and *Train* there is a single "autobiographical" character whose experience and situation has obvious referents to Baldwin's own life, John Grimes and Leo Proudhammer, respectively. Although John and Leo represent different periods of Baldwin's life, each represents a relatively familiar model of the self, that is, the model of the divided self or double-consciousness. Both characters are driven by inner conflicts which have their source in the structures of American racism and sexual fear. In his last novel, however, Baldwin revises this familiar model of the black self. In *Just Above My Head* there is no single character like John or Leo that the reader can readily identify with Baldwin's own experience and positionality. Instead there are four characters, each of whom represent important elements of the author's life: Hall, Arthur, Julia, and Jimmy. If John Grimes and Leo Proudhammer are representations of Baldwin's "divided self," the four characters of *JAMH* suggest a complex model of self-representation that gives play to the multiple positions Baldwin inhabited.

The names of the four main characters suggest an autobiographical relationship to their creator. Jimmy is the name by which Baldwin's friends commonly addressed him. Arthur is Baldwin's middle name. The name Julia alliterates with James or Jimmy. The name Hall rhymes with the accented syllable of Baldwin. Hall suggests a passageway or connection from one place to another, symbolically indicating that Hall's attempt to face his brother's life and death is equally an attempt to face himself. As Baldwin repeatedly argued, one cannot know or embrace the "self" without knowing or embracing the "other," because the "other" is always part of the "self." Hall's life and narrative is informed by the lives and stories of Arthur, Julia, and Jimmy. Together, the four characters comprise Baldwin's complex self-representation.[21]

Through the character of Julia Miller, Baldwin refigures his troubled relationship with his father and his early church experience. Julia, like Baldwin, is a child preacher abused by the daddy she loves. Like Baldwin, she loses faith in the God of her childhood but comes to embrace a vision of human love as she is transformed from a fundamentalist preacher to a modern griot or "obeah woman," as Hall calls her. Her personal disappointment at being childless reflects Baldwin's own disappointment at never having a family and children of his own, and her special role at the center of an extended family compensates for this loss and parallels Baldwin's relationship to his nephews and nieces.[22]

Through the character of Hall Montana, Baldwin explores his desire for safety and gives voice to his own meditations on the problems and deceptions of memory. Hall, like Baldwin, is an older brother who feels tremendous responsibility for his younger siblings. As Arthur's manager, trained in advertising and public relations, Hall is responsible for his brother's public image. Similar to the way in which Leo Proudhammer's public persona compromises his sense of self, Hall's relationship to Arthur has been compromised by his role as Arthur's publicist. Hall says that he has been so busy "covering up for Arthur, strong-arming the press, flying half over the goddam globe—I hardly had time to cry, much less talk."[23] Hall, who is still in "show business,"[24] has created an apparently "safe" (if artificial) life with the resources of his brother's singing and suffering existence. (He bought his house in the Bronx during one of Arthur's "more spectacular years.") Up to this point Hall's "private" story of Arthur's life, and his own, has been constrained by "public" demands. Hall now carries the heavy responsibility of passing on his brother's legacy to his children (much as Baldwin saw himself inheriting the legacy of those black writers and musicians who came before him). Passing on the legacy requires Hall to "talk," to reveal the "private" which threatens Hall's sense of safety.

Through the characters of Arthur and Jimmy, Baldwin explores his homosexuality and its effects on his life as a black creative artist and as a celebrity. Arthur, like Baldwin, is the gifted singer-artist whose song is an expression of his love. Like Baldwin, Arthur comes under criticism for his homosexuality by those he most wishes to represent. At the height of his career Arthur gets "lost" from his song and from those he loves. Since he is filled with self-doubt, his life becomes increasingly chaotic and self-destructive. (Arthur's death at thirty-nine occurs at the same age Leo Proudhammer suffers a heart attack.) However Jimmy, Arthur's accompanist and devoted lover, survives. Unabashed about his homosexuality and unashamed of his love for Arthur, Jimmy is a tougher, more resilient personality than his lover. Like the author, he has come home from a worldwide pilgrimage (to the places he and Arthur performed together, which are all places Baldwin lived and visited) to write a book about his and Arthur's life. Jimmy is the Baldwin who survived the personal and political crises of the sixties, who weathered the storm, who came to express himself and his sexuality more freely, and who is not intimidated by the judgment of others. At the end of the novel, Jimmy's unfinished book is another reminder of the limitation of language to express the totality of human experience. *JAMH* may be the culmination of Baldwin's quest to represent the complexity of his experience in words, but it is not and can never be the whole story.

Julia, Hall, Arthur, and Jimmy are a composite of the author's attitudes, experiences, fears, and hopes. They also contribute to the self-reflexive quality of *JAMH* in that all four characters are engaged in interrelated storytelling-performance actions. Some of the negative criticism *JAMH* received, about its variation from literary to vernacular language style, its repetitiousness, its "melange" of themes, and its "lack of plot" reflect expectations of formal unity that readers bring to modern novels. On the other hand, if we approach *JAMH* as a novel that foregrounds elements of the storytelling tradition we can better appreciate its structure and ethos. In "The Storyteller," Walter Benjamin makes a distinction between the aesthetics and values of storytelling and those of the novel. The art of storytelling originates in oral cultures long predating the art of the novel and is based on the value of sharing experience. According to Benjamin, a storyteller is often a traveler who has returned home from a journey to report his and others' experience in the vernacular to a particular community. He is a "craftsman" who is "rooted in the people," and his story contains something "useful"; a storyteller provides "counsel" for his listeners. "The storyteller takes what he tells from experience—his own or that reported by others. And he in turn makes it the experience of those who are listening to his tale," says Benjamin.[25] Thus, he often leaves his "tracks" in his stories. For example, the storyteller may appear as a character in the story, reporting his experience to an audience of listeners. Storytelling comes from the oral tradition in which "the perfect narrative is revealed through the layers of a variety of retellings."[26] Thus, storytelling is by nature continuous, epic, revisionary, and open ended. As Benjamin says, "Actually there is no story for which the question as to how it continued would not be legitimate."[27]

In contrast to the storyteller, Benjamin says, "the novelist has isolated himself." The novelist is the solitary individual who can no longer counsel himself or others. He carries "the incommensurable to extremes in the representation of human life."[28] The novel strives for unity, for an expression of "the meaning of life," and with such insight reaches an end. To argue that Baldwin employs storytelling techniques is not meant to suggest that *JAMH* is a story rather than a novel. Certainly the attention to realistic detail and the extended descriptions of the characters' interior lives and motives are all elements of the novelistic form. Moreover, *JAMH* does strive for "unity" and for an expression of the "meaning of life," goals Benjamin attributes to the novel. However, by importing elements associated with storytelling, Baldwin opens up the novel form and demonstrates the use of storytelling in sustaining individuals and creating communities. *JAMH* is a novel about the power and process of storytelling.

Black music is the vernacular language of *JAMH,* and the author leaves his "tracks" in the many singing, preaching, and storytelling performances of his characters. In an essay for the *New Edinburgh Review,* published the same year as *JAMH,* Baldwin discusses black music (in this case jazz, although his analysis could be applied to spirituals and blues as well) as a coded language that "redeems[s] a history unwritten and despised" in order to "checkmate the European notion of the world." Baldwin describes jazz as "an exceedingly laconic description of black circumstances: and, as a way, by describing these circumstances, of overcoming them. It was necessary that the description be laconic: the iron necessity being that the description not be overheard."[29] In *JAMH* it is the "laconic" Arthur Montana whose song carries this hidden history (or what Michel Foucault would call "subjugated knowledge"). Certainly Arthur Montana represents many of the qualities that Walter Benjamin ascribes to the storyteller. To use Benjamin's terms, Arthur's music is "useful," it is "rooted in the people," and it provides "counsel." Like the storyteller's story, Arthur's song comes from his own experience. Arthur must "live the song he sings." He tells Hall, "When you sing, . . . you can't sing outside the song. You've got to be the song you sing. You've got to make a confession."[30] Like the storyteller's art, Arthur's song belongs to a communal tradition of which his song is a particular retelling shaped by the expectations of his listeners. Comparing Arthur's relationship to his song as the relationship of the preacher to his sermon, Jimmy tells Hall: "The sermon does not belong to the preacher. He, too, is a kind of talking drum. The man who tells the story isn't making up a story. He's listening to us, and can only give back, to us, what he hears: from us."[31]

Arthur is not the only figure of the African American singer-storyteller in *JAMH*. His death makes the focus of the novel less Arthur's story per se than the challenge of passing on his story (and the stories of the other characters as well) to the next generation. The role of storyteller in *JAMH* is shared by Julia, the child preacher, who as an adult is "more in the pulpit than when she was preaching";[32] by Jimmy, the piano player turned author; and of course, most significantly, by brother Hall, the first-person narrator. Julie Nash points out that *JAMH* is centered on Hall's response to Arthur's tragedy and claims that Hall becomes a blues hero in his own right. The novel is about the communication of Hall's pain, not the objective fact of Arthur's demise, she argues. Nash goes on to illustrate how "Baldwin incorporates this blues style throughout the novel by repeating and italicizing words or phrases for emphasis. As a result, his prose sounds like the gospel and blues songs that are interspersed with the text."[33] Hall's voice, from the opening paragraph, reflects the "spontaneous and emotional qualities along with the structural elements of blues."[34] Nash's observations are perceptive, although Hall's voice does not always exhibit the compact brevity one associates with the blues. Yet the opening of *JAMH* can be described, as Nash says, as a "blues moan." Hall describes his brother's death as though it had just happened:

> The damn'd blood burst, first through his nostrils, then pounded through the veins in his neck, the scarlet torrent exploded through his mouth, it reached his eyes and blinded him, and brought Arthur down, down, down, down, down.
>
> . . . He had been found lying in a pool of blood—why does one say pool?—a storm, a violence, a miracle of blood: his blood, my brother's blood, my brother's blood, my brother's blood! My blood, my brother's blood, my blood, Arthur's blood, soaking into the sawdust of some grimy men's room in the filthy basement of some filthy London pub.[35]

In addition to setting a blues tone, the opening passage suggests, especially with the repetition of the term "blood," the novel's interlocking thematic concerns: the binding ties of kinship, racial, and sexual experience. The "bloody" death scene connotes a terrible internal violence (psychological as well as physical) that kills Arthur and seriously wounds Hall's psyche. Arthur's death in a pool of blood takes on metaphorical dimensions similar to Leo Proudhammer's heart attack, reflecting a crisis in black life. Hall's narrative becomes an effort to stop the blood loss, to repair the wound, and to make vivid the ties of kinship. By reconstituting Arthur's life in memory and story Hall hopes to end his own nightmares and sense of isolation.

Hall experiences Arthur's death as an acute loss of self: "Everything becomes unanswerable, unreadable, in the face of an event yet more unimaginable than one's own death. It is one's death."[36] After receiving the news that Arthur has died, Hall tells us he collapsed while looking into a mirror: "I looked into my eyes: they were someone else's eyes."[37] The profound disassociation that Hall experiences immediately following his brother's death drives home the extent to which Hall's sense of identity is tied to his brother. Hall had thought of Arthur's life paternalistically as an extension and a fulfillment of his own life. Hall had been Arthur's protector and promoter. At the same time Hall received a sense of vicarious pleasure in Arthur's song, there was a limit to what he wished to know of his brother's private life, of the suffering that produced the song. Hall's more conventional life had kept him "outside" the danger, passion, happiness, and sorrow of his brother's experience. That Arthur's death remains terribly unresolved for Hall two years later is evident in his nightmares. Hall dreams that his ceiling has dropped to crush him; it is "just above my head."[38] Then he dreams he is pursuing Arthur across a changing landscape, trying unsuccessfully to locate him and to rescue him. Like Leo Proudhammer and Tish Rivers, Hall Montana begins his narrative at a point of personal crisis. Yet the crisis for Hall is more than personal; it involves his role as the keeper of Arthur's legacy. Up to this point Hall has not really spoken of his brother's death to his family and close friends. Hall's silence has been a "trap" for the others as well as himself: "they can't talk about it until I can talk."[39]

The narrative voice of *JAMH* represents the communal ethos of the oral storytelling tradition, an ethos consistent with blues and gospel. Hall needs both Julia and Jimmy to help him begin and complete the daunting task of telling Arthur's story. There are extended passages where Julia and Jimmy report their experience and perspectives directly. Their assistance is first figured in book 1, "Have Mercy." The scene of Hall's personal anguish and isolation is followed by a family gathering at Julia's house. The family gathering, which is the center episode of book 1, provides Hall with the courage and the context to break his silence and to share his memories with Julia's and Jimmy's memories and to answer his son's question about his uncle Arthur.

The gathering at Julia's house takes on an almost ritualistic quality of parents passing on a sacred heritage to their children through music, dancing, and stories of the past. Echoing a scene that describes a happy family moment in *Tell Me How Long the Train's Been Gone*, parents and children dance together. The dance evokes the continuity of generations and is a prayer for the future. Hall says,

> How strange and beautiful—it must be one of the few real reasons for remaining alive, of desiring to—to dance with your daughter, your son, and your wife; touching, really digging it, laughing, and keeping the beat, free. Odessa is a very aggressive dancer, or so, at least, she is with her father, whom she is using as rehearsal for an event of which she, as yet, knows nothing. Ruth is very gentle with her son, who is at once very mocking and gentle with her—he, too, is involved in a rehearsal. Yesterday, we were the children, Ruth and I and Julia: we're the old folks now, and this is what will happen to Tony and Odessa, please God be willing.[40]

This ritual is a vehicle of both cultural heritage and gender rules. It is a rehearsal of a family's heterosexual expectations for their children. Significantly, the dance is disrupted when Tony takes his father aside and raises the issue of his uncle Arthur's sexuality. In the conversation that follows the reasons for Hall's silence about Arthur become evident. The kids at Tony's school have been talking about Arthur, and Tony wants to know if what they say about Arthur is true: "They say—he was a faggot."[41] Hall's response to his son, while not dishonest, is defensive and, I would argue, misleading, revealing, at the very least, his discomfort with Arthur's sexuality. By confessing his own brief homosexual experience, Hall seeks to identify with his brother, but in effect misrepresents the permanence of Arthur's homosexual desire. The passage which follows has been interpreted to show both Hall's strengths and weaknesses as a father and a brother:[42]

"Okay. Your uncle was my brother, right? And I loved him. Okay? He was a very—lonely—man. He had a very strange—life. I think that—he was a very great singer."

Tony's eyes do not leave my face. I talk into his eyes.

"Yes. I know a lot of men who loved my brother—your uncle—or who thought they did. I know two men—your uncle—Arthur loved—"

"Was one of those men Jimmy?"

Lord. "You mean—Julia's brother?"

"Yes."

Good Lord. "Yes."

Tony nods.

"I know—before Jimmy—Arthur slept with a lot of people—mostly men, but not always. He was young, Tony. Before your mother, I slept with a lot of women"—I do not believe I can say this, his eyes do not leave my face—"mostly women, but—in the army—I was young, too—not always. You want the truth, I'm trying to tell you the truth—anyway, let me tell you, baby, I'm proud of my brother, your uncle, and I'll be proud of him until the day I die. You should be, too. Whatever the fuck your uncle was, and he was a whole lot of things, he was nobody's faggot."[43]

Although Hall had angrily defended Arthur to a white producer who suggested that Arthur's private life was a problem (Hall responded, "If he likes boys, then buy him a bathtubful, you hear? . . . What the fuck do you like?"[44]), Hall's silence following his brother's death is clearly related to his discomfort with his brother's homosexuality. Hall's discomfort exists in spite of, or perhaps because of, Hall's intense adoration of and devotion to Arthur. Hall's awkward conversation with his son, Tony, is the first step to breaking silence. Afterward he feels his "heavy burden [begin] almost imperceptibly to lift."[45]

Hall and Tony then rejoin the women, and Julia takes the lead in talking about the past. The rest of the scene at Julia's house provides not so much a frame for the novel as a doorway or introduction to the people and events that will take up Hall's narrative. Julia's memories and later Jimmy's rather serendipitous arrival are the catalysts for Hall's own reminiscences. They also suggest the particular form and process that Hall will follow in "sorting out" his feelings and expressing his "love song" to Arthur. As Tony and Odessa ask questions, Julia talks about the gospel quartet, the Trumpets of Zion, that launched Arthur's career and her own experience as a child preacher. She brings out pictures of herself and Arthur from thirty years ago. Hall's lingering thoughts over the pictures foreshadow what we later learn of Julia's tragic youth. The pictures of Julia all dressed up with her handsome family are "the hieroglyphics spelling out the root, and the beginning of her sorrow."[46] But these events are barely hinted at as Julia talks to Hall's teenage children.

One picture evokes Julia's story of Bessie Green's funeral, which was the occasion of the last sermon she preached at age fourteen and the occasion of one of Arthur's early singing engagements at fifteen. As she tells the story of how she kept her promise to an old blind woman, and her disillusionment with the corruption of the ministers, Tony listens "with an intensity of wonder," and Odessa listens with "an attitude too intense to be described as shrinking, too eager to be described as fear."[47] Although Hall has known Julia practically all of his life, this story seems to him a new revelation. Hall says,

"You never told me all this—what you've just told me."

"Well. I guess it takes time—more time than anybody wants to imagine—to sort things out, inside, and then try to put them together, and then—try not so much to make sense of it all—as to see. Maybe that's why what seems to be past begins to be clearer than what seems to be present."[48]

The process that Julia describes in this passage is akin to the process upon which Hall is about to embark as he sorts through his and Arthur's past; it is also analogous to Baldwin's description of his journey as an autobiographical writer and witness. The distinction between "seeing" and making "sense," the emphasis on keeping past experience alive by recreating it, as opposed to analyzing the past for its meaning in order to place it at a distance, suggests the distinction Benjamin makes between the storyteller and the novelist.

Encouraged by more questions and responses from Odessa and Tony, Julia continues her story of Bessie's funeral. Julia plays a song on the piano that Arthur sang that long-ago day: "I'm thinking of friends whom I used to know / Who lived, and suffered, in this world below," a song certainly as appropriate in the present context as it was then. The lines of the song in the text are interspersed with Hall's reflections and speculations about the past and the present. Jimmy's unexpected arrival at this point suggests to Tony that there is something magical in the song that Julia has just played: "It was the song that brought you—it was the song."[49] Jimmy's arrival completes the circle of intimate friends and family and is the final catalyst to Hall's ensuing narrative. Hall hasn't spoken with his brother's lover since Arthur's death: "There is a silence between Jimmy and I—not uncomfortable, but tense. With our first words, whatever they may be, we will have begun a journey."[50]

In *The Power of Black Music* Samuel Floyd uses the term "cultural memory" to refer to the "subjective knowledge of a people" that is contained and transferred through specific cultural practices. Floyd's idea of black music as a form of cultural memory is very similar to Baldwin's use of black music in *JAMH*. Floyd believes that African retentions have provided a continuity in black music through the present period. Specifically, he traces this continuity to the ritual of the "ring shout," where drum, dance, and song constitute a form of conflated sacred and secular expression that confirms community solidarity and provides catharsis. The gathering at Julia's house suggests a modern version of such a ritual, where adults pass on memories to children through dance, story, and music. Out of this ritual of cultural memory, Hall gathers the will to break his lonely silence. Yet the specifically heterosexual ritual of the dance between parents and children foreshadows just how fraught with difficulty Hall's effort to speak will be.

The structure of *Just Above My Head* is both repetitious and additive, not unlike the musical forms that inspire the novel. By the end of book 1 the reader has been introduced to all of the major characters and knows in outline what will happen to them. Book 1 functions like the "head" in a jazz performance. It sets out the tune without embellishment. From this point on the narrative moves forward circuitously, revisiting events, filling in some gaps, creating others, adding details and perspectives. Book 1 ends when Hall agrees to become Arthur's manager, which is at least ten years after Bessie Green's funeral and approximately fifteen years before the present gathering at Julia's house. In the last scene of book 1, Hall is listening to Arthur perform in an after-hours joint: "It was the first time I ever watched my brother in a world which was his, not mine."[51]

At the opening of book 2, "Twelve Gates to the City," the reader is plunged back another fifteen years (approximately five years before Bessie Green's funeral). Book 2 covers five years, although the chronology is not filled in, from the time Julia is nine and Arthur eleven to the time they are fourteen and sixteen, respectively. Instead of chronology we get tableaux of family and church experiences—a Christmas dinner, a practice session, a church performance, and others. The scenes contrast the dysfunctional Miller family with the Montana family.[52] Toward the end of book 2, Hall skips ahead to events that occur later when he is in Korea. Hall includes a passage in italics of excerpts from Arthur's correspondence to him during this period, which he introduces by saying, "I'll have to backtrack, presently, and go through this in some detail. Now, I'm just trying to get the sequence together in my mind. I was off the scene for much of this. Arthur was my principal (and unreliable) informer."[53] Book 2 eventually takes us back to the scene of Bessie Green's funeral that was first described in book 1, but this time Julia's sermon, "Set Thine House in Order," is given a much more devastating context from what we have learned about her family life.

In book 3, "The Gospel Singer," Hall fulfills his promise "to go through this in some detail." Hall recreates the intimate details of Arthur's first trip south with the Trumpets of Zion and Arthur's formative love affair with Crunch, events alluded to in book 2 in the context of Arthur's brief and unreliable correspondence. Book 2 ends with Julia's rape by her father, but it's not until the second half of book 3 that Julia and Joel's incestuous relationship is developed. Arthur and Julia violate taboos against homosexuality and incest, experiences which isolate them, because they can not reveal their secrets even to each other, although Arthur recognizes his situation in Julia's: Arthur "held his breath, paralyzed, staring at the girl—staring, in a way, into his mirror."[54] Arthur and Julia are linked by the silence their experiences impose on them as well as by their love for Crunch, and when Crunch leaves for Korea, Hall says that Julia was "the only person in the world, now, who spoke [Arthur's] language. They knew the same things."[55] Yet, paradoxically, Arthur and Julia have no "language" because their stories have not been told, even to each other: "she shared his secret without knowing that she did."[56] It is left to Hall to put secrets into language. Hall's narration in book 3 achieves its most powerful expression as he writes about events of which he could have had no firsthand knowledge. Hall has reconstructed (improvised) the intimate details that were absent from Arthur's correspondence and given explicit language to the love that Arthur could only express in the coded form of his song.

Book 4, "Stepchild," the longest of the five books, covers approximately seven years, beginning with Hall's return from Korea, when Arthur is eighteen, and ending not long before Arthur and Jimmy begin their fourteen-year partnership, when Arthur is twenty-five. In book 4 we once again revisit the scene of Julia's rape, but now we hear about it retrospectively, first as reported to Hall by his mother and then later as reported to Hall by Julia herself. We learn that Julia became pregnant, that her father beat her brutally until she miscarried, and that she finally went south to find her brother, Jimmy, and care for him. Book 4 describes the characters' adult journeys, their separations, dispersal, and return. Hall moves to California to begin a career in advertising, then returns to New York to work for a black advertising firm and has a love affair with Julia, who has become a successful model. Julia then leaves for Africa, leaving Hall brokenhearted. Arthur's career as a gospel singer takes off, and he makes more tours of the South during the Civil Rights movement, including the visit where Peanut disappears (presumably murdered by white racists), an event which had been foreshadowed early in the novel. Arthur travels to Europe, has a love affair with a descendent of the French aristocracy, and is on his way to becoming a famous international performer. Book 4 ends with the imminent return of both Julia and Arthur, whose journeys to Africa and Europe, respectively, have prepared them to once again take up life in America.

At the opening of book 5, "The Gates of Hell," Hall breaks the narrative frame, returns to the present, and addresses the reader directly. This storytelling technique is used only occasionally, but at key moments in the novel (note the earlier example of Hall telling his listeners that he is now going to "backtrack," what in jazz might be called improvisation). In this passage Hall signals his inability to separate himself from the story he is telling. This story will not be a finished product or work of art that shapes experience into a fixed form. Rather this story is a living process that challenges and shapes the man who tries to tell it. Hall tells us,

> You have sensed my fatigue and my panic, certainly, if you have followed me until now, and you can guess how terrified I am to be approaching the end of my story. It was not meant to be my story, though it is far more my story than I would have thought, or might have wished. I have wondered, more than once, why I started it, but—I know why. It is a love song to my brother. It is an attempt to face both love and death.[57]

Hall expresses his fatigue and panic in an increasingly elliptical narrative. Book 5 covers Hall's marriage and the last fourteen years of Arthur's life by developing a few key scenes, including the last trip south where Arthur and Jimmy first perform together, but mostly by summary. Although we know that through Jimmy's encouragement Arthur crossed over from gospel to soul and became an international celebrity with Jimmy as Arthur's accompanist and Hall as his manager, we get no detailed description of these years. As Hall's thoughts return to Arthur's death in the London pub, Hall is unable to reconcile Arthur's happiness with Jimmy (their apparent personal and professional success) with Arthur's death. Hall says, "I'm left with what I don't know."[58]

Then, toward the very end of the novel, Hall relinquishes his text to Arthur's lover. In doing so Hall specifically suggests that *JAMH* has been a group performance. Borrowing a term from jazz which describes the musical segment providing the transition to the end, Hall says that he will now do what he has "most feared to do, surrender my brother to Jimmy for the ultimate solo: which must also now, be taken as the bridge."[59] Jimmy's "bridge" reveals the relentless negative self-judgment, fueled by public attitudes, that destroyed Arthur. In addition, Jimmy does not let Hall off the hook in bearing responsibility for Arthur's fate: "all Arthur wanted was for the people who had made the music, from God knows who, to Satchmo, Mr. Jelly-Lord, Bessie, Mahalia, Miles, Ray, Trane, his daddy, and you, too, motherfucker, you! It was only when he got scared about what they might think of what he'd done to their song—our song—that he really started to be uptight about our love."[60] Jimmy's words, which are the climax of this long novel, throw into relief the limitations of Hall's efforts to tell his brother's story in a way that protects the family and community from complicity in Arthur's death.

While many critics have given lip service to the complexity of James Baldwin's vision, most readings of *Just Above My Head* have been overly simplified. Most of the scholarly response has focused on the theme of reconciliation and has argued that compared to other Baldwin novels, *JAMH* achieves a high degree of resolution.[61] In these readings black music is the vehicle of reconciliation or transcendence, and "home" and "family" represent a secular salvation. Carolyn Wedin Sylvander, Dorothy Lee, Nagueyalti Warren, and Craig Werner all read *JAMH* as a sort of success story for Baldwin-Hall. "In many indirect ways there is not simply resolution in the novel, but affirmation, even cause for joy, " states Sylvander.[62] She argues that for the first time Baldwin is able to embody his idea that suffering is a bridge between people in moving and convincing characters "whose struggles are comprehensive and whose victories are believable."[63] Lee's reading also focuses on the "bridge of suffering" motif, "an image [that] conveys a bonding of opposites."[64] As a black, homosexual artist,

Arthur is an ambivalent figure who becomes an agent of transformation, one who is "dispossessed but [represents] the potential for community."[65] The characters who survive do so because they have learned from Arthur's life and death and have "gotten hold of the rock of the family." Arthur, "the black, gay artist-brother-lover, [is] . . . their redeemer, the agent of their rebirth, in death as in life. We find them at the end where the imagery has been bringing them all along. They are home," states Lee.[66] Similarly, Warren claims "the novel ends with the family, Julia and her extended family, constituting a church as it were."[67] Werner also emphasizes the significance of a revised understanding of faith in Baldwin's work. He explores *JAMH* as "the point of maximum resolution in Baldwin's exploration of the gospel impulse," claiming that the novel moves to a state of "higher innocence" that refuses oppositional categories and an oversimplification of experience.[68] Andrew Shin and Barbara Judson argue that *JAMH* redefines the discourse of family. The hierarchical, paternal family is transformed into an egalitarian family based on brotherly love: "Arthur is the agent who ultimately reintegrates family and community. . . . The picture of the extended family with which *Just Above My Head* concludes is the social manifestation of transformed consciousnesses."[69]

*Just Above My Head* is, however, a considerably more problematic and open-ended text than these interpretations suggest.[70] These critics attribute a larger degree of resolution to *JAMH* than the text warrants either by not discussing the homosexual theme (Warren and Werner), or by oversimplifying it and by idealizing "home" and "family" (Lee). In fact, the novel does not "end with the family" (it ends rather with Hall's dream of the family, which is an important distinction), and the gospel "call-and-response" pattern, that Werner rightly sees as important to the novel, is at critical moments short-circuited. Specifically, the novel does *not* return to the intimate family scene of book 1, which is the catalyst for Hall's memories. When Hall's narrative returns to the present at the beginning of book 5, the only characters who are "home" are Hall and Jimmy. Hall's wife and children have gone to see the *The Wiz*, the black gospel version of *The Wizard of Oz,* while Hall agrees to meet with his brother's lover. Hall says, "The day proposed to me, in short, though somewhat more grueling than the matinee, was, equally, more urgent. Still, I feel a little guilty about not being with Ruth, and the children. But I have something, yet, to work out. I am not reconciled."[71]

Ostensibly Hall sets out to be Arthur's interpreter for his children. He is "the vessel which contains, for them his legacy." Yet Jimmy's "bridge" and, moreover, the children's absence at the novel's end suggest that the full "document" of Arthur's life remains unread in the context of "home" and "family." Moreover, for Tony and Odessa, Arthur's story has been displaced by a much less "grueling" narrative, Broadway's version of gospel. The happy ending of *The Wiz* is a foil to the unhappy ending of Arthur's life and signifies on the gap between Hall's desire for reconciliation and his desire not "to cheat in all that I have tried to say so far."[72] While Hall's wife and children watch Dorothy "ease on down the road" and eventually find her way home, Hall listens to Jimmy tell of the shame and negative self-judgment that finally destroyed Arthur's life and prevented him from coming home to either his lover or his brother. The familial reconciliation that eludes Hall and Arthur in "real life" is made manifest in Hall's final dream. Similar to the ending of *If Beale Street Could Talk,* the ending *of Just Above My Head* juxtaposes a harsh unresolved reality with an uncertain dream of family and community. Interestingly, the images of Hall's dream are derived from *The Wizard of Oz*: the road, the driving rain, the country house, even the dream itself. In Hall's dream his home is a shelter for family and friends, a place where people come to get out of the driving rain. Inside the house they laugh and warm themselves by a fire Hall has built. But throughout the scene Hall is tormented by Arthur's question: "Shall we tell them? What's up the road?" The novel concludes with Hall's response to Arthur followed by Hall's waking moment: "No, they'll find out what's up the road, ain't nothing up the road but us, man, and then I wake up, and my pillow is wet with tears."[73]

Although the novel does lead "home," as so many critics have noted, the home represented at the end is a dream from which Hall Montana awakes alone, mourning the death of his brother. The novel begins with Hall's inability to cry and ends with his tears. Moreover, home is represented ambivalently throughout the novel. While Hall finds comfort from a racist and dangerous city in the home of his youth and later finds simple happiness in his life with Ruth, in contrast, Julia and Jimmy experience pain and betrayal in their childhood homes. Arthur feels alienated from home despite his loving family, and even Hall, who feels exiled in his suburban neighborhood, which he describes as "one of the blood-soaked outposts of hell,"[74] and who finds it very difficult to talk freely to his children, finds "home" and "family" (if defined beyond his relationship to his wife) problematic.

Those critics who have been favorable toward the novel tend to overestimate the achievement of reconciliation and say little, if anything, about the way that Arthur's experience of his homosexuality disrupts Hall's dream of reconciliation. It is, I believe, a mistake to equate Hall's point of view with Baldwin's (or, for that matter, to assume that Hall's limitations as the narrator of Arthur's story are a lapse of authorial control). Through the voice of Hall, Baldwin draws attention to the essentially subjective nature of writing history, of storytelling. Hall's distinctly personal motivation, his struggle with memory and with his fear of self-disclosure, makes him a narrator who deconstructs the idea that an author can have complete control of his text any more than a singer, like Arthur, can have complete control of his song. In the very process of telling his story, Hall's narrative is significantly shaped and informed by others. To use Eleanor Traylor's musical metaphor in a different fashion, we might think of Hall not as a solo blues performer but as the lead singer in a quartet.[75] Hall carries the melody, but the voices of Julia, Jimmy, and Arthur provide both harmony and dissonance.

It is important to separate the story that Hall wishes to tell from the one that emerges over the course of the novel, which is the one that Baldwin has told. Hall struggles for reconciliation with the memory of his brother. However, Baldwin presents Arthur's legacy as an unresolved challenge for those who inherit it. Hall wishes to reintegrate Arthur's story into the family story and to interpret Arthur's legacy for his children, but in order to accomplish this goal he represses uncomfortable truths, in particular his own complicity as a homophobic in Arthur's demise. The story of Hall's struggle to be reconciled with Arthur is Baldwin's vehicle for telling a different story, one that opens up the questions and controversy of Arthur's legacy—and by extension of Baldwin's.

# II.

The "different" story, the one that cannot be contained by Hall, emerges through the gospel song of Arthur Montana: "When a nigger quotes the Gospel, he is not quoting: he is telling you what happened to him today, and what is certainly going to happen to you tomorrow."[76] In *Just Above My Head* gospel music is represented as a protean discourse, in which meanings are derived from the historical experience of a people, reinterpreted by the particular experiences of individual performers, and mediated by the audiences' experiences and expectations.[77] In the novel, traditional black gospel is an expression of personal experience and faith as well as a vehicle of cultural memory for the African American community. It can create a familial bond or inspire communal resistance and solidarity. Gospel music is represented as a coded expression of an oppressed community, but—most important—in Baldwin's work it is also represented as a coded expression of sexual desire. Baldwin's insistence on the relationship between sexual passion and black religious music is heresy for the conventionally religious person and has undoubtedly put off some readers.[78] Yet Baldwin's conflation of religion and sexuality is one of the most important ways in which he signifies on the generation of African American writers that preceded him. In "Alas, Poor Richard" Baldwin writes, "In most of the novels written by Negroes until today (with the exception of Chester Himes' *If He Hollers Let Him Go*) there is a great space where sex ought to be; and what usually fills this space is violence."[79] In this passage Baldwin argues that the gratuitous and compulsive violence in Wright's work has its roots in an unexamined rage at the "sexual horror" that blacks experience as a result of white racism. The absence of representations of sexual desire (and the substitution of violence) in African American fiction is the direct result of white racism, which invests blacks with "hates and longings and . . . sexual paranoia."[80] Thus, Baldwin's descriptions of sexual desire and loving, ecstatic sexual experience between black men, between black men and women, and between blacks and whites are explicitly political revisions that challenge the racism that, in Baldwin's understanding, has limited and distorted African American fiction. By bringing sex into the church, Baldwin is making a political statement. Baldwin connected religious music with sexual desire as early as *Go Tell It on the Mountain*. Yet the depiction of specifically homosexual desire in a religious context was relatively subtle in his first novel, while in *JAMH* it is explicit.[81] For Arthur Montana, whose homosexuality sets him apart from the traditional expectations of black family and community, gospel is a doubly coded form of self-expression, although one that the author makes sure we can read.

In addition to the sexual meanings of gospel, the novel also demonstrates how the popular success of black gospel, and the secular forms it has influenced, such as soul, has brought black music to new audiences who may have little understanding of its traditional roots and meanings and who experience it as spectators rather than participants. Thus, both form and meaning of gospel music change as its audience changes. The explicitly "sacred" language of gospel is revealed to have a variety of "secular" meanings. In a strikingly polyphonic passage early in *JAMH*, Hall describes the harried and hectic world of the gospel singer. He improvises between the beat ("oo-ba oo-ba"), a disconnected collage of sex talk and phrases from gospel songs:

I knew no one who was happy, God knows, in that world of the gospel singer: the musicians, the buses, the costumes, the theater owners, the churches, the pastors, the deacons, the backing choir, booking agents, the hotel rooms, the cars, the buses, sometimes the trains, eventually the planes, the fucked-up schedules, the fucked-up nerves, Red and Crunch and Peanut and Arthur, in their early quartet days when Arthur, at fifteen, was a lead singer. *Jesus is all this world to me motherfucker hold on this little light of mine oo-ba shit man oo-ba oo-ba if I don't get my money hal-ay-lyu-yah! I don't want to hear that noise Jesus I'll never forget you going to have you a brand-new asshole you can't crown him till I oo-ba oo-ba boom-boom-boom yeah and how would you like till I get there a brand-new cock and when the roll is why? you don't like called up yonder oo-ba oo-ba swinging on sweet hour of prayer my old one no hiding place! No more? Jesus I'll never forget man dig them oh the tell me titties man oo-ba oo-ba oh shake it off Mama an uncloudy cat's digging day you down below how did you man feel when you yeah baby keep digging come it ain't half hard yet out the wilderness oh ba oo-ba yeah leaning oh you precious freak you leaning on oh don't it look good to leaning you now on the Lord come on back here 'tis the old yeah you stay ship right there of Zion it going be beautiful my soul I'm going let you have looks up a little taste to Thee.*

Lord. And yet: they walked by faith.[82]

The tone of the concluding statement—"yet: they walked by faith"—is serious. The purpose of Hall's profane description is not to discredit the gospel singer or his message but to reveal the link between religious and sexual passion, between faith in an invisible world and experience in this one, as well as the distorting pressures of commercial performance.

As Eleanor Traylor has pointed out, Arthur Montana is the last of several black musicians or singers in Baldwin's fictional corpus. His predecessors include Rufus and Ida of *Another Country,* Sonny of "Sonny's Blues," Luke of *Amen Corner,* and Richard of *Blues for Mister Charlie.* In *Give Birth to Brightness,* Sherley Anne Williams analyzes Baldwin's musician characters as symbolic of social alienation and of black experience. Although her analysis predated the publication of *JAMH,* her observations are relevant to Arthur Montana as well:

> The musician in the works of James Baldwin is more than a metaphor; he is the embodiment of alienation and estrangement, which the figure of the artist becomes in much of twentieth century literature. Most of his characters have at the center of their portrayal an isolation from the society, the culture, even each other. They are also commentaries upon the brutal, emasculating, feared—and fearing—land from which they are so estranged. The musician is also for Baldwin an archetypal figure whose referent is Black lives, Black experiences and Black deaths. He is the hope of making it in America and the bitter mockery of never making it well enough to escape the danger of being Black, the living symbol of alienation from the past and hence from self and the rhythmical link with the mysterious ancestral past. That past and its pain and the transcendence of pain is always an implicit part of the musician's characterization in Baldwin. Music is the medium through which the musician achieves enough understanding and strength to deal with the past and present hurt.[83]

Williams nicely captures the paradox represented in the figure of the Baldwin musician, who represents both alienation and a vital cultural link to the past. In many respects Arthur Montana is Baldwin's most fully developed treatment of this archetypal musician. In broad symbolic terms he certainly represents the familial and cultural past with which his brother Hall is attempting to come to terms. Hall's narrative voice in all its varied tones of revelation and uncertainty ("what can one really know about the life of another" . . . "I'm left with what I don't know") struggles with the complex reality of his brother's life, which comes to represent, as Williams puts it, "Black lives, Black experiences and Black deaths."

Yet Arthur is more than an archetype for a generalized "black" experience. His story comes to represent the intersection of a public and a private history, one that challenges traditional definitions of masculinity as well as traditional understandings of black resistance. Throughout the novel Arthur's songs signify, simultaneously, in multiple discourses—political, religious, and sexual—and thereby continually suggest the ways in which these discourses are interimplicated in the creation of individual and communal identities. Isaac Julien and Kobena Mercer have argued that contrary to a "revolutionary black nationalism" that ignores more subtle forms of resistance and "depoliticizes the conflicts and contradictions—especially around sexuality and gender . . . sexuality, sexual choices, desires, and identities have always been on the agenda of black politics."[84] They go on to point out that it is through black music in particular that black men have challenged traditional concepts of masculinity:

> While "black macho" images were big box-office in the Blaxploitation movies of the early 1970s, Stevie Wonder and Marvin Gaye undercut the braggadocio to reveal a whole range of concerns with caring, responsibility, and sensitivity. In this period, classic Motown like "I'll be There," by the Four Tops, valued reliability and dependability, while "Papa Was a Rolling Stone," by the Temptations, was critical of certain models of black paternity and fatherhood. Today, artists like Luther Vandross, the Chi-Lites, and the much-maligned Michael Jackson disclose the "soft side" of black manliness. As a way forward to debates on race, sexuality, and culture, we need to reclaim these resources

to make visible the positive ways black men have been involved in a political struggle around the very meaning of masculinity.[85]

Baldwin's story of a homosexual musical artist filtered through the voice of the heterosexual br(other) is indeed a novel that makes visible a personal and political struggle around the meaning of black masculinity. Arthur Montana is the perfect figure to represent this struggle and thereby becomes the most interesting and complex of Baldwin's musician characters. By focusing on the life of a gospel singer, Baldwin creates a character that represents a "mainstream" black experience and history, one that is acknowledged and honored within the black community, and a "hidden" black experience that is not. Arthur Montana occupies a site that is paradigmatically both black and gay.

In "Struggles of a Black Pentecostal," James S. Tinney describes himself as a black, gay Pentecostal who has managed to "reconcile [his] sexual orientation and [his] religion,"[86] although not without difficulty. Pentecostalism, Tinney says, "is reputed to be the 'Blackest' form of religion, as well as the 'gayest.'"[87] It is the "blackest" because it contains more surviving Africanism than any other religion in the diaspora, and it is the "gayest" because of the preponderance of homosexuals, particularly among the musicians and gospel choirs:

> Pentecostalism is the "earthly heaven" for sissies (and closeted homosexuals) of all types. Estimates of the percentage of Pentecostal members who are gay run as high as 70 percent. Who can know for sure? Certainly, there is no quarrel about the fact that obviously gay, flamboyant and queenly males and masculine-type females exist in abounding numbers in Pentecostal churches—more so than in other faiths. If our churches were to instantly get rid of the homosexuals in them, they would cease to remain "Pentecostalist." For the gospel choirs and musicians (the mainstay and pivot of our "liturgy") would certainly disappear.[88]

Pentecostalism demands that gays stay in the closet. Even though many of the spiritual leaders in the church are gay, according to Tinney, the "holiness or hell" judgment is continually applied to homosexuals from the pulpit. Still, Tinney sees a certain practical tolerance of variant sexualities, despite the church's antisexual pronouncements: "The conscious way in which the presence of homosexuality was recognized (whether approved or not) contributed to a feeling that it was really no worse than women wearing open-toe shoes or saints missing a mid-week prayer meeting. In such an atmosphere the mind easily reaches its own conclusions."[89] Yet Tinney acknowledges that the cognitive dissonance for many gays is too great and as a result many leave the church.[90] Although Tinney claimed to have reconciled his faith with his sexuality, not long after writing "Struggles of a Black Pentecostal" he formed the nation's first black, gay Pentecostal church, suggesting the reconciliation could not be complete within existing institutions.[91]

In Hall's narrative of Arthur's journey to becoming the Soul Emperor, Arthur's sexuality is the kind of open secret that Tinney describes in traditional Pentecostal churches. While Arthur's musical journey is emblematic of "Black lives, Black experiences and Black deaths" in the new world, the revelation of Arthur's private life—the loves that actually fuel his journey—creates for Hall a dissonance that calls into question his ability to assimilate Arthur into family history, into "black" history. Arthur's life as a gospel singer makes him a vehicle of black cultural memory and thus a "representative" of African American experience, while his homosexuality reveals the "difference" hidden within that experience.

Of all modern forms of black music, gospel is the most traditionally linked to the early spirituals, to black religion, and to black performance ritual. Joyce Marie Jackson defines gospel music as "an evolving, dynamic, and vernacular art form" that "offers absolute evidence of the existence of a continuum in African American music."[92] She describes how gospel aesthetics and performance styles have developed in relationship to the changing conditions of black America while, at the same time, they have continued to reflect values and structures basic to an originally African-derived aesthetic. Traditional African performance aesthetics require participation by group members and such participation in music is reinforced by the structure of the song itself. Spontaneous songs are sung in an antiphonal style with no predetermined length. The antiphonal style is characterized by a call-and-response or leader-chorus structure in which "the leader spontaneously improvises text, time, and melody," and the group responds with "a short repetitive phrase" which can make changes in one or more of those elements.[93] Jackson argues that while gospel "has evolved to encompass performance practices of several genres of music from spirituals and hymns to blues, jazz, soul and rap," it remains the most distinctively African American musical form, the least influenced by European standards, in its expression of communal and aesthetic values.[94] In *The Power of Black Music* Samuel A. Floyd Jr. makes a similar claim. Even after gospel became entertainment in the 1960s, Floyd says, "the more refined contemporary black gospel music retained the characteristics of its predecessors, and its performance still depended on a performer-audience call-and-response rapport unlike that of any other musical experience."[95]

The beginning of gospel music reflects African American experience from the end of slavery to the great migration to northern cities. Its message speaks to the struggle for freedom in its secular as well as spiritual meanings. Horace Boyer designates the years 1896 to 1920 as the first period of gospel singing.[96] Both Boyer and Jackson describe gospel as a development from the earlier jubilee quartets that began traveling and performing spirituals after the Civil War. Jackson defines gospel as "the modern-day counterpart of the antebellum spiritual."[97] In fact the spiritual from which Baldwin's novel takes its title, "Just Above My Head" (also "Over my head / I hear music in the air"), is one that became associated with the gospel tradition. For example, this song appears in the title of a recording of the Golden Gate Quartet, *I Hear Music in the Air: A Treasury of Gospel Music,* and it was in the repertoire of the Wings Over Jordan Choir (1937–49), a group that Floyd credits as having laid the foundation for the use of spirituals and hymns in church-based protest activity.[98]

The development of gospel music was influenced most significantly in the 1920s by the preaching, praying, and testifying practices of Pentecostal churches, known as Sanctified or Holiness churches, which were the central communal institution for many poor urban blacks. Jackson describes gospel music as coming to fruition during the Great Depression in the context of a new Pentecostal movement. An important catalyst to its development during this period was Dr. Thomas A. Dorsey, a blues musician who decided to dedicate his musical talents to God and brought the rhythms and instrumental accompaniment of the blues into the gospel tradition. As the demand for gospel music increased, more gospel quartets began touring outside their home communities. Competitions or "song battles" became an important component of the quartet tradition, promoting a sense of musical identity and high professional standards. It was also during this period that the lead singer began to assume a more prominent role as soloist.[99] By the late 1940s gospel had become big business and the performance style became increasingly focused on the individual creativity of the lead singer, who was now an independent part of the group. The lead singer performed extended solo passages and "improvised personal statements and testimonies."[100]

The history of gospel reflects the sacred-secular division in black musical traditions and the crossing of that division. From the early part of the century there were quartets who played both sides of the fence, both blues and gospel, but they would often change the name of their group according to the function they were performing, since the sacred-secular division was very important to a group's identity. The period following World War II saw a greater blend of sacred and secular styles. As the popularity of gospel grew, it was performed in an increasing number of sacred and secular settings, and its texts took on more social and political significance. The 1950s saw the proliferation of church and community gospel choirs, and the 1950s and 1960s saw the entrance of gospel into the Civil Rights movement. The secular tradition "soul" was influenced by gospel, and the song "Oh Happy Day" (1969) was the first gospel song to cross over to the soul charts. By the 1970s Broadway saw the advent of gospel-based musicals, such as *The Wiz*.

The development and history of gospel is given a clear fictional representation in the life and career of Arthur Montana. In *Just Above My Head* Baldwin captures many of the above-described elements of the tradition, from its origins in Holiness churches, its participatory aesthetics, its traveling quartets and song battles, to its role in the Civil Rights movement and its changing performance aesthetic which emphasized the role of soloist. Arthur's career in gospel, including his crossover to soul, mirrors the very development of the form itself.

Arthur's music comes from a quotidian black experience. His father, Paul, a blues pianist (who performs in both bars and churches and who has a following on the "hill"), is his first teacher. Arthur's first gospel performance in Julia's Sanctified church parallels the early development of gospel in black Pentecostal churches. His early musical experience in a quartet, the Trumpets of Zion, represents the most common configuration of early gospel groups and the communal and antiphonal qualities inherent in the tradition. The growing popularity of gospel quartets in more "worldly" churches is represented when the Trumpets engage in a "song battle" with quartets from Philadelphia, Newark, and Brooklyn.[101] The importance of gospel to the Civil Rights movement is represented in Arthur's southern tours where, continuing to sing in churches, he discovers the roots of his music and its connection to the freedom struggle. Arthur's decision to go solo and his increasing fame parallels the increased demand for gospel among white as well as black audiences. His decision to crossover to soul and his international fame, coupled with his growing feeling of isolation from his audience and the song he sings, suggest that the commercial success of black music has brought with it a heavy price for the performer who is cut off from the music's communal ethos and its history.

Arthur's training begins at home. He learns from his father, Paul, whose repertoire includes both spirituals and blues, who represents the intersection of sacred and secular in traditional African American music and culture. Paul also represents the combined qualities of his two sons, Arthur and Hall. Like Arthur, Paul is a musician who sings his experience, who carries the story of African American history in his song; like Hall, Paul is a loving family man devoted to his wife and children. Paul combines qualities often irreconcilable in Baldwin's work: depth of feeling and emotional honesty with the ability to provide security and domestic harmony. Baldwin started to revise the figure of the morally rigid and rejecting father that dominates *Go Tell It on the Mountain* with the characterization of Mr.

Proudhammer and the rapprochement of father and son that occurs near the end of *Tell Me How Long the Train's Been Gone*. That revision appears complete in *JAMH* with Paul Montana. Even more than Joseph, the good father of *If Beale Street Could Talk,* Paul represents, at least in the explicit registers of Hall's voice, the ideal father.[102] While Joseph is a captive of an exploitative economic system (he must steal from his job on the docks to meet the needs of his family), Paul, as a blues musician, supports his family financially and emotionally with a vocation that reflects his complex identity as an African American male. As Arthur's first teacher, Paul emphasizes the communal and participatory ethos of black music. He recognizes Arthur's talent, but unlike Julia's father, Joel, who exploits his daughter's talent as a preacher for his own material gain, Paul does not "carry Arthur around."[103] In fact, Paul takes "a very distant attitude toward Arthur's singing."[104] He knows that his son's precocious talent comes from a "deep and unreadable passion" and that one's reaction to this passion can destroy the singer.[105] Paul takes on the task of forming a group of neighborhood boys into a gospel quartet, the Trumpets of Zion, as a way of both teaching and protecting his son:

> Paul marshaled the other boys around his menaced son, for he knew why they were singing. (The boys thought they knew, too.) He knew they would not sing long—something would get in the way. But if anything got in Arthur's way, Paul would be missing a son.
>
> So, he labored every weekend, my old man with the slicked-down hair, Friday, Saturday, and Sunday evening. It was out of jealousy and curiosity that Arthur joined them, and that's how the quartet got started. Arthur wasn't really anxious to surrender his solo status, he really dug being alone up there. But, on the other hand, it was more of a challenge, and more fun, being up there with the others, and he learned more that way. Paul had painted him into a corner, for he would not work with Arthur without the others: and, teaching the others, he was teaching and guiding his son.[106]

That Paul views the traditions of black music as a way of guiding and protecting his sons is developed in relationship to Hall as well as Arthur. The blues that Paul plays for Hall is an acknowledgment of racial oppression and a mode of response and survival. At one point Hall returns home after beating a white boy who calls him "Shine." Hall feels shame and despair over having let his anger get the best of him:

> I looked into [Paul's] eyes, and we smiled. I was so glad to see him, my father, my old man. I thought of the boy who had called me Shine: but my father knew about him already, had known him from a long ways off.
>
> "You're home early," my father said.
>
> Arthur and Peanut stared at me, but said nothing.
>
> "It was a rough day," I said, "down yonder in the dungeon. But everything will be all right if you'll just sit down at that piano and play us a little something."
>
> Paul gave me a look, and Peanut moved from the piano stool. Peanut and Arthur stood at the window, and I sat down in the chair by the door. Paul played Duke's "Across the Track Blues." The boys at the window, me in the chair, Paul with his slicked-down hair as the day began to fade, and the Duke, from wherever he was, smiling all over his face.[107]

The blues musician father intuitively understands the son's experience; his music provides the recognition and support that Hall needs to survive his own anger and frustration. In *Tell Me How Long the Train's Been Gone,* Leo Proudhammer observes the way a Sicilian restaurant owner treats a young Italian customer like a son by virtue of their common ethnic history. By contrast Leo feels the absence of paternal and communal connection. Echoing W. E. B. Du Bois's words that the "American world . . . yields [the negro] no true self-consciousness," Leo says, "My life in effect, had not yet happened in anybody's consciousness."[108] *JAMH,* on the other hand, creates images of a black communal life and consciousness largely missing from *Train.* Paul is the mirror of a "true self-consciousness" for Hall but not, finally, for Arthur.

Hall's memories of his father, Arthur, and the practice sessions of the Trumpets of Zion are tableaux of musical moments that bring together an image of a nurturing familial relationship with an idealized male bond. Hall evokes this bond through his description of the qualities of improvisation, reciprocity, and witnessing that are enacted in the music. Yet the bond Arthur, Peanut, Crunch, and Red have forged through music is mediated by Hall's elegiac tone. Transcendent moments of the past are contextualized through reminders of the rough life the boys lead and foreshadow the future. In a passage similar to one in "Sonny's Blues,"[109] Hall describes how music transforms the faces of "the street boys" who sing it. As the Trumpets practice "Savior, Don't Pass Me by," Hall says, "their faces and their voices held the promise of the Promised Land; but we never see our faces, the singer rarely hears his song."[110] Hall's words foreshadow the tragedy that awaits each member of the quartet. There is sadness rather than irony in Hall's description of the disjunction between transformed faces and dangerous, difficult lives. Hall's comment again suggests the paradoxical position of the black singer-musician in Baldwin's work, a figure unable to hear or translate into his own life the message of hope he carries.

The American South is key to Arthur's musical development and maturity. On his first trip with the Trumpets Arthur discovers the continuity of the black community, the connection between North and South, and the source of his music. After an early performance in a church basement in Tennessee, Arthur feels, "mysteriously, warm and protected. . . . He has never seen any of these people before; and yet, he has, has always known them."[111] The community reminds Arthur of his father, his mother, and his brother, and he knows that between northern cities and southern towns "there was a connection as deep as that inarticulate connection between himself and Peanut and Crunch and Red when they sang."[112] The deeper south the Trumpets go, the more vital the music they hear. In Birmingham they want to get close to "this rough exquisite sound, not yet known as funky—hand out, fall out, try out, get high, and learn: there had been something, as Crunch said, waiting here for them, all along. In spite of their terror, they were tremendously excited, and their terror, after all, had nothing to do with black people."[113] In *JAMH* the South has the potential to destroy—demonstrated most dramatically by the murder of Peanut—but the South also has the potential to heal.[114] Upon his first trip south Hall says, "It was as though something had been waiting here for me, something that I needed."[115] Following her father's attack, Julia goes south to be reunited with her brother. Mama Montana returns to live in New Orleans after Arthur dies because "they've lost the true religion" in the North; she believes New York City robbed her of her son. In the South she can attend church, grieve, pray, and sing and not be "mocked."[116] It is also no accident that Arthur's most important love affairs begin in the South. Arthur's love for Crunch and then for Jimmy is cause, effect, and expression of the music they make together. The music that the singers carry has its origin in the South; the key to its meaning is in southern history. As northern boys taking the music back to the South and relearning it in the context of the Civil Rights movement, they create powerful new connections not only with each other, but with their southern audience and between the past and the present.

The description of Arthur's performance at a civil rights fundraiser in a Richmond church is a climactic scene, similar in spirit (if not in content) to the scene in *Train* when Leo performs the lead role in *The Corn Is Green*. In both cases there is such a rapport between performer and audience that the event becomes less a "performance" than a ritual of communal faith and possibility. The church where Arthur sings is an "ordinary black church," but the times (circa 1963) are anything but ordinary. Inside, the church is packed with black people and a few white supporters; outside, the church is surrounded by police and hostile white motorists. Arthur's hosts, the Reeds, are a respectable, middle-aged, professional black couple who have risked their safety for their commitment to black freedom. They introduce Arthur as a singer from New York who is "singing about us."[117]

Hall describes the event by interspersing commentary between the lines of the song Arthur sings; Hall's focus is not on Arthur, but on the song and the response it evokes from him as well as from the congregation. Hall's manner of description parallels the call-and-response pattern of the event. Arthur's song evokes the historical experience of a people revealing "a design long hidden. . . . He is us."[118] Arthur sings, "God leads His dear children along," describing God's supportive presence through safety and danger, happiness and sorrow. The song sets a tone of assurance for the listeners who are reminded that the immediate danger outside is not new and that they have survived. Hall tells his readers that the song sounds, "at this moment and in this place, older than the oldest trees."[119] Throughout Hall's narration trees have been symbolic of a threatening and threatened masculinity. At the beginning of the novel Hall describes a dream in which "laughing" trees prevent him from rescuing Arthur.[120] Later he describes "exiled" and "expiring" trees around his suburban home in New York as a metaphor for his own sense of alienation and displacement. Trees in the South evoke images of lynching and castrations. The statement that the song is "older than the oldest trees" implies that its power transcends an embattled masculinity and is the sustaining force of black life.

Hall's careful description of the congregation's response supports Samuel A. Floyd Jr.'s observation that gospel continues to retain much of its original performance aesthetic and continues to depend on a "performer-audience call-and-response rapport unlike that of any other musical experience."[121] First Hall hears the "hum of approbation and delight" and feels "the power of the people" as he watches his brother perform. During the beginning of the song the church is quiet, but the quietness suggests an intensity where every line is being anticipated, as though "their passion were coming through that one voice."[122] As Arthur gets to the end of the beginning of his song, there's a "collective exhaling," and then the call-and-response begins when an "old woman [says], as out of the immense, the fiery cloud of the past, yes *child,* sing it."[123] Then Arthur, as caller, sings out the questions about trials and tribulations, and the audience replies with expressions such as "yes, Lord." Organ, drum, people, and choir all respond as witnesses confirming the truth of the song. Although the ritual is old, Hall makes it clear that its power comes from the way it has been "made new" in this particular time and place. At the end there is no applause, because, as Hall says, "spectators applaud, but there are no spectators in the church."[124]

As Arthur starts performing for more diverse audiences, he experiences the power of black music to cross racial and national boundaries, but at the same time he experiences a shift in the performer-audience relationship, from that of leader-participant to entertainer-spectator. Arthur's European debut occurs in a Paris jazz joint where he has gone to hear an American blues trio with his French lover, Guy Lazare. The audience in the jazz joint is from Europe, Africa, and America and represents a microcosm of the world's racial and national divisions. All have come to hear black music, but what they hear and how they feel about it are not the same. Arthur observes Sonny Carr, a very old and legendary American blues performer, sitting in with the trio. After Sonny performs, the place "explodes with applause."[125] Arthur reflects on the meaning of the applause:

> He hears, in their applause, a kind of silent wonder, inarticulate lamentations. They might, for example, be willing to give "anything" to sing like that, but fear that they haven't "anything" to give: but, far more crucially, do not suspect that it is not a matter of being "willing." It is a matter of embracing one's only life even though this life so often seems to be, merely, one's doom. And it is, in a way, though not "merely." But to refuse the doom of one's only life is to be trapped outside all nourishment; their wonder, then, is mixed with, and their lamentations defined by, that paralyzing envy from which what we call "racism" derives so much of its energy. Racism is a word which describes one of the results—perhaps the principal result—of our estrangement from our beginnings, from the universal source.
>
> And the applause functions, then in part, to pacify, narcotize, the resulting violent and inescapable discomfort.[126]

When these audience members (or at least some of them) hear Sonny, they do not experience "he is us" like the congregation in the Richmond church. They experience "he is not us." In their sense of Sonny's otherness there is a mixture of relief and envy. They are relieved that the past and the condition from which the songs comes is not theirs, but they are envious of the power of the song. Sonny's song reminds them not of their past, but of the aspects of their experience they have denied and the resulting sense of self-estrangement. "Arthur wonders what he would feel like before this audience"[127] and soon gets an opportunity to find out.

Sonny recognizes Arthur as the son of Paul Montana and invites Arthur to perform with him and the trio. Arthur sings a gospel song about the prophet Daniel. During the performance "everything comes together, he and the trio and the beat. Sonny's black face and Guy's white face, and all the other faces. . . . It is all right. Sonny is clapping his hands: 'Well, let's have a little church in here!' Guy's face is burning. The other, darker faces meet him with the intensity and the beauty of the beat he rides, and the faces beyond this circle seem to come forward with a mute appeal."[128]

When Arthur finishes, "applause washes over him, like the sound of a crumbling wall."[129] In the scene in the Paris jazz joint the applause represents the complex relationship between the black performer and his audience. In observing the response to Sonny's blues performance, Arthur perceives a strain of envy and discomfort masked by the loud applause. After his own gospel performance, Arthur hears the applause "like the sound of a crumbling wall," which suggests that he has conquered his audience or that his song has brought this diverse group of people together for a moment. In either case, however, applause represents an altered relationship between the performer and his audience. The blues and gospel performances in the Paris jazz joint do not function as a communal ritual in the way that Arthur's earlier church based performances do; the dynamic of call-and-response is replaced by applause. As opposed to being an integral member of a community, the gospel singer becomes a kind of ambassador to foreign nations. His song may be lauded, it may even provide water for the thirsty, but it may not be understood by an audience who lacks the experience of the context from which the song comes and thereby is unable to respond with the caring and the "correction" the singer needs.[130]

Song is a form of human communication. When the singer is in rapport with others the potential of the song is realized. The power of Arthur's music in the Paris jazz joint comes from the rapport he has with Sonny Carr, the legendary blues singer and father figure, and with the trio who backs them up. During Arthur's rise to fame it is Jimmy, Arthur's lover-accompanist, who is the anchor and inspiration in Arthur's life. Hall says, "It is very largely because of Jimmy that Arthur became: a star. . . . Jimmy made Arthur happy. There is no other way to put it. I saw my brother happy, for the first time in our lives."[131] Yet the relationship is difficult, and

Jimmy's departure is a contributing factor in Arthur's death. Arthur's final performance on a London stage contrasts the roaring approval of the audience with the singer's isolation and the distortion of his song:

> He had sung that, as an encore, on the Paris music hall stage, for Jimmy, who had not been there. He had played his own piano, he had not, after all, been bad, not as far, in any case, as his audience had been able to hear. He had been drunk, stoned, in a state of fury and anguish and panic, and had certainly not, as far as he had heard himself, been good.
>
> He had been certain that Jimmy was ashamed of him, and should have been ashamed of him, and that was the reason that Jimmy had not been there.
>
> Yet the people—that void beyond him—roared. He was imprisoned, blinded, by the light, and had completely lost the sense of humor which had been his key to [the song].[132]

Arthur Montana's overwhelming sense of alienation at the height of his public career is similar to the experience of Leo Proudhammer. As Leo is "trapped in [his] role," Arthur is "blinded by the light." Both feel diminished by their public images and both experience alienation as a separation from family and from the black community. For both characters the problem isn't so much "fame" per se as the interlocking racial and sexual dynamics that produce both fame and alienation. In *Train* this dynamic is presented somewhat schematically through Leo's bisexuality and his dual attachment to the white liberal, Barbara King, and to the black revolutionary, Christopher Hall. In *JAMH* Arthur's alienation and his downfall is ultimately attributed to a corrosive, internalized homophobia that separates him from the source of his creativity, damages his personal life, and compromises his relationship to his family, to his community, and, most important, to his place in a history of resistance defined by his real and spiritual fathers.

Some critics felt that the reasons for Arthur's decline and death were insufficiently developed, because the novel provides little information about Arthur's life once he becomes famous. In fact, Hall's narrative attempts to conceal the role of homophobia in Arthur's demise until close to the end when Hall finally admits that he cannot explain Arthur's death, and that he is unable to reconcile it with Arthur's apparent personal happiness and professional success. It is to Hall's credit that he recognizes his limitations and allows Jimmy's voice to penetrate this fiction of Arthur's life. It is Jimmy who reveals the extent of Arthur's internalized homophobia, and his fear that those he loved most are ashamed of him. Jimmy tells Hall that his brother was "such a tired, black Puritan. . . . Sometimes I thought he hated me for the way—the ways, all the ways I loved him. I couldn't hide it, where was I to hide it? Every inch of Arthur was sacred to me."[133] Arthur's negative self-judgment stems from his fear that his father, his brother, and the tradition they represent ("the people who had made the music") disapprove of what he has done to "their song."[134] Fear of disapproval cuts Arthur off from his love for Jimmy. Unable to love and be loved, Arthur loses his song.

The panic that Hall feels in telling his brother's story can be attributed to the difficulty Hall has coming to terms with his own feelings of guilt and responsibility for Arthur's death. Hall concludes that Arthur has been an accomplice in his own doom, which while true, is also a rather self-serving conclusion for Hall to make: "For [Arthur] knows that it is he, and only he, who so relentlessly demands the judgment, assembles the paraphernalia of the Judgment Day, selects the judges, demands that the trumpet sound."[135] Hall sees his brother's death as the "massive consequence" of Arthur's anguish, which is fueled by his own relentless, negative self-judgment. Hall insists that Arthur's fear that his father and brother are ashamed of him has no basis in reality; however, between the lines of Hall's story, which strives to reconnect and celebrate home and family, a more complex tale emerges.

In spite of Hall's description of Paul as an ideal father, the subtext of Hall's story reveals that the relationship between Paul and Arthur is not ideal. While Hall explains the "distant attitude" that Paul adopts toward Arthur's talent as motivated by a fatherly desire to "protect" his son, Paul's cautiousness also suggests the emotional distance between Arthur and his father. That Arthur's homosexuality is at the root of this distance is never made explicit by Hall, but is strongly suggested at more than one point. In telling the story Hall idealizes his father, because it is Hall who has had the best relationship with Paul. Hall accompanies his father to his favorite haunts and is treated like an equal. Although Hall is not a musician, the fact that his father was proud of him fills him with "a happiness [he] feel[s] until today."[136] Hall knows that he never did anything to make his father feel "ashamed," and "thank[s] God, [he] can say that," but Hall also knows "if [he's] honest, that Arthur didn't feel he could say that."[137] The passage is oblique; the reasons for Arthur's sense of shame are not made explicit. Hall believes that Arthur has misunderstood their father: "I know better, but I would: I knew our father better than he did. That was because my life as a man had begun, my suffering had begun. I had my father to turn to, but Arthur had only me, and I was not enough."[138]

Hall's explanation for Arthur's "misinterpretation" of the father is not very satisfactory. Why can't Arthur turn to his father? And why isn't Hall "enough"? Hall implies that Arthur didn't know his father because he was still a "boy," and he hadn't suffered. Yet Arthur (like Hall) does grow up in his father's house, and if it is suffering that makes a man, as Hall implies, Arthur certainly suffers. Yet Arthur's suffering (unlike Hall's) is not a bridge that connects him to his father. Nor does Arthur's suffering initiate him into "manhood" as it does Hall. In fact Arthur suffers all the more because his experience as a homosexual does not allow him the consolation of the bond that Hall has with his father.

That Arthur's homosexuality is the basis for the emotional distance between Arthur and his family becomes more clear in the contrast between the events which follow Arthur's break up with Crunch and Hall's break up with Julia. In the latter case Hall's mother and father acknowledge and sympathize with his grief. Their "respect" for "[Hall's] life and [his] pain"[139] are essential to Hall's recovery: "I looked at my father and I opened my mouth and I couldn't catch my breath, I felt my father grab one of my hands in his, and that was all, all, I swear to you, that held me in this world."[140] On the other hand, Arthur cannot confide his love for Crunch to anyone. After Crunch is drafted, Arthur mourns his lover deeply but keeps the truth of their relationship secret. His father, Paul, refuses to acknowledge its true significance, viewing the attachment to Crunch as a sign of his son's immaturity and as a substitute for Hall who has also gone to war.

"Yeah," said Paul. "You latched onto him like he was Hall—like he was your big brother."

Arthur felt immediately disloyal. "Why no sir," he said. "Not exactly." Paul looked at him, and Arthur blushed. "Hall's my brother." Arthur said lamely. "Crunch—Crunch—he's my friend."

"Just the same, he's older than you, and you always been the younger brother and so you needed another older brother. Somebody you could trust," and Paul looked at Arthur again. "Ain't nothing wrong with it—the youngest always needs the oldest. Until," he added, after a devastating pause during which he lit his pipe again, "the youngest grows up enough to realize he's his own man and can't keep running to his older brother no more." He paused again, and looked at Arthur. "Especially if he's not really the older brother but just the older friend."

"But can't a friend," Arthur dared, "be as important as a brother?"

"He can be more important. I'm just saying they're not the same."

He sat down in the chair near the window.

"When you get married, for example"—here he paused for another examination of his pipe—"if you do, and I hope you do, that woman you marry, she going to have be more important than your mama or your daddy. You ain't going to be living with us. You going to be living with her, and raising your children with her. We can't hold on to you—we leaving. We did what we could. And you can't hold on to us—can't nobody move backward, not far, anyhow. They come to grief." He smiled, but something in the smile frightened Arthur. "And I don't want you to come to grief."

Arthur sensed a warning: he did not want to hear it. To hear it would be to confess. Something in him longed to break his silence, to ask *What's happening to me?* He longed to lay his burden down, and end his tormented wonder. But he could not incriminate, menace Crunch—his "heart": he sat silent, looking down at the keyboard.[141]

Paul's association of "manhood" with heterosexuality couldn't be more clear. Arthur is expected to grow up, which means taking a wife and raising a family. His attachment to Crunch is a sign of his youth, his status as the younger brother. It is not something to be "concerned about"; "only time could indicate to what extent it was 'normal.'"[142] Paul and Hall speak in what David Bergman has described as a "patriarchal discourse" that tries to deny the permanence and genuineness of homosexuality. This patriarchal discourse manifests itself in modern psychoanalytic theory that posits homosexuality as "arrested sexual development." Homosexual behavior (or what Bergman calls "intramale sexuality") is conceived as a normal transitional phase of development which, if it becomes prolonged, becomes an abnormal state.[143] It is no wonder Arthur wants to leave home: "It was as though, at home, he found himself trapped in a play, acting a role he had played too long."[144] Neither Paul (nor Hall for that matter) can reconcile Arthur's "manhood" with his "homosexuality." At home Arthur is always the younger brother who needs protection, and yet neither Paul nor Hall can protect Arthur, because they can't in effect admit him into the community of "men." Arthur can find no mirror, no "true self-consciousness" within this heterosexual family.

David Bergman distinguishes a patriarchal discourse of intramale sexuality from a distinctive homosexual discourse.[145] Paul, Hall, and even Crunch (who advises Arthur to have sexual relations with a woman) describe Arthur's love for Crunch in a patriarchal discourse that denies the permanence and genuineness of Arthur's homosexuality. Yet Arthur's actual life experience disrupts this discourse and reflects the characteristics Bergman identifies as belonging to the structure of homosexual experience. The most significant characteristic of homosexual discourse, according to Bergman, is a profound and categorical sense of "otherness." While the experience of "otherness" creates a sense of boundaries and ego identity in heterosexuals, it creates a sense of "egolessness" in homosexuals:

The homosexual's separateness occurs with neither firm boundaries nor with heightened identification with the father. He is distanced without definition. . . . This negativity of self mirrors the sociological fact that no homosexual is raised as such; he finds no likeness in the family circle. Thus, the homosexual misses the bonding and identification which for the heterosexual bridges the gap between himself and others. Indeed the family reminds the homosexual of his own "unlikeness."[146]

Arthur's emotional and physical isolation from his family is a salient aspect of his character that is, paradoxically, foregrounded by the objective of Hall's narrative, which is to "return Arthur within the orbit of family."[147] Hall's narrative is posthumous compensation for his inability to provide a home for Arthur during his lifetime. Hall tells us he bought the house he lives in "with Arthur in mind." It was to be a place where his brother "could always crash. [Arthur] didn't see it that way, though, he didn't want his sorrow to corrode my life, or menace my children's lives."[148] Arthur, the man of sorrow, dies alone, far away from home, separated from Jimmy due to a lover's quarrel and afraid that his father and brother are ashamed of him.

Other characteristics that Bergman identifies with a distinct homosexual discourse are also substantiated by Arthur's life, including homosexuality as a "lifelong condition," the experience of homosexual desire as genuine (as opposed to a substitute for a "normal" or "adult" heterosexual desire), and homosexual relationships that are based on equality rather than on rigidly polarized roles of a dominant and a subordinate partner.[149] Arthur Montana is Baldwin's only adult main character who is not described as bisexual. Despite what Hall tells his son, Tony ("Arthur slept with a lot of people—mostly men, but not always. He was young . . ."), at no point in the course of Arthur's life is he portrayed as sexually interested in a woman. Despite Hall's patriarchal discourse, the novel offers glimpses that Arthur from a young age acknowledges the basic difference, the "genuineness," of his sexual orientation:

> I told my brother that the way he wore his hair made him look like a sissy, and that may be the first time I ever really looked at my brother. He cracked up, and started doing imitations of all the most broken-down queens we knew, and he kept saying, just before each imitation. "But I am a sissy." He scared me—I hadn't known he was so sharp, that he saw so much—so much despair, so clearly.[150]

That Arthur can only express the "genuineness" of his homosexual experience in his brother's inauthentic language—"But I am a sissy"—and then by imitating a stereotype of homosexuality—is central to Arthur's dilemma and to the novel's theme of incomplete reconciliation.

Significantly, Hall first observes that his brother looks like a "sissy" at Arthur's public singing debut in Julia's Pentecostal church. Arthur's song is soon to become his means of expressing his hidden sexual identity. Following his first love affair with Crunch, Arthur longs to "confess," but he cannot. Instead, Hall says, "Arthur hid a secret and he hated having anything to hide; he had never had a secret before. He poured it all into his song, and Paul watched him, and listened, striving to become reconciled" (263). (The sentence makes it ambiguous about who is striving to become reconciled to whom: Arthur to himself, Paul to Arthur, Arthur to Paul.) Arthur's song is a doubly coded means of expression, reflecting Arthur's double marginalization as a black American and as a homosexual. Arthur adopts and revises the musical tradition his father represents, which is itself "coded." As observers since Frederick Douglass have pointed out, the sorrow songs spoke of black suffering and resistance to white oppression through Christian stories and language that said one thing to the slave owner and another to fellow slaves. Songs like "Steal Away to Jesus" or "Follow the Drinking Gourd" not only expressed a love of God, but plans for secret meetings or escape.[151] Mary Ellison has argued:

> The spirituals were far more revolutionary than most people, until recently, have imagined. Close examination shows just how subversive they were, and it is not surprising that so many were used as "freedom songs" by the civil rights movement of the 1950s and 1960s. Songs like "Go Tell It on the Mountain," "We'll Never Turn Back," "Walk with Me, Lord," "Been in the Storm So Long," and "Freedom Train" were all spirituals being used a second time to stir up a spirit of resistance.[152]

To this already "coded" musical tradition, Arthur brings his own experience as a homosexual who, in the context of family and community, cannot directly "confess" his love for another man. Throughout the novel Arthur and his lovers, first Crunch and then Jimmy, express their love and desire in the public language of spirituals and gospel. In a Florida church Jimmy tells Arthur how he feels by singing "Just a Closer Walk with Thee," and Hall says, "I had no idea, then, of course, how direct, and as it were, sacrilegious, Jimmy was being."[153] "Just a Closer Walk with Thee" becomes Arthur and Jimmy's song, "a sacrament, a stone marking a moment on their road: the point of no return, when they confessed to each other."[154] Only after Arthur embraces Jimmy is the full power of his song released; Arthur's subsequent fame depends on Jimmy's love.

Symbolically, this moment near the end of *JAMH,* where Arthur and Jimmy are united in spirit and song, represents the critical role of sexual self-acceptance and love in the life and work of the author, James Arthur Baldwin.[155] Jimmy and Arthur's expression of love in a traditional religious song resonates with Baldwin's lifelong project of filling the "empty bottles" of his father's texts and songs with new meaning, of writing his double marginalization as black and homosexual into the "gospel" of American and African American discourse. That project in *JAMH* is the free expression of homosexual love within a black context and the self-acceptance that the Jimmy and Arthur love song symbolizes. The lesson that Baldwin learns from his father's texts, "nothing is ever escaped," is the lesson that Hall Montana learns from telling his brother's story. Throughout the text Hall works hard to minimize, even conceal, not Arthur's homosexuality itself, but the effects of homophobia on Arthur's life and the extent to which Arthur's alienation from his family is deeply connected to the silence imposed by attitudes toward homosexuality. What Hall can't face is the question of his own complicity in Arthur's troubles. Only Jimmy can tell this story, and so it is Jimmy's "bridge" that Hall must cross to finish the story of Arthur's life. Jimmy's testimony to the impact of homophobia on Arthur's life ("it was only when he got scared about what they might think of what he'd done to their song—that he really started to be uptight about our love"[156]) is Baldwin's testimony, as well, and a challenge to those who inherit and pass on his legacy.

Lee Edelman argues that by appropriating the language of gospel hymns Arthur gains access to a "'manhood' whose meaning is decisively rewritten."[157] According to Edelman, Arthur's relationship with Crunch (and later with Guy and Jimmy) not only reinterprets "manhood," but the very construction of identity through difference upon which a western notion of "manhood" is based. Edelman works at length with Baldwin's reoccurring image of container and contained. Describing Arthur and Crunch's love-making, Hall says, "each contained the other."[158] Baldwin evokes this same image in a different context at the conclusion of "Here Be Dragons": "But we are all androgynous, not only because we are all born of a woman impregnated by the seed of a man but because each of us, helplessly and forever, contains the other—male in female, female in male, white in black and black in white. We are part of each other. Many of my countrymen appear to find this fact exceedingly inconvenient and even unfair, and so, very often, do I. But none of us can do anything about it."[159]

Edelman argues that the idea of "each containing the other" disrupts the terms of a cultural logic that defines manhood in relation to phobic exclusions. The idea that one simultaneously contains the other and is contained by the other appears to deconstruct the very idea of "identity"—as something fixed, bounded, and separate. Through their lovemaking, Arthur and Crunch experience a new sense of identity—one that is "mutually determining and relational, effected not through a fortification of boundaries but through a willingness to allow the boundaries of their identities to be penetrated."[160] This new sense of identity finds expression in the same gospel songs Arthur and Crunch sang before their erotic involvement. Edelman points out,

> as Arthur and Crunch contain each other, so, too, do the various 'meanings' of their apparently identical songs. . . . The "same" text now exhibits discontinuous, potentially contradictory, meanings that reflect its determination through contiguity to different parts of the context that contains it. . . . So the experience of singing in the novel comes to figure the erotic exchange of inside and outside, the taking in and giving back of a language seen as the prototype of the foreign substance that penetrates, and constitutes identity.[161]

Melvin Dixon claims that in *Just Above My Head* "readers are brought back to Baldwin's central dilemma: how to reconcile an aberrant sexuality with a religion that condemns it as sin. Yet most artists are living paradoxes: products of, critics to, and supporters of a cultural community. An artist belongs to a community, a language, a historical experience."[162]

Baldwin himself might have defined the "dilemma" more broadly. The conflict between homosexuality and religion is an aspect of the conflict between all sexuality and a puritanical religion that told its adherents to mortify the flesh, and has parallels to the conflict between the struggle for black dignity and freedom and a religion that slaveholders used to justify white supremacy. In appropriating religious song to express human desire for freedom, dignity, and love in this world as well as the next, Baldwin conflated sacred and secular meanings in a manner consistent with a long African American tradition of representation. What Baldwin brought that was new to this tradition and what continues to make him controversial is his insistence on the importance of sexuality in all human and creative relationships. While Baldwin was, as Dixon says, both product and critic of a particular language and experience, I think Baldwin clearly recognizes this insider-outsider paradox and makes of it less a "dilemma" to be solved than an opportunity to express a complex subjectivity. In *JAMH* this complex subjectivity is informed by the struggle of all four main characters to become reconciled with their experience through music, narrative, preaching, and journeys to foreign and native lands. While the desire for reconciliation motivates the singer, artist, traveler, and writer, Baldwin's work does not sentimentalize such desires but shows them in relation to human limitations and life's irreconcilable experiences. In *Just Above My Head* reconciliation is a creative act of the imagination, not an empirical condition, an idea which finds its representation in the gospel song from which *JAMH* takes its title:

> Just above my head,
> I hear music in the air;
> Just above my head,
> I hear music in the air;
> Just above my head,
> I hear music in the air;
> There must be a God somewhere.[163]

# Coda

I t is my hope that this study results in an appreciation of James Baldwin's undervalued later work. His last three novels, in particular, reveal that Baldwin continued to be a profound witness to the American experience. He gave testimony to the racial struggles of the 1960s and 1970s by exploring the relationship between private life and political realities in ways no one has done since. As a witness he described not only the social landscape, but also the human heart, giving testimony to our desires and dreams for a new identity and a new nation.

A serious evaluation of Baldwin's contribution to American letters cannot be undertaken without understanding that his later novels are a continuation and expansion of his earlier work. Beginning with Leo Proudhammer's return home in *Tell Me How Long the Train's Been Gone*, Baldwin's novels explore the possibilities of resistance to a racially and sexually divided American landscape from within black experience and culture. Baldwin explores the family relationship as a potential site of resistance and black music as a language of cultural resistance. Moreover, he refigures the Du Boisian concept of "double-consciousness." Double-consciousness is more than a "negro problem"; it is a universal human condition. Our "double-consciousness," which is how we experience the "other" in the "self," is the most fundamental human challenge. Hall Montana is Baldwin's last character who represents the struggle to understand the life of the br(other) and thus himself. By viewing "double-consciousness" as a human condition, Baldwin alters the discourse of black and white in American letters. Clearly, Baldwin extends the double-consciousness descriptor to his white characters. Some, such as Barbara King (*Train*) or Guy Lazare (*JAMH*), are aware that they, too, are caught in a history of racism and sexual oppression that has divided them from the "other" and thus cut them off from part of the "self." Other white characters, such as Officer Bell of *If Beale Street Could Talk*, repress their self-division, insist on their identity as "whites," and become predators driven by anxieties and desires they can neither face nor articulate. What Baldwin's lovers and brothers discover at their best moments is the interdependency of personal identity. Recognizing that each contains the other, and is contained by the other, becomes a personal and a political statement of resistance.

Hall Montana's struggle to tell the story of his br(other) is a metaphor for the necessity and the hazards of inscribing history—be it American history, African American history, gay history, straight history, or James Baldwin's history. Baldwin asks us: can we write our history, tell our stories, without denying the "other"? For that matter, can we pass on James Baldwin's legacy to America, insisting on his multiply connected identities as an American, a black American, a homosexual, a political activist, a novelist, an essayist, a preacher, a brother? Hall's reflection on the embattled nature of "history" near the end of *Just Above My Head* sums up the challenge:

> To overhaul a history, or to attempt to redeem it—which effort may or may not
> justify it—is not at all the same thing as the descent one must make in order to
> excavate a history. To be forced to excavate a history is, also, to repudiate the
> concept of history, and the vocabulary in which history is written; for the

written history is, and must be, merely the vocabulary of power, and power is history's most seductively attired false witness.

And yet, the attempt, more the necessity, to excavate a history, to find out the truth about oneself! is motivated by the need to have the power to force others to recognize your presence, your right to be here. The disputed passage will remain disputed so long as you do not have the authority of the right-of-way—so long, that is, as your passage can be disputed: the document promising safe passage can always be revoked. Power clears the passage, swiftly: but the paradox, here, is that power, rooted in history, is also, the mockery and the repudiation of history. The power to define the other seals one's definition of oneself—who, then, in such a fearful mathematic, to use Guy's term, is trapped?

Perhaps, then after all, we have no idea of what history is: or are in flight from the demon we have summoned. Perhaps history is not to be found in our mirrors, but in our repudiations: perhaps, the other is ourselves. History may be a great deal more than the quicksand which swallows others, and which has not yet swallowed us: history may be attempting to vomit us up, and spew us out: history may be tired. Death, itself, which swallows everyone, is beginning to be weary—of history, in fact: for death has no history.

Our history is each other. That is our only guide. One thing is absolutely certain: one can repudiate, or despise, no one's history without repudiating and despising one's own. Perhaps that is what the gospel singer is singing. (*Just Above My Head,* 480–81)

# Notes, Works Cited, and Index

# Notes

**PREFACE**

1. James Baldwin, "The Devil Finds Work," in *The Price of the Ticket: Collected Nonfiction, 1948–1985* (New York: St. Martin's and Merk, 1985), 559.
2. Ibid., 570.
3. Interview with Orilla Winfield, 1989. All quotations from Winfield that follow come from this source.


**INTRODUCTION**

1. Dwight McBride, *James Baldwin Now* (New York: New York University Press, 1999); D. Quentin Miller, ed., *Re-Viewing James Baldwin: Things Not Seen* (Philadelphia: Temple University Press, 2000).
2. I use the terms "signify" and "signifying" throughout this book in the sense they are used by Henry Louis Gates as a metaphor for black literary criticism. Gates describes the ways in which black texts are concerned with their antecedents through patterns of formal revision and intertextuality, patterns that repeat with a "signal difference." See Gates' *The Signifying Monkey* (New York: Oxford University Press, 1988), especially page 51. I find this concept particularly useful in analyzing Baldwin's relation-

ship to earlier African American writers as well as the relationship of his later work to his own earlier work.

3. David Leeming, *James Baldwin: A Biography* (New York: Alfred A. Knopf, 1994).

4. For a well-balanced discussion of Baldwin's attitudes toward the church and religion, see Michael Lynch's "Staying out of the Temple," in *Re-viewing James Baldwin: Things Not Seen*, ed. D. Quentin Miller (Philadelphia: Temple University Press, 2000), 33–71. Lynch argues that "Baldwin could neither end his argument with the church nor break totally his emotional ties with the faith whose ideals had formed his vision" (34). In *"Just Above My Head*: James Baldwin's Quest for Belief," *Literature and Theology* 11, no. 2 (1997): 284–98, Michael Lynch argues that Baldwin should be regarded as a "theological writer" whose vision evolved "from fear to self-affirmation and from emphasis on the individual to the community."

5. Orilla (Miller) Winfield, who had left New York during World War II, had lost touch with her former pupil until she saw her name in print in "Me and My House" in *Harper's* 211 (November 1955): 251–59. She then got in touch with Baldwin through his literary agent and they stayed in contact throughout the rest of his life. Mrs. Winfield had been surprised to learn of the resentment that the elder Baldwin had felt toward her; she said that he had always been very "dignified," never revealing his feelings, and she had been young and "naive." "Me and My House" was later reprinted as "Notes of a Native Son." Orilla Winfield interview by author, Manistee, Mich., August 1989.

6. James Baldwin, "The Devil Finds Work," in *The Price of the Ticket: Collected Nonfiction, 1948–1985* (New York: St. Martin's and Marek, 1985), 558–59.

7. There were a number of teachers with Ph.D.s at Clinton during the depression who were unable to find university jobs. See Leeming, *James Baldwin*, 26.

8. Ibid.

9. Ibid., 27.

10. Baldwin, "Notes of a Native Son," in *The Price of the Ticket*, 133.

11. As quoted in Leeming, *James Baldwin*, 43.

12. Ibid., 49.

13. Although Baldwin writes about masculinity and racial mythology in his nonfiction, he only discusses the subject of homosexuality in three essays: "The Preservation of Innocence" *Zero* 1, no. 2 (1949): 14–22; "The Male Prison"; and "Here Be Dragons." The later two are reprinted in *The Price of the Ticket*. "The Male Prison" was originally published in *The New Leader* 13 (December 1954) as "Gide as Husband and Homosexual" and was later collected in *Nobody Knows My Name*. "Here Be Dragons" was originally published in *Playboy* (January 1985) as "Freaks and the American Ideal of Manhood." "The Preservation of Innocence" has not been included in collections of Baldwin's essays, but it was reprinted in *Out/Look: National Lesbian and Gay Quarterly* 6 (fall 1989): 40–45, with an introduction by Melvin Dixon.

14. Baldwin, "Here Be Dragons," in *Price of the Ticket*, 684.

15. Kobena Mercer and Isaac Julien, quoted in Lynne Segal's *Slow Motion: Changing Masculinities: Changing Men* (London: Virago Press, 1990), 201.

16. Baldwin, introduction to *The Price of the Ticket*, xi.

17. Ibid.

18. Leeming, *James Baldwin*, 33

19. Ibid., 34

20. Ibid., 49–50.

21. Baldwin, "The Discovery of What It Means to Be an American," in *Price of the Ticket*, 171.

22. Emmanuel S. Nelson, "Continents of Desire: James Baldwin and the Pleasures of Homosexual Exile," *James White Review: A Gay Men's Literary Quarterly* 13, no. 4 (1996): 8.

23. See n. 13 above for the original publication and reprint data for "The Preservation of Innocence." Roderick Ferguson points out that Baldwin published "Everybody's Protest Novel"—and "The Preservation of Innocence" as companion pieces. Both were published in the same issue of *Zero* magazine. The first analyzed the image of the Negro in literature and the second analyzed the image of the homosexual in literature. See "The Parvenu Baldwin and the Other Side of Redemption: Modernity, Race, Sexuality and the Cold War," in *James Baldwin Now*, ed. Dwight McBride (New York: New York University Press, 1999), 233.

24. Leeming, *James Baldwin*, 142.

25. Ibid., 217.

26. Ibid., 188.

27. Ibid., 245.

28. Ibid., 301.

29. Ibid., 298.

30. According to Leeming, Baldwin reached a low point in the winter of 1969 and took an overdose of sleeping pills just before abandoning the Hollywood project. Fortunately, he was rushed to the hospital in time. Ibid., 301.

31. Ibid., 257.

32. As quoted in ibid., 269.

33. Ibid., 289.

34. Ibid., 293. Leeming's description of Baldwin's contacts with the Black Panthers is on pages 292–94.

35. For an analysis of Baldwin's refiguring of the term "witness" see Joshua Miller, "The Discovery of What It Means to Be a Witness," in *James Baldwin Now*, 331–59.

36. For example, see Michel Fabre's "Fathers and Sons in James Baldwin's *Go Tell It on the Mountain*," in *James Baldwin: A Collection of Critical Essays*, ed. Keneth Kinnamon (Englewoods Cliffs, N.J.: Prentice-Hall), 120–38; and Michael Lynch's "The Everlasting Father: Mythic Quest and Rebellion in Baldwin's *Go Tell It on the Mountain*," *CLA Journal* 37, no. 2 (1993): 156–75.

37. Trudier Harris, *Black Women in the Fiction of James Baldwin* (Knoxville: University of Tennessee Press, 1985), 194.

38. Trudier Harris has commented on the frequency of incestuous overtones in Baldwin's fiction. See ibid., 193–200.

39. Fern Marja Eckman, *The Furious Passage of James Baldwin* (New York: M.Evans and Co., 1966), 68.

40. James Baldwin, *Go Tell It on the Mountain* (New York: Dial, 1953; New York: Laurel-Dell, 1985), 19.

41. Ibid., 35.

42. James Baldwin, *Just Above My Head* (New York: Dial, 1979; New York: Laurel-Dell, 1990), 559.

43. James Baldwin, interview by Ida Lewis (1970), in *Conversations with James Baldwin*, Fred L. Standley and Lewis H. Pratt, eds. (Jackson, Miss.: University Press of Mississippi, 1989), 89.

44. Leeming, *James Baldwin*, 55. Also see Baldwin's own description of leaving home in "Every Good-Bye Ain't Gone" (1977), reprinted in *The Price of the Ticket*, 641.

45. James Baldwin, "Everybody's Protest Novel," reprinted in *The Price of the Ticket*, 31.

46. Ibid., 33.

47. "Black Boys and Native Sons," originally published in *Dissent* 10 (autumn, 1963), reprinted in Irving Howe, *A World More Attractive* (New York: Horizon, 1963), 99.

48. *The Journey Back: Issues in Black Literature and Criticism* (Chicago: University of Chicago Press, 1980), 60–61.

49. Houston A. Baker Jr., *Blues, Ideology, and Afro-American Literature: A Vernacular Theory* (Chicago: University of Chicago Press, 1984), 142. See Roderick Ferguson for a completely different interpretation of Baldwin's use of the aesthetic values of the fifties: "The avant-garde's complicity in the production of masculinity and in the U.S. government's effort to spread American economic, political, and cultural hegemony suggests that Baldwin's use of the avant-garde aesthetics is a 'signifying(g)' strategy. That Baldwin would use an aesthetic that privileged the individual as a means to promote non-essentialist representations of gays suggests he is using that aesthetic for 'essentially polemic and subversive strategies,' that he is 'revising the received sign' of the American avant-garde to critique the heterosexist nature of the American national narrative." In "The Parvenu Baldwin and the Other Side of Redemption," in *James Baldwin Now*, 242.

50. Horace Porter, *Stealing the Fire: The Art and Protest of James Baldwin* (Middletown, Conn.: Wesleyan University Press, 1989), 82.

51. Baldwin, "Many Thousands Gone," reprinted in *The Price of the Ticket*, 72.

52. See Keith Clark's "Baldwin, Communitas, and the Black Masculinist Tradition," in *New Essays on "Go Tell It on the Mountain,"* ed. Trudier Harris (Cambridge: Cambridge University Press, 1996), 127–58. Clark notes that Baldwin's critique of *Native Son* "informs his aesthetic aims." He reads *Go Tell It* as a repudiation of Wright's discourse and the protest tradition.

## CHAPTER 1

1. Clyde Taylor, "Celebrating Jimmy," in *James Baldwin: The Legacy*, ed. Quincy Troupe (New York: Touchstone-Simon and Schuster, 1989), 30.

2. Ibid., 37

3. Toni Morrison, "Life in His Language," in *James Baldwin: The Legacy,* 76.

4. Barbara Smith, "We Must Always Bury Our Dead Twice," *Gay Community News,* 20–26 December 1987: center and 10.

5. Patricia Holland addresses the way in which discursive boundaries have made the black gay subject invisible: "The disciplines of feminist, lesbian-gay, and African American studies have imagined for themselves appropriate subjects to be removed, at least theoretically, from such a contentious space into the place of recognition. These bodies/subjects are either white but not heterosexual or black but not homosexual. In the crack between discourses, the black and queer subject resides." See "(Pro)Creating Imaginative Spaces and Other Queer Acts," in *James Baldwin Now,* ed. Dwight McBride (New York: New York University Press, 1999), 266.

6. Taylor, "Celebrating Jimmy," 33–34.

7. James Baldwin, "The Discovery of What It Means to Be an American," in *The Price of the Ticket: Collected Nonfiction, 1948–1985* (New York: St. Martin's and Marek, 1985), 171.

8. Morrison, "Life in His Language," 75.

9. Biographies of James Baldwin include David Leeming, *James Baldwin: A Biography* (New York: Alfred A. Knopf, 1994); James Campbell, *Talking at the Gates: A Life of James Baldwin* (New York: Penguin, 1991); W. J. Weatherby, *James Baldwin: Artist on Fire* (New York: Dell, 1989); and Fern Marja Eckman, *The Furious Passage of James Baldwin* (New York: M. Evans, 1966). Juvenile biographies include Lisa Rosset, *James Baldwin* (New York: Chelsea House, 1989); Randall Kenan, *James Baldwin* (New York: Chelsea House, 1994); Ted Gottfried, *James Baldwin: Voice from Harlem* (New York: F. Watts, 1997); and James Tachach, *James Baldwin* (San Diego: Lucent Books, 1997).

10. Single author, book-length studies that focus solely on Baldwin's work include Rosa Bobia, *The Critical Reception of James Baldwin in France* (New York: Peter Lang, 1997); Horace Porter, *Stealing the Fire: The Art and Protest of James Baldwin* (Middletown, Conn.: Wesleyan University Press, 1989); Trudier Harris, *Black Women in the Fiction of James Baldwin* (Knoxville, Tenn.: University of Tennessee Press, 1985); Carolyn Wedin Sylvander, *James Baldwin* (New York: Frederick Ungar, 1980); Louis H. Pratt, *James Baldwin* (Boston: Twayne Publishers, 1978); and Stanley Macebuh, *James Baldwin: A Critical Study* (New York: Third Press, 1973). European monographs on Baldwin's work include Karin Möller, *The Theme of Identity in the Essays of James Baldwin: An Interpretation* (Goteborg, Sweden: Acta Universitatis Gothoburgensis, 1975); and Peter Bruck, *Von der "Storefront Church" zum "American Dream": James Baldwin und der amerikanische Rassenkonflikt* (Amsterdam: n.p., 1975).

11. Edited collections of critical essays on Baldwin's work include D. Quentin Miller, ed., *Re-viewing James Baldwin: Things Not Seen* (Philadelphia: Temple University Press, 2000); Dwight A. McBride, ed., *James Baldwin Now* (New York: New York University Press, 1999); Trudier Harris, ed., *New Essays on "Go Tell It on the Mountain"* (New

York: Cambridge University Press, 1999); Jakob Kollhofer, ed., *James Baldwin: His Place in American Literary History and His Reception in Europe* (New York: Peter Lang, 1991); Fred L. Standley and Nancy V. Burt, eds., *Critical Essays on James Baldwin* (Boston: G. K. Hall, 1988); Harold Bloom, ed., *James Baldwin* (New York: Chelsea House Publishers, 1986); Therman B. O'Daniel, ed., *James Baldwin: A Critical Evaluation* (Washington, D.C.: Howard University Press, 1977); and Keneth Kinnamon, ed., *James Baldwin: A Collection of Critical Essays* (Englewood Cliffs, N.J.: Prentice-Hall, 1974). Tributes to James Baldwin include Quincy Troupe, ed., *James Baldwin: The Legacy* (New York: Touchstone-Simon and Schuster, 1989); Jules Chametzky, ed., *Black Writers Redefine the Struggle: A Tribute to James Baldwin* (Amherst, Mass.: University of Massachusetts Press, 1989); and Ralph Reckley, ed., *James Baldwin in Memoriam: Proceedings of the Annual Conference of the Middle Atlantic Writers' Association, 1989* (Baltimore: Middle Atlantic Writers' Association Press, 1992).

12. For the most complete listing of Baldwin's published work, see David Leeming and Lisa Gitelman's "Chronological Bibliography of Printed Works by James Baldwin," in David Leeming's *James Baldwin*, 405–17. To get a picture of the initial reception of Baldwin's work through *If Beale Street Could Talk* and the first three decades of critical response, see Fred L. Standley and Nancy V. Standley's *James Baldwin: A Reference Guide* (Boston: G. K. Hall, 1980), which provides an annotated bibliography of writings about James Baldwin from 1946 to 1978. Also see Daryl Dance's "James Baldwin," in *Black American Writers Bibliographical Essays*, vol. 2, ed. Thomas Inge et al. (New York: St. Martin's, 1978), 73–119. While no one has matched the thoroughness of the Standleys' *Reference Guide*, there have been subsequent bibliographic lists and essays, including the introduction to Fred L. Standley and Nancy V. Burt's *Critical Essays on James Baldwin*; and Jeffrey W. Hole, "Select Bibliography of Works by and on James Baldwin," in *James Baldwin Now*, 393–409. Among other things, Hole lists seventy-five essays published on the work of James Baldwin between 1985 and 1997 and thirty-eight dissertations that include a significant discussion of Baldwin's work published during the same years.

13. See, for example, Cassandra M. Ellis, "The Black Boy Looks at the Silver Screen: Baldwin as Moviegoer," in *Re-viewing James Baldwin*, 190–214; and D. Quentin Miller, "James Baldwin, Poet," in *Re-viewing James Baldwin*, 233–54.

14. See, for example, Yasmin Y. DeGout, "'Masculinity' and (Im)maturity: 'The Man Child' and Other Stories in Baldwin's Gender Studies Enterprise," in *Re-viewing James Baldwin*, 134. De Gout argues that "any reading of Baldwin's fiction reveals him to be progenitor of many of the theoretical formulations currently associated with feminist, gay, and gender studies. . . . Baldwin ultimately reveals in his fiction how sexism and heterosexism affect women and men in a gendered society and how gender constructs are inseparably linked to race, class, and other identity categories."

15. An exception to the focus on Baldwin's earlier work is Nicholas Boggs, "Of Mimicry and (Little Man Little) Man: Toward a Queer Sighted Theory of Black Childhood," in *James Baldwin Now*, 122–60. Boggs reads Baldwin's 1976 *Little Man Little Man: A*

*Story of Childhood* in the contexts of metaphors of African Americanist criticism and queer theory.

16. Harris, *Black Women in the Fiction of James Baldwin*, 3–4.

17. Craig Werner, "James Baldwin: Politics and the Gospel Impulse," *New Politics: A Journal of Socialist Thought* 2, no. 2 (1989): 107.

18. Ibid.

19. Eric Savoy, "Other(ed) Americans in Paris: Henry James, James Baldwin, and the Subversion of Identity," *English Studies in Canada* 18, no. 3(1992): 3.

20. Houston A. Baker Jr., *Blues, Ideology, and Afro-American Literature: A Vernacular Theory* (Chicago: University of Chicago Press, 1984), 140–42.

21. Houston A. Baker Jr., *The Journey Back: Issues in Black Literature and Criticism* (Chicago: University of Chicago Press, 1980), 60–61.

22. Lawrie Balfour has also recently argued that Baldwin's critique of *Native Son* is not "purely an aesthetic one." Baldwin's objection is moral in that he argues the protest novel helps perpetuate what he has called "the myth of innocence." See her essay "Finding the Words: Baldwin, Race Consciousness, and Democratic Theory," in *James Baldwin Now*, 76–77.

23. Werner, "James Baldwin," 111.

24. Porter, *Stealing the Fire*, 160. Houston A. Baker Jr., however, came to the defense of Baldwin's later work. See "The Embattled Craftsman: An Essay on James Baldwin," *The Journal of African-Afro-American Affairs* 1, no. 1 (1977): 28–51, where Baker argues that Baldwin needs a new kind of critic who understands his relationship to African American literature and culture. See the following chapter for further discussion.

25. Henry Louis Gates Jr., "What James Baldwin Can and Can't Teach America," *New Republic*, 1 June 1992, 42.

26. Hilton Als, "The Enemy Within," *New Yorker*, 16 February 1998, 72, 78. Also see Henry Louis Gates Jr. and Nellie McKay's introduction to Baldwin in *The Norton Anthology of African American Literature* (New York: W. W. Norton and Co., 1997) for a summary of the negative assessment of Baldwin's later work.

27. Werner, "James Baldwin," 106.

28. In *Blues People: Negro Music in White America* (New York: William Morrow, 1963), 30–31, LeRoi Jones's description of Charlie Parker's relationship to his alto saxophone had great resonance for me as I thought about the relationship between Baldwin and many of the characters he created (especially the four autobiographical characters in *Just Above My Head*, each of whom are named after Baldwin).

    Jones says, Parker produced a sound that "would literally imitate the human voice with his cries, swoops, squawks, and slurs. . . . Parker did not admit that there was any separation between himself and the agent he had chosen as his means of self-expression."

29. Chametzky, *Black Writers Redefine the Struggle*, 66.

30. As quoted in ibid., 6–7.

31. Eldridge Cleaver, *Soul on Ice* (New York: Delta-Dell, 1968), 99.

32. Ibid., 105

33. Ibid., 109–10.

34. Robert Bone as quoted in David Bergman, *Gaiety Transfigured: Gay Self-Representation in American Literature* (Madison: University of Wisconsin Press, 1991), 164–65.

35. David Leeming says that Baldwin knew that "people were wary of his reputation as a homosexual and he was disappointed that he had not been asked to participate [in the March on Washington] in any meaningful way" (*James Baldwin*, 228). Lee Edelman deconstructs the barely coded homophobic language that was used to describe Baldwin in *Time Magazine* and in other public arenas, language that marginalized or negated Baldwin's role as a civil rights leader. He points out that such "humorous" descriptions of Baldwin as "Martin Luther Queen" combined racism and homophobia to discredit King and the movement as well as Baldwin. See *Homographesis: Essays in Gay Literary and Cultural Theory* (New York: Routledge, 1994), 42–44.

36. Emmanuel S. Nelson, "Critical Deviance: Homophobia and the Reception of James Baldwin's Fiction," *Journal of American Culture* 14, no. 3 (1991): 91–96.

37. Ibid., 91.

38. Bryan R. Washington, *The Politics of Exile: Ideology in Henry James, F. Scott Fitzgerald, and James Baldwin* (Boston: Northeastern University Press, 1995), 97.

39. Stephen Adams, *The Homosexual as Hero in Contemporary Fiction* (New York: Harper and Row, 1980), 36.

40. Ibid., 54.

41. Bergman, *Gaiety Transfigured*, 168.

42. Ibid., 166.

43. Melvin Dixon, *Ride out the Wilderness: Geography and Identity in Afro-American Literature* (Urbana: University of Illinois, 1987); Edelman, *Homographesis*.

44. Cleaver, *Soul on Ice*, 97.

45. Ibid., 98

46. Werner, "James Baldwin," 112.

47. James Baldwin, "The Last Interview (1987)," interview with Quincy Troupe, in *James Baldwin: The Legacy*, 184.


CHAPTER 2

1. David Leeming, *James Baldwin: A Biography* (New York: Alfred A. Knoff, 1994), 263–83.

2. James Campbell, *Talking at the Gates: A Life of James Baldwin* (New York: Penguin Books, 1991), 226.

3. Granville Hicks, "From Harlem with Hatred," review of *Tell Me How Long the Train's Been Gone*, by James Baldwin, *Saturday Review*, 1 June 1968, 23–24; Irving Howe, "At Ease in Apocalypse," review of *Tell Me How Long the Train's Been Gone*, by James Baldwin, *Harper's* 237 (September 1968): 94–100, reprinted in *James Baldwin: A Collection of Critical Essays*, ed. Keneth Kinnamon (Englewood Cliffs, N.J.: Prentice-

Hall, 1974), 96–108; Nelson Algren, "Sashaying Around," review of *Tell Me How Long the Train's Been Gone,* by James Baldwin, *The Critic* 27 (October-November 1968): 86–87; Mario Puzo, "His Cardboard Lovers," review of *Tell Me How Long the Train's Been Gone,* by James Baldwin, *New York Times Book Review,* 23 June 1968, 5, 34, reprinted in *Critical Essays on James Baldwin,* ed. Fred L. Standley and Nancy V. Burt (Boston: Hall, 1988), 155–58.

4.  There were a couple of important exceptions to *Tell Me How Long the Train's Been Gone's* negative reception. David Llorens described *Train* as "the most important novel of this crucial decade in American history" and argued that the cool reception was indicative of an audience's unwillingness to hear a story which disrupts its "fantasy-like version of the American reality" (51–85). John Thompson described *Train* as "a masterpiece by one of the best living writers in America" that provides expert testimony on the present social crisis. Thompson went on to claim that *Train* was not a "protest novel," because "it avoids melodrama and explores human motivation on the deepest level." David Llorens, review of *Tell Me How Long the Train's Been Gone,* by James Baldwin, *Negro Digest* 17, no. 10 (1968): 51–52, 85–86; John Thompson, "Baldwin: The Prophet as Artist," review of *Tell Me How Long the Train's Been Gone,* by James Baldwin, *Commentary* 45, no. 6 (June 1968): 67–69.

    There has been little subsequent critical attention given to Baldwin's fourth novel. Of the full-length studies of Baldwin's fiction, only Pratt and Sylvander discuss the novel. Pratt defends *Train* against Irving Howe's claim that the characters' language and behavior are unrealistic, but agrees with Calvin Hernton's criticism (see n. 77) that the themes are repetitive of Baldwin's earlier fiction. Sylvander believes the theme of the estrangement of the black intellectual is "carried to a positive (or happy) resolution." See Louis H. Pratt, *James Baldwin* (Boston: Twayne Publishers, 1978), 71–76; and Carolyn Wedin Sylvander, *James Baldwin* (New York: Frederick Ungar, 1980), 67–83.

    Donald B. Gibson, "James Baldwin: The Anatomy of Space," In *The Politics of Literary Expression: A Study of Major Black Writers,* Contributions in Afro-American and African Studies, no. 63 (Westport, Conn.: Greenwood Press, 1981), 99–123; and Craig Werner, "The Economic Evolution of James Baldwin," in *Critical Essays on James Baldwin,* 87–88, are among the few scholars who have written on *Train.* Gibson argues that *Train* is Baldwin's "most directly political novel" and that it develops a tension between "inner space" and "public space" which is not resolved. Leo Proudhammer's "problem has no solution in the framework of his politics. He is American to the core and a liberal democrat. Liberal democratic politics has not successfully solved the problems that Baldwin addresses, explaining his towering rage." Werner also focuses on the novel's politics, but argues that *Train* reflects Baldwin's developing interest in economics and class, "a new willingness to speak in institutional rather than individual terms." While I would agree with Gibson that *Tell Me How Long the Train's Been Gone* is Baldwin's "most directly political novel," I would disagree that the protagonist's politics are "liberal democratic." I would also disagree that *Train* represents a shift in Baldwin's political sensibility from the "individual" to the "institutional," since these realms are closely linked in all of Baldwin's work. In this chapter I argue that *Train* exposes the failure of American liberalism to end racism and puts such liberal ideals as upward mobility and the opportunity for individual success under pressure. I also argue that Baldwin's politics in *Train* (as well as in the rest of his work) must be understood in terms of the relationship between American racism and sexual hierarchies as they are played out on the black male body.

5. More black Americans were unemployed in 1964 than in 1954, and the unemployment gap between the races was higher. It was becoming increasingly clear to civil rights workers that abolishing segregation, alone, would not address the problems of urban blacks. See Lee Rainwater and William L. Yancey, *The Moynihan Report and the Politics of Controversy* (Cambridge, Mass.: MIT Press, 1967), 11.

6. The FBI compiled a large file on James Baldwin, more than 1,700 pages, which Natalie Robins obtained under the Freedom of Information Act. See Natalie Robins, *Alien Ink: The FBI's War on Freedom of Expression* (New York: William Morrow, 1992), 345–49. Also see Maurice Wallace, "'I'm Not Entirely What I Look Like': Richard Wright, James Baldwin, and the Hegemony of Vision; or, Jimmy's FBEye Blues," in *James Baldwin Now*, ed. Dwight McBride (New York: New York University Press, 1999), 305. Robins says that Baldwin is first mentioned in Wright's FBI file in 1951 as a young Negro writer who "attacked the hatred themes of the Wright writings." By 1960 the FBI had classified Baldwin as "dangerous." Robins says, "The FBI employed a great many confidential informants to shadow Baldwin, people who attended rallies and meetings with him, and reported what he said and did, as well as neighbors who were willing to keep a surveillance on him, or monitor his mail for any change of address. The FBI also telephoned him under various pretexts to ascertain his whereabouts, and photographed him." In 1964 he was targeted in a COINTELPRO operation. The files show that the Bureau was not only interested in Baldwin as a political activist, but in the possible "obscenity" of his writing and in his lifestyle. A note of J. Edgar Hoover reads: "Isn't Baldwin a well known pervert?"

   Although Baldwin never saw his file, he was aware that he was often followed: "Later, after the assassinations of the Kennedys and Martin Luther King, Jr., and Malcolm X, [Baldwin] took the FBI's activities very seriously and often spoke of fearing for his own life" (Leeming, *James Baldwin*, 225–26). Also see Baldwin's conversations with Margaret Mead and Ida Lewis for his own description of how he was affected by the assassinations. Margaret Mead and James Baldwin, *A Rap on Race* (Philadelphia: J. B. Lippincott, 1971), 10, 244; James Baldwin, interview by Ida Lewis (1970), in Standley and Pratt, *Conversations with James Baldwin*, 85.

7. See Ward Churchill and Jim VanderWall, *Agents of Repression: The FBI's Secret Wars against the Black Panther Party and the American Indian Movement* (Boston: South End Press, 1988). For an early description of federal and local authorities' actions against the Black Panthers, including a document from the FBI counterintelligence, see Steve Weissman's *Big Brother and the Holding Company: The World Behind Watergate* (Palto Alto, Calif: Ramparts Press, 1974), 28–30, 317–19.

8. For an example of disgust at the novel's sexual themes, see William Edward Farrison's

"If Baldwin's Train Had Not Gone," in *James Baldwin: A Critical Evaluation,* ed. Therman B. O'Daniel (Washington, D.C.: Howard University Press, 1977), 70. Farrison complains about the "plethora of sexual acts . . . in which the story needlessly abounds" and describes the Proudhammer-Black Christopher relationship as "not the kind that deserves the approval of normal, healthy-minded people."

9. Emmanuel S. Nelson, "Critical Deviance: Homophobia and the Reception of James Baldwin's Fiction," *Journal of American Culture* 14, no. 3 (1991): 91. Stephen Adams also makes this argument: "There would seem to be some correlation between this decline in critical esteem and the increasing prominence given to the homosexual theme in his novels." Stephen Adams, *The Homosexual as Hero in Contemporary Fiction* (New York: Harper and Row, 1980), 45.

10. All page numbers refer to James Baldwin, *Tell Me How Long the Train's Been Gone* (New York: Dial, 1968; New York: Dell, 1969). Over the course of the novel we learn, somewhat cryptically at first, that Barbara has had a sexual relationship with Leo's lover, Christopher, in order to rekindle her relationship with Leo. Symbolically the lovers-friends are represented as a family where familial bonds take precedence over sexual competition. When they are young, Leo and Barbara refer to each other as brother and sister (218). Leo's interest in Christopher is clearly paternal as well as sexual. (At one point Leo sees him as an orphan needing to be rescued [344].) Christopher refers to Leo as "Big Daddy" (350). Barbara refers to Leo as a "stubborn child" and is maternally protective of him (239). Barbara's interest in Christopher is motivated by her desire to reexperience her love for Leo (362–63). Although Barbara says that Christopher represents "our journey through hell," she also believes that the relationship with Christopher has "redeemed" something between herself and Leo (80). In addition, Barbara believes that the affair showed Christopher that "love is possible" (363). Christopher wonders why Leo and Barbara, lifelong best friends, never married (351).

11. Irving Howe read *Train* as a conventional success story: "buried deep within this seemingly iconoclastic writer is a very conventional sensibility, perfectly attuned to the daydream of success." I argue, on the contrary, that Baldwin's reading of the American success story is not at all conventional. See Howe, "At Ease in Apocalypse," 103.

12. Leeming, *James Baldwin,* 278.

13. W. J. Weatherby, *James Baldwin: Artist on Fire* (New York: Dell, 1989), 313–14.

14. Baldwin, *Tell Me How Long the Train's Been Gone,* 356–58.

15. Ibid., 250.

16. Puzo, "His Cardboard Lovers," 156.

17. Houston A. Baker Jr. attributed the increasingly negative reception of Baldwin's later work not to an alleged "artistic decline" but to Baldwin's "renewed" interest in black culture, and noted that there "are too few critics versed in black American culture to testify to [Baldwin's] present stance." Baker, "The Embattled Craftsman: An Essay on James Baldwin," *The Journal of African-Afro-American Affairs* 1, no. 1 (1977): 28. Reviews such as Puzo's provide much credence to Baker's argument, and the continued paucity of work done on Baldwin's later fiction suggests that Baker's call for a new kind of critic remains relevant.

18. Robert B. Stepto, *From behind the Veil: A Study of Afro-American Narrative* (Urbana: University of Illinois Press, 1979). For an overview of the influence of the slave narrative on African American literary forms, see Charles T. Davis and Henry Louis Gates Jr.'s *The Slave's Narrative* (Oxford: Oxford University Press, 1985), xviii–xxxiv.

19. Stepto, *From behind the Veil,* 132.

20. Frederick Douglass, *Narrative of the Life of Frederick Douglass, an American Slave, Written by Himself,* ed. Houston A. Baker Jr. (1845; reprint, New York: Penguin American Library, 1982), 75.

21. Richard Wright, *Black Boy* ( New York: Perennial-Harper and Brothers, 1945; New York: Perennial Classics, 1966), 42.

22. Ibid., 43.

23. Douglass, *Narrative,* 151.

24. William Andrews, *To Tell a Free Story: The First Century of Afro-American Autobiography, 1760–1865* (Urbana: University of Illinois Press, 1985), 127.

25. Douglass, *Narrative,* 121.

26. Charles T. Davis, "From Experience to Eloquence: Richard Wright's *Black Boy* as Art (1979)," in *Black Is the Color of the Cosmos: Essays on Afro-American Literature and Culture, 1942–1981* (New York: Garland Publishing, 1982), 288.

27. Baldwin, *Tell Me How Long the Train's Been Gone,* 7

28. Ibid., 31.

29. Ibid.

30. Ibid., 32.

31. *Spirituals and Gospels* (New York: Wise Publications, 1975), 30.

32. Baldwin, *Tell Me How Long the Train's Been Gone,* 55.

33. Ibid., 54.

34. Ibid., 63–64.

35. Ibid., 75.

36. Ibid., 76.

37. Ibid., 106–7.

38. Ibid., 107.

39. Ibid., 332.

40. Ibid., 84.

41. Ibid., 84–85.

42. Ibid., 84.

43. Ibid., 87.

44. Ibid., 334.

45. Ibid., 362.

46. Stepto, *From behind the Veil,* 167.

47. W. E. B. Du Bois, *The Souls of Black Folk* (1903; reprint, New York: Signet-New American Library Edition, 1969), 45.

48. Ibid., 49.

49. Baldwin, *Tell Me How Long the Train's Been Gone,* 143.

50. Ibid., 154.

51. Ibid., 216–18.

52. Ibid., 124.

53. Ibid., 144.

54. Stepto, *From behind the Veil*, 68.

55. Baldwin, *Tell Me How Long the Train's Been Gone*, 145.

56. "I have often been been utterly astonished, since I came to the north, to find persons who could speak of the singing, among slaves, as evidence of their contentment and happiness. It is impossible to conceive of a greater mistake. Slaves sing most when they are most unhappy. The songs of the slave represent the sorrows of his heart; and he is relieved by them, only as an aching heart is relieved by its tears" (Douglass, *Narrative*, 58).

57. Baldwin, *Tell Me How Long the Train's Been Gone*, 146.

58. Victor Turner, as quoted in Stepto, *From behind the Veil*, 69.

59. Baldwin, *Tell Me How Long the Train's Been Gone*, 365.

60. Ibid., 366.

61. Ibid., 368.

62. Ibid., 369.

63. Ibid.

64. See James Baldwin's *No Name in the Street* (New York: Dial Press, 1972; New York: Delta-Dell, 1973), 179–89, for a nonfictional description of San Francisco in the late sixties where Baldwin reflects on race relations and the possibility of *communitas*. The chaos and fragmentation of *Train's* dance hall scene is revoiced in the following passage:

> In this place, and more particularly, in this time, generations appear to flower, flourish, and wither with the speed of light. I don't think that this is merely the inevitable reflection of middle age: I suspect that there really has been some radical alteration in the structure, the nature, of time. One may say that there are no clear images; everything seems superimposed on, and at war with something else. There are no clear vistas: the road that seems to pull one forward into the future is also pulling one backward into the past. I felt, anyway, kaleidoscopic, fragmented, walking through the streets of San Francisco, trying to decipher whatever it was that my own consciousness made of all the elements in which I was entangled, and which were all tangled up in me.

65. Baldwin, *Tell Me How Long the Train's Been Gone*, 7–8.

66. Ralph Ellison, *Invisible Man* (New York: Random House, 1952; New York: Vintage-Random House, 1972), 33.

67. Ibid., 552–53.

68. James Baldwin says in the introduction to *Nobody Knows My Name* (New York: Dial, 1961; New York: Dell, 1963), 12: "Havens are high-priced. The price exacted of the haven-dweller is that he contrive to delude himself into believing that he has found a haven." Baldwin is discussing his return to America from Europe. The statement is consistent with Baldwin's representation of the artist as an involved political figure and may, in fact, be a response to Ellison's image of hibernation in *Invisible Man*.

69. Stepto, *From behind the Veil*, 163–94.

70. Ibid., 168.

71. Ellison, *Invisible Man*, 568.

72. Ibid., 345–46.

73. Ibid., 568.

74. Baldwin, *Tell Me How Long the Train's Been Gone*, 107.

75. Ibid., 243.

76. Ibid., 370.

77. For example, the reviewer for *Time* stated that *Tell Me How Long the Train's Been Gone* "rambles like a milk train over the same run that Baldwin covered *in Another Country*, creaks over the same hard ground, sounds the same blast about the Negro's condition, rattles the same rationale for homosexuality." See "Milk Run," review of *Tell Me How Long the Train's Been Gone*, by James Baldwin, *Time*, 7 June 1968, 104. Also see Calvin C. Hernton's description of *Train* as "nothing but a reshuffling of the same old cards on the same old games" ("A Fiery Baptism," in *James Baldwin*, 119).

78. Campbell, *Talking at the Gates*, 228.

79. Baldwin, *Tell Me How Long the Train's Been Gone*, 108.

80. Ibid., 213.

81. Ibid., 209

82. Baker, "Embattled Craftsman," 40; James Baldwin, *The Fire Next Time* (New York: Dial, 1963), 141.

83. Following are the lyrics to "Go Tell It on de Mountains," in *Spirituals and Gospels*, 19. Originally copyrighted in 1975 by Dorsey Brothers Music Limited.

> When I was a lear-ner, I sought both night and day,
> I ask the Lord to help me, An' He show me the way.
> Go tell it on de mountains, O-ver de hills an' ev-'ry where.
> Go tell it on de mountains, Our Je-sus Christ is born.
>
> \* \* \*
>
> He made me a watch-man, Up on the city wall,
> An if I am a Christian, I am the least of all.
> [Repeat: Go tell . . . ]
>
> \* \* \*
>
> While shepherds kept their watching, O'er wand'ring flock by night;
> Behold! from out the heavens, There shone a holy light.
> [Repeat: Go tell . . . ]
>
> \* \* \*
>
> And lo! when they had seen it, They all bowed down and prayed;
> Then travel'd on together, To where the babe was laid.
> [Repeat: Go tell . . . ]

84. George D. Kelsey, "George D. Kelsey preaches and leads congregation in gospel music in Washington, D.C," recorded 22 August 1948, Voice Library, M579 bd.2, Michigan State University, East Lansing, Mich.

85. Shirley Allen, "Religious Symbolism and Psychic Reality in Baldwin's *Go Tell It on the Mountain*," *CLAJ* 19 (December 1975): 175.

86. Houston A. Baker Jr., *Blues, Ideology, and Afro-American Literature: A Vernacular Theory* (Chicago: University of Chicago Press, 1984), 1–14.

87. Following are the lyrics to "Mary Had a Baby, Yes Lord," in Erskine Peters, ed., *Lyrics of the Afro-American Spiritual: A Documentary Collection* (Westport, Conn.: Greenwood, 1993), 28.

> Yes, Lord!
> Mary had a baby,
> Yes, Lord!
> Mary had a baby,
> Yes, Lord!
> The people keep a-coming
> And the train done gone.
>
> \* \* \*
>
> Mary had a baby,
> Yes, Lord!
> What did she name him?
> She named him King Jesus,
> She named him Mighty Counselor.
> Where was he born?
> Born in a manger,
> Yes, Lord.
>
> \* \* \*
>
> Mary had a baby,
> Yes, Lord!
> The people keep a-coming
> And the train done gone.

88. Baldwin, *Tell Me How Long the Train's Been Gone,* 368.

89. James Baldwin, *Go Tell It on the Mountain* (New York: Dial, 1953; New York: Laurel-Dell, 1985), 19.

90. Ibid.

91. Ibid, 33.

92. Baldwin, *Tell Me How Long the Train's Been Gone,* 171.

93. Ibid., 174

94. Baldwin, *Go Tell It on the Mountain,* 33.

95. Ibid., 34.

96. Baldwin, *Tell Me How Long the Train's Been Gone,* 366.

97. Ibid., 11–12.

98. Ibid, 170.

99. Calvin Hernton completely missed the revision of the father-son relationship in *Train,* claiming that "the obsession with the father comes across as nothing less than Patricidal Mania." See Hernton, "A Fiery Baptism," 188.

100. Leeming, *James Baldwin,* 280.

101. Baldwin, *Tell Me How Long the Train's Been Gone*, 165.

102. Ibid., 90

103. Ibid.

104. Ibid., 157.

105. Ibid., 370

106. Ibid., 335.

107. Ibid.

108. Ibid., 19.

109. Ibid., 370.

110. For an excellent analysis of Baldwin's depiction of the connection between racism and homophobia in *Another Country,* see Susan Feldman's "Another Look at *Another Country*: Reconciling Baldwin's Racial and Sexual Politics," in *Re-viewing James Baldwin: Things Not Seen,* ed. D. Quentin Miller (Philadelphia: Temple University Press, 2000), 88–104.

111. Baldwin, *Tell Me How Long the Train's Been Gone*, 179.

112. Ibid., 182.

113. Ibid., 185–86.

114. Ibid., 180.

115. Ibid., 159.

116. Ibid., 157.

117. Ibid., 163.

118. For a critique of Freud's construction of homosexuality as immaturity, see Jonathan Ned Katz, *The Invention of Heterosexuality* (New York: Plume Penguin, 1996), 73–79.

119. See especially Leslie Fiedler's "The Failure of Sentiment and the Evasion of Love," chapter 11 of *Love and Death in the American Novel*, rev. ed. (1966; New York: Third Scarborough Books Edition, 1982), 337–90.

120. The "unusual door" is Baldwin's metaphor for homoerotic love. In the introduction to *The Price of the Ticket: Collected Nonfiction, 1948–1985* (New York: St. Martin's and Marek, 1985) Baldwin describes the importance of his friendship with the black, homosexual artist Beauford Delaney: "*Lord,* I was to hear Beauford sing, later, and for many years, *open the unusal door.* My running buddy had sent me to the right one, and not a moment too soon" (x; italics in the original). Near the beginning of *Tell Me How Long the Train's Been Gone*, Leo imagines "how Christopher must have sometimes felt" and goes on discuss love as the doorway to the self: "And yet—one would prefer, after all, not to be locked out. One would prefer, merely, that the key unlocked a less stunningly unusual door" (7)

# CHAPTER 3

1. As quoted in David Leeming, *James Baldwin: A Biography* (New York: Alfred A. Knopf, 1994), 321.

2. James Baldwin, "Come out the Wilderness," in *Going to Meet the Man* (New York: Dial, 1965; New York: Laurel-Dell, 1976), 187.

3. Ibid.

4. Adrienne Rich, "When We Dead Awaken: Writing as Revision (1971)," reprinted in *The Norton Anthology of Literature by Women: The Tradition in English*, ed. Sandra M. Gilbert and Susan Gubar (New York: W. W. Norton and Co., 1985), 2045–46.

5. Ibid., 2046. Rich was calling for a feminist critique of male texts, and I'm aware of the irony of using her definition of "re-vision" to describe Baldwin's novel *If Beale Street Could Talk*, a novel that some feminist critics have persuasively described as both sexist and heterosexist. However, I do believe that Baldwin's work in *Beale Street* was re-visionist in relationship to his own earlier work and to social discourses on race and literature in much of the manner that Rich describes.

6. Ivan Webster, review of *If Beale Street Could Talk*, by James Baldwin, *New Republic*, 15 June 1974, 26.

7. James Baldwin, *If Beale Street Could Talk* (New York: Dial, 1974), 193–94.

8. Ibid., 86.

9. Houston A. Baker Jr., "The Embattled Craftsman: An Essay on James Baldwin," *The Journal of African-Afro-American Affairs* 1, no. 1 (1977): 48.

10. Leeming, *James Baldwin*, 323.

11. For sources on the Tony Maynard case, see W. J. Weatherby, *James Baldwin: Artist on Fire* (New York: Dell Publishing, 1989), 328–29; Leeming, *James Baldwin*, 289–90, 296, and 301; and James Baldwin, *No Name in the Street* (New York: Dial, 1972; New York: Delta-Dell, 1973), 109–16.

12. Baldwin, *No Name in the Street*, 196.

13. Ibid., 109.

14. Leeming's chronological bibliography of Baldwin's writing and interviews lists thirty-three entries between *Train* and *Beale Street* (*James Baldwin*, 412–13).

15. Ibid., 316–17.

16. For example, see Baldwin's interviews by Eve Auchincloss and Nancy Lynch (1969), 64–82; by Ida Lewis (1970), 83–97; and by John Hall (1970), 98–107; all can be found in Standley and Pratt, *Conversations with James Baldwin*.

17. James Baldwin, interview by Eve Auchincloss and Nancy Lynch (1969), in Standley and Pratt, *Conversations with James Baldwin*, 68.

18. Baldwin, *No Name in the Street*, 135.

19. Ibid, 165.

20. James Baldwin, interview by Herbert R. Lottman (1972), in Standley and Pratt, *Conversations with James Baldwin*, 112.

21. Ibid., 85.

22. Margaret Mead and James Baldwin, *A Rap on Race* (Philadelphia: J. B. Lippincott, 1971), 10.

23. Ibid., 244.

24. James Baldwin, interview by Eve Auchincloss and Nancy Lynch (1969), Standley and Pratt, *Conversations with James Baldwin*, 82.

25. James Baldwin, interview by David Frost (1970), Standley and Pratt, *Conversations with James Baldwin*, 96.

26. James Baldwin and Nikki Giovanni, *A Dialogue* (Philadelphia: J. B. Lippincott, 1973), 26–27.

27. James Baldwin, interview by Herbert R. Lottman (1972), Standley and Pratt, *Conversations with James Baldwin*, 110.

28. James Baldwin, interview by Joe Walker (1972), Standley and Pratt, *Conversations with James Baldwin*, 140.

29. Ibid., 141.

30. Mead and Baldwin, *A Rap on Race*, 248.

31. Ibid., 249.

32. Ibid.

33. Ibid., 251.

34. James Baldwin, interview by *The Black Scholar* (1973), Standley and Pratt, *Conversations with James Baldwin*, 157–58.

35. Weatherby, *James Baldwin*, 357.

36. James Baldwin, "An Open Letter to My Sister, Miss Angela Davis," *New York Review of Books*, 7 January 1971, 15.

37. Baldwin and Giovanni, *A Dialogue*, 16.

38. James Baldwin, interview by *The Black Scholar* (1973), Standley and Pratt, *Conversations with James Baldwin*, 143.

39. Ibid.

40. Also see LeRoi Jones's "Brief Reflections on Two Hot Shots," in *Home: Social Essays* (New York: William Morrow, 1966), 117, where Jones takes Baldwin to task for his "individualism," describing Baldwin as "shriek[ing] the shriek of a fashionable international body of white middle class society . . . a Joan of Arc of the cocktail party." Comparing Baldwin to a black South African writer Jones says, "If Abrahams and Baldwin were turned white . . . there would be no more noise from them. Not because they consciously desire that, but because then they could be sensitive in peace" (120). David Leeming also refers to an alleged insult from Ishmael Reed and others (*James Baldwin*, 304). In "The Last Interview (1987)" Baldwin tells Quincy Troupe that Reed insulted him: "it seemed to be beneath him, his anger and contempt for me," in *James Baldwin: The Legacy*, ed. Quincy Troupe (Touchstone-Simon and Schuster, 1989), 202.

41. As quoted in Leeming, *James Baldwin*, 316.

42. Henry Louis Gates Jr., "What Baldwin Can and Can't Teach America," *New Republic*, 1 June 1992, 40.

43. Ibid., 42.

44. Baldwin and Giovanni, *A Dialogue*, 59.

45. Ibid., 62–63.

46. James Baldwin, interview by Eve Achincloss and Nancy Lynch (1970), Standley and Pratt, *Conversations with James Baldwin*, 81.

47. James Baldwin, "The Discovery of What It Means to Be an American," in *The Price of the Ticket: Collected Nonfiction, 1948–1985* (New York: St. Martin's and Merk, 1985), 171.

48. James Baldwin, interview by *The Black Scholar* (1973), Standley and Pratt,

*Conversations with James Baldwin,* 154.

49. In a 1979 interview with Kalamu ya Salaam, "James Baldwin: Looking toward the Eighties," reprinted in Fred L. Standley and Nancy V. Burt's *Critical Essays on James Baldwin* (Boston: G. K. Hall, 1988), 36–37, Baldwin discusses his life as a "commuter" between the United States and Europe in terms of a double (but not incompatible) responsibility as an activist-teacher and as a writer.

> Baldwin: For a very long time until Martin died, I was operating as a public speaker in the context of the civil rights movement. And when Martin died, something happened to me and something happened to many people. It took a while for me and for many people to pull ourselves back together. Then I had to find another way to discharge what I considered to be my responsibility. I've been working on college campuses and in prisons; which is why I don't bring my typewriter across the ocean.
>
> Salaam: The responsibility on the other side of the ocean is to be a writer in the sense of a craftsperson who puts words on the page. The responsibility on this side is what?
>
> Baldwin: On this side my responsibility is, well, it's very difficult to answer that because it involves being available, it involves being visible, it involves being vulnerable, it involves my concept of my responsibility to people coming after me and to people who came before me. . . .
>
> Salaam: To, in a sense, tell their story, so that others can understand from whence they came.
>
> Baldwin: Yes. I consider myself to be a witness.
>
> Salaam: On one side of the ocean you can write about what you have witnessed, and on this side of the ocean you bear witness to that which you would write about.
>
> Baldwin: That puts it about as well as it can be put.

50. James Baldwin, interview by James Hall (1970), Standley and Pratt, *Conversations with James Baldwin,* 104.

51. Ibid., 157.

52. James Baldwin, "The Black Situation Now," interview, *Washington Post,* 21 July 1974, C4.

53. Baldwin, "An Open Letter," 16.

54. Baldwin and Giovanni, *A Dialogue,* 20.

55. Ibid., 21.

56. For a discussion of Baldwin's construction of complex subjectivity in *Go Tell It on the Mountain,* see Vivian M. May's "Ambivalent Narratives, Fragmented Selves: Performative Identities and the Mutability of Roles in James Baldwin's *Go Tell It on the Mountain,*" in *New Essays on "Go Tell It on the Mountain,"* ed. Trudier Harris (New York: Cambridge University Press, 1996), 97–126.

57. The most negative reviews of *If Beale Street Could Talk* were John Aldridge's "The Fire Next Time?" *Saturday Review World,* 15 June 1974, 20, 24–25; Pearl K. Bell's "Blacks and the Blues," *New Leader,* 27 May 1974, 3–5; Anatole Broyard's "No Color Line in Cliches," *New York Times,* 17 May 1974, 37; Thomas R. Edwards's "Can You Go Home Again?" *New York Review of Books,* 13 June 1974, 37–38; and June Jordan's "If Beale Street Could Talk," *Village Voice,* 20 June 1974, 33–35.

John Aldridge's review was not only devastating but off the mark. For example, his claim that "Baldwin's artistry has frequently been placed beyond judgment because of the sacredness of his subject" (20) is not supported by even a cursory look at the reception Baldwin's work actually received. He viewed *Beale Street* as the proof of Baldwin's long slide into sentimentality and describes the novel as "junk" which promotes the illusion that "ghetto blacks are very happy with their lot" (26). In conclusion he claimed that Baldwin has one great novel left to write: the story of a talented black writer "who achieves world-wide success on the strength of his anger and, in succeeding, gradually loses his anger and comes to be loved by everybody" (25). Aldridge's commentary on Baldwin's "anger" is confused. He seems to arguing that Baldwin's "success" has made him less angry and that without anger Baldwin is no longer able to write well (hence his slide into "sentimentality"). Most critics who speculated on the relationship between Baldwin's anger and his art came to quite different conclusions. Donald B. Gibson, *The Politics of Literary Expression: A Study of Major Black Writers*, Contributions in Afro-American and African Studies, no. 63 (Westport, Conn.: Greenwood Press, 1981), viewed *Beale Street* as a novel which "expresses a lot of frustration and anger" and claimed that "the intensity of [Baldwin's] moralizing rhetoric is in direct proportion to the degree of his frustration with the country that has, fate of fates, given him his success" (118). Carolyn Wedin Sylvander, *James Baldwin* (New York: Frederick Ungar, 1980), wrote that some of "the lack of control and the anger" of *Beale Street* was "perhaps . . . generated by the personal experience Baldwin was dramatizing." Of course Baldwin had not lost his anger. In the face of the increasing setbacks in the struggle for black freedom, he was quite unwilling to make the separate peace that Aldridge says he did. If anything Baldwin's work in the seventies is inflected by more anger rather than less, but he faced an audience that had become increasingly less willing to believe in or listen to his jeremiad.

Pearl K. Bell described *Beale Street* as Baldwin's "shallowest work of fiction," committing "those very atrocities of distortion and stereotyping that [Baldwin] long ago deplored in *Native Son*" and the tradition of the "protest" novel in general. An "ethnic soap opera," the plot was "factitious," the characters, "one-dimensional," and Tish's voice "inconsistent," ranging from "a tough and brutal Harlem idiom into sudden inexplicable flights of highly sophisticated literary imagery—the intrusive ventriloquist's voice, in fact, of James Baldwin" (4–5). Anatole Broyard objected to the "siren sounds of terror" and wondered how nonblack readers received Tish's often uncompromising language, such as "we live in a nation of pigs and murderers" (37). Dismissing *Beale Street* as sentimental fiction, an "urbanized 'Perils of Pauline,'" Broyard flippantly characterizes the story as containing "the most Heralded pregnancy since the Annunciation" (37).

Thomas R. Edwards found it impossible to read the novel "as accurate social drama" because he did not believe Fonny's case would have gone so badly: "In the real world, one wonders if even the most officious Assistant DA would touch such a case, or if even the most bigoted examining magistrate would bind over the defendant without even allowing bail" (38). (Actually, bail is set for Fonny near the end and an important element of the plot is the family's struggle to raise it.) Edwards found the novel "bitter" and disturbing; blackness becomes "a condition of helpless passivity . . . persecution and violation are emphasized so insistently and despairingly that enduring them becomes a kind of acceptance" (38).

Mary Fair Burks's "James Baldwin's Protest Novel," *Negro American Literature Forum* 10, no. 3 (1976): 83–95, was generally negative in tone. While she acknowledged that *Beale Street* has moments of "moving, unforgettable beauty," she found it generally disappointing.

The most positive reviews were Joyce Carol Oates's "A Quite Moving and Very Traditional Celebration of Love," *New York Times Book Review,* 26 May 1974, reprinted in *Critical Essay on James Baldwin,* ed. Fred L. Standley and Nancy V. Burt (Boston: G. K. Hall, 1988), 158–61; John McCluskey's "If Beale Street Could Talk," *Black World,* December 1974, 51–52, 88–91; Ivan Webster's review in *New Republic,* 15 June 1974, 25–26; Louis D. Mitchell's review in *Best Sellers,* 15 May 1974, 106–7; and Michael Joseph's "Blacks and Blues," *Times Literary Supplement,* 21 June 1974, 656. Ivan Webster dubbed *Beale Street* a "major work of black American fiction" and Baldwin's "best novel yet" (25). Webster liked the theme of hope, represented by Tish's unborn child, which he thought of as uncharacteristic of Baldwin, and he was particularly impressed by the women characters, whom he found to be "extraordinary," and who "carry the book" (26). Louis D. Mitchell also praised *Beale Street* as "a fine exercise in the many possibilities of Negro life in America" (106). He described the plot as a "struggle against impossible odds . . . resolved in the typical blues transcendence" and the style as "straight, simple, powerful and never dull" (107). Comparing *Beale Street* to *Love Story,* Joseph praised Baldwin's novel for "balanc[ing] the ledger on the side of truthfulness" (656).

In the British press the reception was fairly negative except for Michael Joseph's review above. Other British reviews were Peter Straub's "Happy Ends," *New Statesman,* 28 June 1974, 930; Peter Ackroyd's "A Little Black Magic," *Spectator,* 6 July 1974, 22; and David Thomas's "Too Black, Too White," *Listener,* 25 July 1974, 125. Straub conceded that the novel contains "much affecting writing" but claimed that "Baldwin's hate collapses everything into a rigid scheme." Ackroyd judged the novel harshly for its "mawkish" style, lack of detail, and "cardboard" characters, but also observed that Baldwin "has never aspired to casual, Yankee mimetism, and the model for his black allegories lies somewhere around D. H. Lawrence." Thomas read *Beale Street* as a "fable" celebrating the Negro American's "new-found capacity for self-creation" and "quest for cultural freedom." Yet he believed that Baldwin created this new image of blackness in "opposition to everything white" and charged him with cartoon portrayals of whites: "It is as if the black American must now begin to invent the white American, his white American, in order to discover his own identity" (125).

Following its initial reception, *If Beale Street Could Talk* has received somewhat more critical attention than *Tell Me How Long the Train's Been Gone.* Critics writing in the later seventies regarded *Beale Street* as a significant new development in Baldwin's representation of love and the family, and some thought it reflected an "evolution" in Baldwin's politics. Their arguments will be taken up in the course of this chapter. See Baker, "The Embattled Craftsman"; Louis H. Pratt, *James Baldwin* (Boston: Twayne Publishers, 1978); Gibson, *Politics of Literary Expression*; and Craig Werner "The Economic Evolution of James Baldwin," in *Critical Essays on James Baldwin*, 78–93. Friederike Hajek "James Baldwin: Beale Street Blues," *Weimarer Beitrage: Zeitschrift fur Literaturwissenschaft, Asthetik und Kulturtheorie* 23, no. 6 (1977): 137–50, saw a shift in Baldwin's approach from internalizing and subjectivizing social relationships to a direct confrontation with society where individuals act in solidarity with one another. She compared Baldwin's answer to racial oppression in *Beale Street* to Malcolm X's injunction that the oppressed must fight for their freedom "by any means necessary."

58. McCluskey ("If Beale Street Could Talk") described *Beale Street* as ending hopefully, with the bail money raised, Fonny released from jail, and the birth of the child signaling "the return and the resurrection" (88). Reading the novel as a tribute to the black family's ability to resist oppression, Pratt, in *James Baldwin*, also believed the novel ends optimistically: "Although he continues to dwell in legal limbo, Fonny has been released from prison, and he has been united with Tish and the baby" (80). Yoshinobu Hakutani, "If the Street Could Talk," in *James Baldwin's Search for Love and Understanding: The City in African-American Literature,* ed. Yoshinobu Hakutani and Robert Butler (London: Associated University Presses, 1995), claimed Baldwin ends the novel "on a triumphant note" with Fonny out of jail "however temporary it may be" (164). On the other hand, Sylvander, in *James Baldwin*, wrote that the ending of *Beale Street* is "not clear," although given the "heroism" of the family, the ending suggests that "it will all turn out all right, whatever all right is" (85–86). Gibson, in *Politics of Literary Expression*, argued that the ending is ambiguous, because we don't know if the final scene is "real, fantasy, or a combination of these," but the title of the last section, "Zion," suggests a positive ending (119). Robert Detweiler, in "Blues Lament" review of *If Beale Street Could Talk*, by James Baldwin, *Christian Century*, 31 July 1974, wrote that the lack of plot resolution "frustrates the reader [and] mirrors the frustration of the black families in their efforts to free Fonny" (752). Burks, in "James Baldwin's Protest Novel," claimed Fonny is still in jail when the novel ends (159). Oates, in "A Quite Moving Celebration," wrote "at the novel's end, Fonny is out on bail, his trial postponed indefinitely" and read the novel as a "parable stressing the irresolute nature of our destinies." Aldridge, in "The Fire Next Time?" thought the novel ends with Fonny still in prison and the trial indefinitely postponed. Straub, in "Happy Ends," believed that Fonny "abandons hope" and that the ending "suggest[s] that the only release is in art or childbearing, a profoundly despairing, profoundly shocking implication."

59. Aldridge, "The Fire Next Time?" and Edwards, "Can You Go Home Again?" See n. 57, above.

60. Jordan, "If Beale Street Could Talk," 34.

61. Ibid.

62. Oates, "A Quite Moving Celebration," 159.

63. Ibid., 161.

64. Ibid., 159.

65. McCluskey, "If Beale Street Could Talk," 89.

66. Ibid., 89–90.

67. Ibid., 91.

68. Trudier Harris, "The Eye as Weapon in *If Beale Street Could Talk*," *MELUS* 5, no. 3 (1978): 63. The passage Harris refers to in *Beale Street* where Tish first makes love with Fonny reads: "I was in his hands, he called me by the thunder at my ear. I was in his hands: I was being changed; all that I could do was cling to him" (78). As Harris notes, Baldwin's language alludes to the first verse of "Steal Away to Jesus," which begins: "My Lord, He calls me, / He calls me by the thunder, / The trumpet sounds within-a my soul" (for the full text see Erskine Peters, ed., *Lyrics of the Afro-American Spiritual: A Documentary Collection* (Westport, Conn.: Greenwood Press, 1993), xxi). Harris finds the Christian allusion as evidence of the novel's patriarchal values through the association of Fonny with "the Lord" and Tish with "the converted." However, Harris doesn't mention the more secular associations of the song, which seem relevant here. During the antebellum period "Steal Away" was sung as a coded call to escape from slavery. Read this way, Fonny is less associated with the Lord than with a free man whose love promises to lead Tish to freedom. This reading is consistent with Baldwin's substitution of sexual, human love for the dogma and abstraction of religious belief and practice. In addition, spirituals are used to express not only heterosexual love, but homosexual love as well in Baldwin's work. For example, in *Just Above My Head*, Jimmy lets Arthur know he loves him by singing "Just a Closer Walk with Thee."

69. Hortense Spillers, "The Politics of Intimacy: A Discussion," in *Sturdy Black Bridges: Visions of Black Women in Literature*, ed. Roseann P. Bell, Bettye J. Parker, and Beverly Guy Sheftall (Garden City, N.Y.: Anchor Books, 1979), 88.

70. Ibid., 99.

71. Ibid., 94–95.

72. Ibid., 99.

73. Baldwin and Giovanni, *A Dialogue*, 88–89.

74. In "Preservation of Innocence," reprinted *Out/Look: National Lesbian and Gay Quarterly* 6 (fall 1989), Baldwin argues that the present debasement of the homosexual in our society "corresponds to the debasement of the relationship between the sexes" (41). Baldwin implies that maturity (as opposed to false innocence) requires discarding distorted concepts of masculinity and femininity and acknowledging that people possess complex traits: "In the truly awesome attempt of the American to at once preserve his innocence and arrive at a man's estate, that mindless monster, the tough guys have been created and perfected whose masculinity is found in the most infantile and elemental externals and whose attitude towards women is the wedding of the most abysmal romanticism and the most implacable distrust" (43).

75. Cora Kaplan, "'A Cavern Opened in My Mind': The Poetics of Homosexuality and the Politics of Masculinity in James Baldwin," in *Representing Black Men*, ed. Marcellus

Blount and George P. Cunningham (New York: Routledge, 1996). Kaplan states that "Baldwin's central project is not to retool femininity" and that "women are, like Eve, the bearers of important but bitter knowledge for men, not the agents or vehicles of hope" (34). While her reading of gender in Baldwin's early fiction is very perceptive, she does not examine Baldwin's later fiction. Tish is certainly a bearer of hope, and "retooling femininity" does appear to be one of Baldwin's projects in *Beale Street,* although, as I will argue later in this chapter, it remains subordinate to Baldwin's primary concern, which is to save the black male and the family.

76. Kaplan, "'A Cavern Opened,'" argues that in Baldwin's late essay he makes a "turn toward a new paradigm" (48) through the inclusion of the grotesque, leading him to a less binary construction of gender.
77. Baldwin and Giovanni, *A Dialogue,* 54–55.
78. Ibid., 40.
79. Baldwin, *If Beale Street Could Talk,* 162.
80. Ibid., 3.
81. James Baldwin, *Giovanni's Room* (New York: Dial, 1956; New York: Dell, 1964), 223.
82. Baldwin, "Sonny's Blues," in *Going to Meet the Man* (1965; reprint, New York: Laurel-Dell, 1976), 86.
83. James Baldwin, *Go Tell It on the Mountain* (New York: Dial, 1953; New York: Laurel-Dell, 1985), 27.
84. James Baldwin, *Just Above My Head* (New York: Dial, 1979; New York: Laurel-Dell, 1990), 15.
85. Baldwin, *Giovanni's Room,* 221.
86. Baldwin, *If Beale Street Could Talk,* 3.
87. Ibid.; see in particular the passage on 122–26.
88. Ibid., 177.
89. Ibid., 178.
90. See n. 58.
91. Baldwin, *If Beale Street Could Talk,* 197.
92. Ibid., 197.
93. W. C. Handy and Edward Abbe Niles, *Blues: An Anthology,* ed. Jerry Silverman (1949; reprint, New York: Macmillan, 1972), 116–19.
94. Ibid., 27.
95. Walter P. Adkins, quoted in Margaret McKee and Fred Chisenhall, *Beale Black and Blue: Life and Music on Black America's Main Street* (Baton Rouge, La.: Louisiana State University Press, 1981), 2.
96. Nat D. Williams, quoted in McKee and Chisenhall, *Beale Black and Blue,* 3.
97. Langston Hughes, *Selected Poems of Langston Hughes* (New York: Knopf, 1959; New York: Vintage-Random House, 1974), 70.
98. Ibid., 4. See Langston Hughes, "The Negro Speaks of Rivers," in *The Collected Poems of Langston Hughes* (New York: Alfred A. Knopf, 1994).
99. Trudier Harris, *Black Women in the Fiction of James Baldwin* (Knoxville, Tenn.: University of Tennessee Press, 1985), 129.

100. Baldwin and Giovanni, *A Dialogue,* 36.
101. James Baldwin interview with Kalamu ya Salaam, "James Baldwin," in *Critical Essays on James Baldwin,* 40.
102. Baldwin, *No Name in the Street,* 187.
103. Baldwin and Giovanni, *A Dialogue,* 37–38.
104. Leeming, *James Baldwin,* 3.
105. Book of Job 18:5, 16, 17. King James Bible.
106. Baldwin, *No Name in the Street,* 196.
107. Ibid., 197.
108. Baldwin, *If Beale Street Could Talk,* 197.
109. Ibid.
110. "Notes of a Native Son" was originally published in the November 1955 issue of *Harper's Magazine* as "Me and My House."
111. Baldwin, "Notes of a Native Son," in *Price of the Ticket,* 145.
112. Barbara K. Olson, "'Come-to-Jesus Stuff' in James Baldwin's *Go Tell It on the Mountain* and *The Amen Corner,*" *African American-Review* 31, no. 2 (1997): 295–301.
113. See, for example, Baldwin's discussion of his adolescent church conversion in *The Fire Next Time* (New York: Dial, 1963), 45:

> For many years, I could not ask myself why human relief had to be achieved in a fashion at once so pagan and so desperate—in a fashion at once so unspeakably old and so unutterably new. And by the time I was able to ask myself this question, I was also able to see that the principles governing the rites and customs of the churches in which I grew up did not differ from the principles governing the rites and customs of other churches, white. The principles were Blindness, Loneliness, and Terror, the first principle necessarily and actively cultivated in order to deny the two others. I would love to believe that the principles were Faith, Hope, and Charity, but this is clearly not so for most Christians, or for what we call the Christian world.

Later interviews with Nikki Giovanni (*A Dialogue*) and Kalamu ya Salaam ("James Baldwin: Looking toward the Eighties"), 40, show a shift in Baldwin's characterization of the black church, which he comes to describe as fundamentally different from the white church and as central to a distinctive American black history and culture. Even in *Fire* Baldwin pays tribute to the powerful influence the church had on him:

> The church was very exciting. It took a long time for me to disengage myself from this excitement, and on the blindest, most visceral level, I never really have, and never will. There is no music like that music, no drama like the drama of the saints rejoicing. . . . I have never seen anything to equal the fire and excitement that sometimes, without warning, fill a church, causing the church, as Leadbelly and so many others have testified, to "rock." Nothing that has happened to me since equals the power and the glory that I sometimes felt when, in the middle of a sermon, I knew that I was somehow, by some miracle, really carrying, as they said, "the Word"—when the church and I were one. (47)

114. Baldwin, *If Beale Street Could Talk,* 16.
115. Ibid., 25.

116. Ibid., 26.

117. Ibid., 68.

118. Ibid., 74.

119. Ibid., 19.

120. As a character type, Mrs. Hunt could be described as a combination of the beautiful Geraldine and the sanctified Mrs. Breedlove, two characters that appeared four years earlier in Toni Morrison's first novel, *The Bluest Eye* (New York: Holt, Rinehart and Winston, 1970; New York: Pocket Books-Washington Square Press, 1972). Both Mrs. Hunt and Mrs. Breedlove are enamored with white standards of beauty and morality. Mrs. Hunt also shares the coldness and class pretensions of Geraldine and the hypocritical religious fervor of Mrs. Breedlove. Among the considerable number of female characters that populate Baldwin's fiction, Mrs. Hunt stands out as singularly unsympathetic.

121. Baldwin, *If Beale Street Could Talk*, 37.

122. Baldwin, "The Black Situation Now," C4.

123. Baldwin, *If Beale Street Could Talk*, 27.

124. Ibid., 28.

125. Ibid., 23.

126. Ibid., 21.

127. Ibid., 33.

128. Ibid., 89.

129. Ibid., 84.

130. Baldwin, *Go Tell It on the Mountain*, 165

131. Ibid., 166.

132. Ibid., 169.

133. Ibid.

134. Ibid., 133.

135. Ibid., 167.

136. Baldwin, *If Beale Street Could Talk*, 4–5.

137. Baldwin, *Go Tell It on the Mountain*, 204.

138. Ibid., 206.

139. James Baldwin, interview by *The Black Scholar* (1973), Standley and Pratt, *Conversations with James Baldwin*, 157.

140. Ibid.

141. Baldwin, *If Beale Street Could Talk*, 36.

142. Ibid., 24.

143. Lee Rainwater and William L. Yancey, *The Moynihan Report and the Politics of Controversy* (Cambridge, Mass.: MIT Press, 1967), 3.

144. Ibid., 5

145. Ibid., 7.

146. Ibid., 416.

147. For a "wholistic" analysis of the resilience of African American families, see Andrew Billingsley's *Climbing Jacob's Ladder: The Enduring Legacy of African-American*

Families (New York: Touchstone-Simon and Schuster, 1992). Also see Andrew Hacker's *Two Nations: Black and White, Separate, Unequal* (New York: Scribners, 1992) for comparisons between racial groups in the areas of divorce, out-of-wedlock births, and households headed by women. By showing the increase of these phenomena among all groups, Hacker demonstrates that changes in traditional family life are caused by recent social and economic pressures rather than by a racial pathology dating back to slavery.

148. As quoted in Rainwater and Yancey, *The Moynihan Report*, 408.

149. As quoted in ibid., 403.

150. Baldwin, *If Beale Street Could Talk*, 191.

151. Ibid., 8.

152. Ibid., 70.

153. Ibid., 171.

154. Ibid., 172.

155. Ibid.

156. Ibid., 172–73.

157. Ibid., 174.

158. Werner, "The Economic Evolution of James Baldwin," in *Critical Essays on James Baldwin*, 89. Werner is correct in pointing out that from the late sixties on that Baldwin increasingly emphasizes the role of economic exploitation in his analyses of racism in his essays, interviews, and speeches. However, the way these ideas are manifested in *Beale Street* may be less radical than Werner would have one believe. June Jordan's remark that the characters are "weirdly isolated" has merit. The solidarity portrayed in *Beale Street* is based on ties of kinship, love, and friendship and not on any organized social or political response. Werner's argument that the "good" characters have disassociated themselves from the system and rejected an "economic perception of value" is based on their willingness to risk their own economic interest to get Fonny out of jail. Although the protagonists are more outspoken about the economic roots of oppression than earlier Baldwin characters, I would argue that their individual responses call into question the degree to which it is possible for anyone to "disassociate" themselves from the system. While the "good" characters of *Beale Street* may be freer psychologically from internalized racism, their modes of action do not seem freer. Their actions (like stealing from their jobs) are desperate, necessary, and reminiscent of John Grimes's conversion. The Rivers family, like John Grimes, negotiates some power within the terms set before it, but it does not "disassociate" itself from the economic system any more than John Grimes disassociates himself from his father's church.

159. Gibson, *Politics of Literary Expression*, 118.

160. Baldwin, "Everybody's Protest Novel," in *The Price of the Ticket*, 32.

161. Ibid., 30.

162. Ibid.

163. Ibid., 32.

164. Ibid., 28.

165. Ibid., 30.

166. Edwards, "Can You Go Home Again?" 37.

167. Burks, "James Baldwin's Protest Novel," 86.

168. Richard Wright performs a careful negotiation around the subject of theft in *Black Boy* (New York: Harper and Brothers, 1945; New York: Perennial Classic, 1966); see chapter 10. Wright indicts southern culture by arguing that it forces blacks into violating its putative moral values, while at the same time Wright appeals to those values to distinguish himself from the general dishonesty around him. In order to raise enough money to leave the South, Wright sells bootleg liquor, participates in a ticket scam, and sells stolen items from a neighbor and a Negro college. Convinced that he will not survive if he stays in the South, and careful to elaborate the absence of other options to earn money, Wright presents his "crimes" as necessary for his survival. At the same time he uses the subject of theft to distinguish himself from other blacks and to appeal to conventional moral values. Describing theft as a way of life ("all about me, Negroes were stealing," 218), as a way to address the inequities of a racist society, Wright says: "But I who stole nothing, who wanted to look them straight in the face, who wanted to talk and act like a man, inspired fear in [whites]" (219). Crime, thus, becomes its own punishment for Wright, because he associates it with being a "nonman": "In that moment I understood the pain that accompanied crime and I hoped that I would never have to feel it again. I never did feel it again, for I never stole again; and what kept me from it was the knowledge that, for me, crime carried its own punishment" (227).

169. Baldwin's invention of a family whose love and loyalty to each other involve eschewing conventional middle-class manners and goals made some readers uncomfortable. William Edward Farrison, "If Baldwin's Train Has Not Gone," in *James Baldwin: A Critical Evaluation*, ed. Therman B. O'Daniel (Washington, D.C.: Howard University Press, 1977), 79, found Tish and Fonny to be lacking in socially and morally respectable ideals, poorly educated, and unsophisticated. Carolyn Wedin Sylvander stated that "anyone with conventional standards of morality will have a hard time seeing the Rivers family as Baldwin evidently intends for the reader to see them as loving and heroic" (*James Baldwin*, 86).

170. Baldwin, *If Beale Street Could Talk*, 33.

171. Ibid., 125.

172. Ibid., 36.

173. Pratt, *James Baldwin*, 80.

174. Baldwin, *If Beale Street Could Talk*, 58.

175. Ibid., 58.

176. Ibid., 59.

177. Ibid., 59.

178. Ibid., 59–60.

179. Ibid., 27.

## CHAPTER 4

1. James Baldwin, *Just Above My Head* (New York: Dial, 1979; New York: Laurel-Dell, 1990), 498.

2. James Baldwin, interview by Wolfgang Binder (1980), in *Conversations with James Baldwin,* Fred L. Standley and Lewis H. Pratt, eds. (Jackson, Miss.: University Press of Mississippi, 1989), 191.

3. Edmund White, "James Baldwin Overcomes," review of *Just Above My Head,* by James Baldwin, *Washington Post Book World,* 23 September 1979, 9. Other very positive reviews included Hoyt Fuller, "Books," review of *Just Above My Head*, by James Baldwin, *Black Collegian,* February-March 1980, 26, 28; Margo Jefferson, "There's a Heaven Somewhere," review of *Just Above My Head,* by James Baldwin, *Nation,* 3 November 1979, 437–38; and Faith Julian, review of *Just Above My Head,* by James Baldwin, *The Critic* 38, no. 11 (1980): 2, 8. Fuller stated: "In *Just Above My Head,* perhaps the novelist has fulfilled his own promise, triumphed, for this rich, violent, convoluted, tender, searching novel speaks truths beyond the ability of the most eloquent of his essays. The novel is an achievement" (26). Jefferson found *JAMH* "wholly successful" in its treatment of homosexual love and responding to those critics who continued to complain that Baldwin's fiction lacked a social, economic, or political vision, Jefferson explained that Baldwin's sense of history is "apocalyptic, not analytic. History provides the landscape and weapons for our spiritual battles" (437). Julian claimed, "The power, lyricism and tenderness of *Just Above My Head* are Baldwin at his best" (8).

4. Three of the more negative reviews were written by Richard Gilman, review of *Just Above My Head,* by James Baldwin, *New Republic,* 24 November 1979, 30–31; Pearl K. Bell, "Roth and Baldwin: Coming Home," review of *The Ghost Writer,* by Philip Roth, and *Just Above My Head,* by James Baldwin, *Commentary,* December 1979, 72–75; and Darryl Pinckney, "Blues for Mister Baldwin," review of *Just Above My Head*, by James Baldwin, *New York Review of Books,* 6 December 1979, 32–33. Gilman described *JAMH* as "stuck halfway between life and art" and complained of a "bitter anti-white strain that runs spasmodically and inelegantly through the book" (30). Both Bell and Pinckney attributed what they viewed as an unfortunate turn in Baldwin's work to "intimidation" by Cleaver and other black nationalists.

5. Stanley Crouch, "Cliches of Degradation," review of *Just Above My Head*, by James Baldwin, *Village Voice,* 29 October 1979, judged one-third to one-half of *JAMH* to be good, containing "some of the finest scenes in recent American literature" (42). Anthony Thwaite, "Apocalyptic Gospel," review of *Just Above My Head*, by James Baldwin, *Observer,* 28 October 1979, praised the scenes that take place in the South as "a superb dramatized documentary of the Freedom Movement," although he found much of the novel to be "too diffuse, unstoppably expansive" (38). Alan Wald, "The Writer as Witness," review of *Just Above My Head,* by James Baldwin, *In These Times,* 5–11 December 1979, praised *JAMH* for its "moments of drama and passion," and its "vignettes of middle-class black life," although he viewed the novel as a whole to be "a throwback . . . reminiscent of the lonely '50's" (20). James Rawley, review of *Just Above My Head,* by James Baldwin, *Saturday Review,* 5 January 1980, argued that the novel's strength is not in the more sensational aspects of Julia and Arthur's lives, "but in sequences in which Baldwin is building the less-sensational structure of day to day

family life" scenes like the Montanas' Christmas dinner, which "rival Dickens" (49). Edmund White, "James Baldwin Overcomes," also compared Baldwin to Dickens: "though in Dickens the happy moments are all to often bathetic, whereas in Baldwin they glow with the steadiness and a clarity of a flame within a glass globe" (5).

6. See for example Roderick Nordell, "Baldwin's World of Black Gospel Singers and Evangelists," review of *Just Above My Head,* by James Baldwin, *Christian Science Monitor,* 26 September 1979, who found parts of the novel "joyfully, instructively alive," but objected to the description of homosexual experience (16). Also see Robert Fleming, "Baldwin's Gospel: Treading Stagnant Waters," review of *Just Above My Head,* by James Baldwin, *Encore American and Worldwide News,* 1 October 1979, who saw *JAMH* as "a [bow] to commercialism" and a "moral retreat" and looked forward to a Baldwin novel where "homosexuality will cease to be an essential theme" (40–41). Also see Stanley Crouch, "Cliches of Degradation," whose faint praise of *JAMH* came belatedly after a lengthy polemic against the novel's homosexual content. Crouch argued that black thinking on homosexuality is "shaped by the threat of rape" and "homosexuality is a form of identity so interwoven with exploitation and oppression that very few black Americans would connect it with liberation" (39). Paul Levy, "American Giants," review of *The Executioner's Song,* by Norman Mailer, *Just Above My Head,* by James Baldwin, *Sophie's Choice,* by William Styron, *Birdy,* by William Wharton, and *Chamber Music,* by Doris Grumbach, *Books and Bookmen,* December 1979, claimed he "did not even squirm too much while reading the pages of explicit lovemaking between Arthur and Crunch," but he found it disturbing that the heterosexual brother, Hall narrates them. He described the result as "unjustified narrative voyeurism" and he dismisses *JAMH* as "more fart than art" (14).

7. Those disappointed in and critical of Baldwin's representation of homosexuality in *JAMH* included Andrea Loewenstein, "James Baldwin and His Critics," *Gay Community News,* 9 February 1980, 10, 11, 17; Darryl Pinckney, "Blues for Mister Baldwin," 161–66; and Melvin Dixon, *Ride out the Wilderness: Geography and Identity in Afro-American Literature* (Urbana: University of Illinois, 1987), 123–40. On the other hand, a number of writers and critics have found much to praise in Baldwin's representation of homosexuality in *JAMH,* including Emmanuel S. Nelson, "James Baldwin (1924–1987)," in *The Gay and Lesbian Literary Heritage,* ed. Claude J. Summers (New York: Henry Holt, 1995), 71–73; White ("James Baldwin Overcomes"); Jefferson ("There's a Heaven Somewhere"); and Joseph Beam "Not a Bad Legacy Brother," *Gay Community News,* 20–26 December 1987, reprinted in *Brother to Brother: New Writings By Black Gay Men,* ed. Essex Hemphill (Boston: Alyson Publications, 1991), 184–88. Loewenstein judged the novel to be "for the most part a failure" due to an "inauthenticity of voice." She viewed the portrayal of the family to be "wooden and sentimental" and complained, "there is even a place within this bland nuclear paradise for Arthur, the gay son and brother, who is neatly swept up and contained by it" (10). Darryl Pinckney and Melvin Dixon also felt *JAMH* lacked power and authenticity. Pinckney viewed the novel as a retreat because in Baldwin's earlier novels "homosexuality is symbolic of a liberated condition" whereas in *JAMH* the

"homosexual characters imitate heterosexual behavior" (164). Pinckney saw Baldwin attempting " a sentimental truce between the outcast [homosexual] and the family, meaning the black community" (163). Similarly, Dixon implied that Baldwin's desire for reconciliation to family and community caused him to adopt an inadequate and inauthentic voice to tell Arthur's story. The novel is "beyond the reach" of Hall, the heterosexual brother and narrator (135): "Hall's heterosexuality seems a poorly constructed shelter in his retreat from the moral 'wilderness' of Arthur's life and sexuality" (138). On the other hand, Emmanuel S. Nelson has applauded *JAMH* for the very reasons Pinckney and others were critical of the novel. While Baldwin cast the homosexual in a "redemptive role" in his earlier fiction, he treats homosexuality "less self-consciously and less polemically" in his last novel: "The gay theme, in fact, is more smoothly integrated into the narrative, and it is presented as an essentially unsensational, though problematic, aspect of Arthur's search for identity, meaning, and love" (73). Similarly, Edmund White praised Baldwin for "successfully plac[ing] the black homosexual back into the context of black society," and finds Baldwin's "decision to bring homosexuality and blackness together is courageous, given the tense political situation" (5, 9). Joseph Beam singled out *Just Above My Head* for liberating black male writing from stereotype: "Heretofore, Black male writers suffered from a kind of 'nationalistic heterosexism.' Homophobia always limited the depths to which we could relate, reducing us to stereotypes speaking slang and aphorisms. In *Just Above My Head,* in plain view of the Black family it was possible for two Black men to be lovers, and be political, and be cherished for who they were" (12). White, Jefferson, Loewenstein, and other critics found the love scenes between Arthur and Crunch to be sensitive and powerfully written, some of the very best scenes in the novel.

8.  While a few reviewers complained that Baldwin's treatment of the family was sentimental (see, for example, Loewenstein, "James Baldwin and His Critics," and Pinckney, "Blues for Mister Baldwin,"), the majority found Baldwin's vignettes of middle-class life to be one of the novel's strengths. See, for example, John Romano, review of *Just Above My Head*, by James Baldwin, *New York Times Book Review,* 23 September 1979, 3, 33; Rawley, review; Fleming, "Baldwin's Gospel"; White, "James Baldwin Overcomes"; and Wald, "The Writer as Witness."

9.  Anthony Thwaite's complaint that Baldwin loses control of the point of view by having Hall relate erotic passages which he "couldn't know about" was typical of a number of reviews (38). On the other hand, John Romano was one of the few critics who liked Hall's narrative voice and described it as a "modest breakthrough" for Baldwin. Over the course of my analysis I will argue that Baldwin's choice of Hall for a narrator is appropriate to what I understand Baldwin's purpose to be in this novel, which is less about Arthur's story per se or an attempt to forge a truce between the homosexual and the family, as some have argued, than about the question of how Arthur's "legacy" (and thereby Baldwin's legacy) will be read by future generations.

10. James Campbell, "Sweet Memory," review of *Just Above My Head*, by James Baldwin, *New Statesman,* 16 November 1979, 771.

11. James Campbell, *Talking at the Gates: A Life of James Baldwin* (New York: Penguin

Books, 1991), states: "In *Just Above My Head*, Baldwin attempted to graft the black oral tradition, to which he felt he belonged, on to the Western literary tradition in which he had studied; the introduction of the parallel, 'alternative' narrative—the gospel—was his attempt to move the realist novel, the great edifice of words, beyond words" (253).

12. Eleanor Traylor, "I Hear Music in the Air: James Baldwin's *Just Above My Head*," *First World* 2, no. 3 (1979): 42.

13. Ibid., 43.

14. James Baldwin, interview by Wolfgang Binder (1980), in *Conversations with James Baldwin*, Standley and Pratt, *Conversations with James Baldwin*, 205.

15. James Baldwin, "James Baldwin Back Home," report of interview by Robert Coles, *New York Times Book Review*, 31 July 1977, 22.

16. Mel Watkins, "James Baldwin Writing and Talking," *New York Times Book Review*, 23 September 1979, 3.

17. James Baldwin, interview by Wolfgang Binder (1980), Standley and Pratt, *Conversations with James Baldwin*, 190–91.

18. James Baldwin, interview by David C. Estes (1986), Standley and Pratt, *Conversations with James Baldwin*, 278.

19. James Baldwin, *Go Tell It on the Mountain* (New York: Dial, 1953; New York: Laurel-Dell, 1985), 221.

20. Michael Lynch, "*Just Above My Head*. James Baldwin's Quest for Belief," *Literature and Theology* 11, no. 3 (1997): 284–98. Lynch offers an important corrective to those critics who see Baldwin's relationship to Christianity as simply one of protest against a corrupt church. Lynch argues that Baldwin's "identity as a moralist owes much to his training in Christianity," and that his ideal of community also has Christian roots (292). Lynch argues that Baldwin's theology evolves from "fear to self-affirmation and from emphasis on the individual to the community," and that this evolution is most evident in his last novel, *Just Above My Head* (292, 294).

21. David Leeming, *James Baldwin: A Biography* (New York: Alfred A. Knopf, 1994), compares the major characters of *JAMH* to James Baldwin's and his brother David Baldwin's lives: "Hall, who has children, has fought in the Korean War and is his brother's manager, has his source in David Baldwin, but he also mirrors the Baldwin driven to tell the story of his nation. . . . Jimmy, whose name suggests a connection with Jimmy Baldwin, is also in some ways a reflection of David Baldwin. Both David and the fictional Jimmy were sent away in childhood to live for a while with southern relatives, for example" (346). Baldwin wrote to his brother David that *JAMH* was about "one man's attempt to understand his brother—an attempt by one side of human experience to make its peace with another. . . . In *Just Above My Head* Hall must learn to face Arthur's inner world—and his 'love'—in such a way as to be able to see Arthur in himself. The people Jimmy Baldwin had loved in his life, he reminds his brother, were all reflections in some way of him [David Baldwin]. 'Life' was based on 'recognitions,' and this was what *Just Above My Head* was about" (349).

22. In "Go the Way Your Blood Beats," interview with Richard Goldstein, in *James*

*Baldwin: The Legacy,* ed. Quincy Troupe (New York: Touchstone-Simon and Schuster, 1989), James Baldwin said that his only real regret was not having children (182). Baldwin maintained a close relationship with his large family throughout his life and was particularly close to his brother David, who was his confidant and protector. *JAMH* is dedicated to all eight of Baldwin's siblings, and many of his other books include family members in their dedications. *Go Tell* was dedicated to his mother and father; "My Dungeon Shook" (the first essay in *The Fire Next Time*) was conceived as a letter to his nephew, James; *No Name in the Street* is dedicated to Berdis Baldwin (his mother); *Train* is dedicated to brother David; and *The Devil Finds Work* is dedicated to his youngest sister, Paula Maria, to whom he felt a special responsibility in that she was born just after his father's death.

23. Baldwin, *Just Above My Head,* 23.
24. Ibid., 22.
25. Walter Benjamin, "The Storyteller," in *Illuminations,* trans. Harry Zohn, ed. Hannah Arendt (New York: Schocken, 1968), 87.
26. Ibid., 93.
27. Ibid., 100.
28. Ibid., 87.
29. James Baldwin, "Of the Sorrow Songs: The Cross of Redemption," *New Edinburgh Review* 47 (August 1979): 19, 20.
30. Baldwin, *Just Above My Head,* 59.
31. Ibid., 553.
32. Ibid., 33
33. Julie Nash, "'A Terrifying Sacrament': James Baldwin's Use of Music in *Just Above My Head,*" *MAWA Review,* December 1990, 110. Developing Traylor's approach to *JAMH,* Julie Nash points out that music operates on "several levels": "First, the novel is saturated with lyrics from traditional blues and gospel songs and has a music-focused plot, which centers around the life and death of Arthur Montana, a famous gospel and blues singer. . . . Second, music is employed as a metaphor for 'living right.' Finally, the book itself is much more than the story of Arthur's life. It is a blues song" (107).
34. Ibid., 109.
35. Baldwin, *Just Above My Head,* 13–14.
36. Ibid., 14.
37. Ibid., 15.
38. Ibid., 24. Leeming, *James Baldwin,* writes that Hall's dreams which open and close the novel were based on real dreams that Jimmy Baldwin and his brother David Baldwin had in the middle seventies and were important to the novel's initial inspiration. The last dream is attributed to David. In David's dream he asks Jimmy the question, "Shall we tell them what's up the road?" to which Jimmy replies, "They'll find out." The first dream about the ceiling descending "just above my head" is attributed to Jimmy. Leeming says, "He told David he thought their dreams must have something to do with each other; the people in David's were looking for an author, crowding into his head, demanding to tell their story" (345).

39. Baldwin, *Just Above My Head*, 16.

40. Ibid., 35.

41. Ibid., 36.

42. Warren J. Carson, "Manhood, Musicality, and Male Bonding in *Just Above My Head*," in *Re-viewing James Baldwin: Things Not Seen*, ed. D. Quentin Miller (Philadelphia: Temple University Press, 2000), reads this passage as evidence of the strength of Hall's bond with his son, Tony. Hall can "look his son in the face and answer his questions without making excuses" (228). On the other hand, Melvin Dixon, *Ride out the Wilderness*, reads this passage as an example of Hall's evasiveness: "Although the details of Hall's answer to Tony are revealing, Hall fails to satisfy Tony's honest question (137). My reading of this passage is closer to Dixon's.

43. Baldwin, *Just Above My Head*, 36–37.

44. Ibid., 22.

45. Ibid., 38.

46. Ibid., 44.

47. Ibid., 48.

48. Ibid.

49. Ibid., 49.

50. Ibid., 54.

51. Ibid., 65.

52. The foil relationship of the two families in *JAMH* is similar to that of the Rivers and the Hunts in *If Beale Street Could Talk*.

53. Baldwin, *Just Above My Head*, 159.

54. Ibid., 227.

55. Ibid., 263.

56. Ibid.

57. Ibid., 497.

58. Ibid., 546.

59. Ibid., 550.

60. Ibid., 553.

61. Although *JAMH* has received somewhat more critical attention than either *Tell Me How Long the Train's Been Gone* or *If Beale Street Could Talk*, compared to Baldwin's early work, it continues to receive relatively little critical attention.

62. Carolyn Wedin Sylvander, *James Baldwin* (New York: Frederick Ungar, 1980), 125.

63. Ibid., 141.

64. Dorothy Lee, "The Bridge of Suffering," *Callaloo* 6, no. 2 (1983): 92.

65. Ibid., 97.

66. Ibid., 98.

67. Nagueyalti Warren, "The Substance of Things Hoped for: Faith in *Go Tell It on the Mountain* and *Just Above My Head*," *Obsidian II* 7, nos. 1 and 2 (1992): 31.

68. Craig Werner, "James Baldwin: Politics and the Gospel Impulse," *New Politics: A Journal of Socialist Thought* 2, no. 2 (1989): 118.

69. Andrew Shin and Barbara Judson, "Beneath the Black Aesthetic: James Baldwin's Primer

of Black American Masculinity," *African American Review* 32, no. 2 (1998): 258.

70. There are some notable exceptions to the above readings of *JAMH*. See Saadet Bozkurt, "Harmony within and without: James Baldwin's Quest for Humanity," *American Studies International* 20, no. 1 (1981). Bozkurt states: "The ultimate truth, as it emerges from Baldwin's fiction, seems to be that there is no reconciliation in life whatsoever. Even a nearly complete harmony within the individual, not to mention between the individual and the society, remains an illusion" (50). While Bozkurt believes *JAMH* to be "exceptionally successful," others have argued that the novel is unsuccessful precisely because the reconciliation theme fails or isn't believable. Peter Bruck, "Dungeon and Salvation: Biblical Rhetoric in James Baldwin's *Just Above My Head*," in *History and Tradition in Afro-American Culture,* ed. Gunter H. Lenz (Frankfurt: Campus Verlag, 1984), argues that Hall's salvation is a sham and the novel is a "retreat from political commitment" into a "sheltered individual happiness and a cozy life" (141–42). Trudier Harris, *Black Women in the Fiction of James Baldwin* (Knoxville, Tenn.: University of Tennessee Press, 1985), argues that the reconciliation Hall experiences in telling this story is really a kind of voyeurism in which Hall successfully represses the one truth he can't admit to himself, his latent homosexual desire toward his brother (201). Melvin Dixon, *Ride out the Wilderness,* defines the novel's central theme as reconciliation, but argues that the novel "fail[s] to address the central paradox in most of Baldwin's fiction: the inability to reconcile the emotional (affectional) needs of a homosexual artist who expresses himself in a verbal art based in the religion that ultimately condemns him" (135). Dixon concludes that Baldwin's long-promised homecoming "may not be as complete or as honestly fulfilling as he would have us think" (135).

The conflicting views over the question of reconciliation in *JAMH* are reminiscent of the controversy over the meaning of John's conversion in *Go Tell* that have preoccupied many critics. Is John's conversion "real" or is it a "trick"? Similarly, has Hall finally come to terms with his brother's life and death or is he fooling himself? I propose that both novels are constructed to suggest that there is no obvious answer to these questions. I argue that the dissonance in Hall's reconciliation is not a symptom of the novel's failure to achieve its purpose, but, if we separate Hall's narrative project from Baldwin's, that dissonance becomes fundamental to Baldwin's complexity.

71. Baldwin, *Just Above My Head,* 498.

72. Ibid.

73. Ibid., 559.

74. Ibid., 26.

75. The French translation of *Just Above My Head* is titled *Harlem Quartet.* The novel was highly praised in France. See James Baldwin, "The Last Interview (1987)," interview with Quincy Troupe, in *James Baldwin,* 207.

76. Baldwin, *Just Above My Head,* 113.

77. Craig Werner, *Playing the Changes: From Afro-Modernism to the Jazz Impulse* (Urbana: University of Illinois Press, 1994), argues that *Just Above My Head* is Baldwin's most complete expression of the "gospel impulse." Werner describes the gospel impulse as a "process [which] parallels William Blake's vision of morality as a movement from inno-

cence through experience to a higher innocence" (224). While I would agree with Werner that Baldwin refuses to accept the oppositional structures of sacred and secular or church and street, I think the meaning of gospel music in *JAMH* is more cacophonous and overdetermined than Werner's image of "higher innocence" suggests.

78. As previously noted, Tish and Fonny's sexual relations in *If Beale Street Could Talk* and Arthur's sexual relations with Crunch and later Jimmy in *Just Above My Head* are described in the language of spirituals and gospels. Michael Lynch, "*Just Above My Head*: James Baldwin's Quest For Belief," writes, "though often attacked as preaching sexual immorality and libertinism in his work, Baldwin does celebrate sexuality of whatever orientation but always subordinates its expression to the ethic of respecting and loving the other as oneself" (292).

79. Baldwin, "Alas, Poor Richard!" in *Price of the Ticket*, 273.

80. Ibid.

81. See Carson, "Manhood, Musicality, and Male Bonding in *Just Above My Head*," for a discussion of the clearly sexual overtones in the gospel performances of Arthur and Crunch.

82. Baldwin, *Just Above My Head*, 23–24.

83. Sherley Anne Williams, *Give Birth to Brightness: A Thematic Study in Neo-black Literature* (New York: Dial Press, 1972), 146.

84. Isaac Julien and Kobena Mercer, "True Confessions: A Discourse on Images of Black Male Sexuality," in *Brother to Brother: New Writings by Black Gay Men*, ed. Essex Hemphill (Boston: Alyson Publications, 1991), 172.

85. Ibid., 172–73.

86. James S. Tinney, "Struggles of a Black Pentecostal," in *Black Men/White Men: A Gay Anthology* (San Francisco: Gay Sunshine Press, 1983), 171.

87. Ibid., 169.

88. Ibid.

89. Ibid., 170.

90. Although Baldwin, to my knowledge, never specifically described the church's prohibition against homosexuality as his reason for leaving—in fact he told Richard Goldstein in "Go the Way Your Blood Beats" that he never heard any antigay rhetoric in the church he grew up in (*James Baldwin*, 179)—he does describe his first feelings of homosexual desire as occurring within the church context: "It hit me with great force while I was in the pulpit. I must have been fourteen. I was still a virgin. I had no idea what you were supposed to do about it. I didn't really understand any of what I felt except I knew I loved one boy, for example. But it was private. And by the time I left home, when I was seventeen or eighteen and still a virgin, it was like everything else in my life, a problem which I would have to resolve myself" (174–75). Baldwin generally spoke about his break from the church as a result of his recognition of its lack of love and hypocrisy, which included its attitude toward all sexuality. In an interview with Charles Fort Jr. (*The Penny Dreadful*, English Dept., Bowling Green State University, winter 1978), Baldwin attributes his final break to a particular conflict with a pastor who turned away an eighty-one-year-old woman. In *Just Above My Head*

Julia's final break with the church is attributed to a similar incident.

91. See James S. Tinney's "Why a Black Gay Church?" in *In the Life: A Black Gay Anthology,* ed. Joseph Beam (Boston: Alyson Publications, 1986), 70–86. Although Tinney's claim that black Pentecostalism is the "blackest" form of religion (i.e., it has more African retentions than non-Pentecostal denominations) has been substantiated by religious scholars and music scholars, the validity of his claim that black Pentecostalism is the "gayest" religion is hard to determine, since there have been no studies on this subject to my knowledge.

92. Joyce Marie Jackson, "The Changing Nature of Gospel Music: A Southern Case Study," *African American Review* 29, no. 2 (1995): 186.

93. Ibid., 188

94. Ibid., 193.

95. Samuel A. Floyd Jr., *The Power of Black Music: Interpreting Its History from Africa to the United States* (New York: Oxford University Press, 1995), 197.

96. Ibid., 63–64.

97. Jackson, "The Changing Nature of Gospel Music," 188.

98. Floyd, *The Power of Black Music,* 64–65 and 171–72.

99. Jackson, "The Changing Nature of Gospel Music," 191–92.

100. Ibid., 192.

101. Baldwin, *Just Above My Head,* 111.

102. Warren Carson, "Manhood, Musicality, and Male Bonding in *Just Above My Head,*" argues that an important issue in *JAMH* is the "necessary bonding between fathers and sons." He claims that "Paul Montana . . . is in many ways a model father for Hall and Arthur" (227). As I will argue later in this chapter, Hall's idealization of the father is part of the dissonance in Hall's presentation, because Arthur and his father finally do **not** bond.

103. Baldwin, *Just Above My Head,* 91.

104. Ibid., 92.

105. Ibid.

106. Ibid.

107. Ibid., 88.

108. Baldwin, *Tell Me How Long the Train's Been Gone,* 124.

109. Baldwin, "Sonny's Blues," 86–122. The narrator describes watching a revival from his window in Harlem: "As the singing filled the air the watching, listening faces underwent a change, the eyes focusing on something within; the music seemed to soothe a poison out of them; and time seemed, nearly, to fall away from the sullen, belligerent, battered faces, as though they were fleeing back to their first condition, while dreaming of their last" (111).

110. Baldwin, *Just Above My Head,* 94.

111. Ibid., 179.

112. Ibid.

113. Ibid., 196.

114. Trudier Harris, "The South as Woman: Chimeric Images of Emasculation in *Just Above*

*My Head,"* in *Studies in Black American Literature,* vol. 1, ed. Joe Weixlmann and Chester J. Fontenot (Greenwood, Fla.: Penkevill, 1984), argues that in *JAMH* the South emerges as "a full-fledged character in terms of its monstrous potential to destroy" (90). However, Harris's single focus on emasculation and terror distorts the full range of meanings the South has in *JAMH.* For a very different analysis of the south in *JAMH* see Andrew Shin and Barbara Judson, "Beneath the Black Aesthetic" They argue that Arthur's gospel performances in the South "present a series of erotic images that rewrite the cultural mythology of the south" and generate "an alternative vernacular of black American masculinity" (256).

115. Baldwin, *Just Above My Head,* 396.
116. Ibid., 15–16.
117. Ibid., 392.
118. Ibid., 393.
119. Ibid.
120. Ibid., 18.
121. Floyd, *The Power of Black Music,* 197.
122. Baldwin, *Just Above My Head,* 394.
123. Ibid.
124. Ibid., 395.
125. Ibid., 486.
126. Ibid., 486–87.
127. Ibid., 487.
128. Ibid., 491.
129. Ibid.
130. In his interview with Mel Watkins, "James Baldwin Writing and Talking," Baldwin offers insight into Arthur's alienation by comparing his own early experience in Paris with that of his character: "When I went to Paris as a young boy, I learned a great deal. One of the things I learned was how much I needed people who knew me—I mean, in particular, black Americans—how much I needed them to correct me. When I first arrived there, no one I was moving with knew enough about me to do that. In a sense, you can say no one loved me enough to correct me. In the same sense, when Arthur's on stage in Paris, in the world in which he moves, he is simply a star. They don't know where he came from; they don't know what nourishes him. And they can't nourish him. I'd like to deal with this more fully in something else someday, but, at least implicitly, that situation is central to the novel" (3).
131. Baldwin, *Just Above My Head,* 534.
132. Ibid., 554.
133. Ibid., 552.
134. Ibid., 553.
135. Ibid., 555.
136. Ibid., 95.
137. Ibid.
138. Ibid.

139. Ibid., 380.

140. Ibid., 381.

141. Ibid., 259–60.

142. Ibid., 262.

143. David Bergman, *Gaiety Transfigured: Gay Self-Representation in American Literature* (Madison: University of Wisconsin Press, 1991), 37.

144. Baldwin, *Just Above My Head*, 262.

145. Bergman, *Gaiety Transfigured*, 26–43.

146. Ibid., 30.

147. Dixon, *Ride out the Wilderness*, 138.

148. Baldwin, *Just Above My Head*, 22.

149. Bergman, *Gaiety Transfigured*, 30–31.

150. Baldwin, *Just Above My Head*, 29.

151. Jackson, "The Changing Nature of Gospel Music," 187.

152. Mary Ellison, *Lyrical Protest: Black Music's Struggle against Discrimination* (New York: Praeger, 1989), 49.

153. Baldwin, *Just Above My Head*, 539.

154. Ibid.

155. Baldwin stated: "The question of human affection, of integrity, in my case, the question of trying to become a writer, are all linked with the question of sexuality. Sexuality is only a part of it. I don't know even if it's the most important part. But it's indispensable." See "Go the Way Your Blood Beats," interview with Richard Goldstein, in *James Baldwin*, 176.

156. Baldwin, *Just Above My Head*, 553.

157. Lee Edelman, "The Part for the (W)hole: Baldwin, Homophobia, and the Fantasmatics of 'Race,'" in *Homographesis: Essays in Gay Literary and Cultural Theory* (New York: Routledge, 1994), 69. Edelman applies Lacanian psychoanalytic theory and deconstructive method to argue that sexual differentiation and racial discrimination have the same psychological-discursive dynamic in a racist and patriarchal society. He goes on to analyze the construction of both "homosexuality" and "homophobia" in racial discourse. Edelman argues that Baldwin revises both Franz Fanon's identification of white racism with homosexuality and W. E. B. Du Bois's goal of "self-conscious manhood" in *JAMH*. In essence Edelman claims that the homosexual relationships in the novel deconstruct a culturally received idea of "manhood": "To the extent, then, that Arthur and Crunch reinterpret 'manhood,' and thus, in Western terms, subjectivity in its paradigmatic form, as the ability to incorporate what is 'foreign' without experiencing a loss of integrity, and without being constrained by the (hetero)sexist either/or logic of active and passive, they point to the partial understanding of 'manhood' that passes in dominant culture for the whole, and they disarticulate the coercive 'wholeness' of an identity based on fantasmatic identification with a part. They thus make visible to the novel's reader the invisible operation of *differance* that destabilizes every signifier, offering a glimpse of the process through which a signifier like 'manhood' can communi-

cate the singularity of a fixed identity only where a community of 'readers' has learned how not to see the differences within that identity and its signifier both" (70–71).

158. Baldwin, *Just Above My Head*, 213.
159. Baldwin, "Here Be Dragons," in *The Price of the Ticket*, 690.
160. Edelman "The Part for the (W)hole," in *Homographesis*, 69.
161. Ibid., 71.
162. Dixon, *Ride out the Wilderness*, 136.
163. Erskine Peters, ed., *Lyrics of the Afro-American Spiritual: A Documentary Collection* (Westport, Conn.: Greenwood Press, 1993), 179–80.

# Works Cited

Ackroyd, Peter. "A Little Black Magic." Review of *If Beale Street Could Talk,* by James Baldwin. *Spectator,* 6 July 1974, 22.

Adams, Stephen. *The Homosexual as Hero in Contemporary Fiction.* New York: Harper and Row, 1980.

Aldridge, John W. "The Fire Next Time?" Review of *If Beale Street Could Talk,* by James Baldwin. *Saturday Review World,* 15 June 1974, 20, 24–25.

Algren, Nelson. "Sashaying Around." Review of *Tell Me How Long the Train's Been Gone,* by James Baldwin. *The Critic* 27 (October–November 1968): 86–87.

Allen, Shirley. "Religious Symbolism and Psychic Reality in Baldwin's *Go Tell It on the Mountain.*" *CLAJ* 19 (December 1975): 173–99.

Als, Hilton. "The Enemy Within." *New Yorker,* 16 February 1998, 72, 78.

Amiel, Barbara. "A 597-Page Doom." Review of *Just Above My Head,* by James Baldwin. *MacCleans,* 1 October 1979, 54.

Andrews, William. *To Tell a Free Story: The First Century of Afro-American Autobiography, 1760–1865.* Urbana, Ill.: University of Illinois Press, 1985.

Bailey, Paul. "Coming on Strong." Review of *Just Above My Head,* by James Baldwin. *Times Literary Supplement,* 21 December 1979, 150.

Baker, Houston A. Jr. *Blues, Ideology, and Afro-American Literature: A Vernacular Theory.* Chicago: University of Chicago Press, 1984.

———. "The Embattled Craftsman: An Essay on James Baldwin." *The Journal of African-Afro-American Affairs* 1, no. 1 (1977): 28–51. Reprinted in *Critical Essays on James Baldwin,* edited by Fred L. Standley and Nancy V. Burt, 62–77. Boston: G. K. Hall, 1988.

———. *The Journey Back: Issues in Black Literature and Criticism.* Chicago: University of Chicago Press, 1980.

———. *Workings of the Spirit: The Poetics of Afro-American Women's Writing.* Chicago: University of Chicago Press, 1991.

Baldwin, James. "Alas, Poor Richard!" In *The Price of the Ticket: Collected Nonfiction, 1948–1985,* 557–636. New York: St. Martin's and Merk, 1985.

———. *Another Country.* New York: Dial, 1962; New York: Dell, 1963.

———. "Are We on the Edge of Civil War?" Interview by David Frost. In *Conversations with James Baldwin,* edited by Fred Standley and Louis Pratt, 93–97. Jackson, Miss.: University Press of Mississippi, 1989.

———. "The Black Scholar Interviews James Baldwin, 1973." In *Conversations with James Baldwin,* edited by Fred Standley and Louis H. Pratt, 142–58. Jackson, Miss.: University Press of Mississippi, 1989.

———. "The Black Situation Now." Interview. *Washington Post,* 21 July 1974, C1.

———. *Blues for Mister Charlie.* New York: Dell, 1964.

———. "Come out the Wilderness." In *Going to Meet the Man,* 170–97. New York: Dial, 1965; New York: Laurel-Dell, 1976.

———. "Conversation: Ida Lewis and James Baldwin." In *Conversations with James Baldwin,* edited by Fred L. Standley and Louis H. Pratt. 83–97. Jackson, Miss.: University Press of Mississippi, 1989.

———. "The Devil Finds Work." In *The Price of the Ticket: Collected Nonfiction, 1948–1985,* 557–636. New York: St. Martin's and Merk, 1985.

———. "The Discovery of What It Means to Be an American." In *The Price of the Ticket: Collected Nonfiction, 1948–1985,* 171–76. New York: St. Martin's and Merk, 1985.

———. "Disturber of the Peace: James Baldwin—An Interview." Interview by Eve Auchincloss and Nancy Lynch. In *Conversations with James Baldwin,* edited by Fred Standley and Louis H. Pratt, 64–82. Jackson, Miss.: University Press of Mississippi, 1989.

———. "Everybody's Protest Novel." In *The Price of the Ticket: Collected Nonfiction, 1948–1985,* 27–33. New York: St. Martin's and Merk, 1985.

———. "Every Good-Bye Ain't Gone." In *The Price of the Ticket: Collected Nonfiction, 1948–1985,* 641–47. New York: St. Martin's and Merk, 1985.

———. "Exclusive Interview with James Baldwin." Interview by Joe Walker. In *Conversations with James Baldwin,* edited by Fred Standley and Louis H. Pratt, 127–41. Jackson, Miss.: University Press of Mississippi, 1989.

———. *The Fire Next Time.* New York: Dial, 1963.

———. *Giovanni's Room.* New York: Dial, 1956; New York: Dell, 1964.

———. "Going to Meet the Man." In *Going to Meet the Man,* 198–218. New York: Dial, 1965; New York: Laurel-Dell, 1976.

———. *Go Tell It on the Mountain.* New York: Dial, 1953; New York: Laurel-Dell, 1985.

———. "Go the Way Your Blood Beats." Interview with Richard Goldstein. In *James Baldwin: The Legacy*, edited by Quincy Troupe, 173–85. New York: Touchstone-Simon and Schuster, 1989.

———. "Here Be Dragons." In *The Price of the Ticket: Collected Nonfiction, 1948–1985*, 677–90. New York: St. Martin's and Merk, 1985.

———. *If Beale Street Could Talk.* New York: Dial, 1974.

———. "An Interview with James Baldwin." Interview by David C. Estes. In *Conversations with James Baldwin*, edited by Fred Standley and Louis H. Pratt, 270-280. Jackson, Miss.: University Press of Mississippi, 1989.

———. Interview with Charles Fort Jr. *The Penny Dreadful,* winter 1978, 25–32. English Dept. Bowling Green State University.

———. "It's Hard to be James Baldwin." Interview by Herbert R. Lottman. In *Conversations with James Baldwin*, edited by Fred Standley and Louis H. Pratt, 108-126. Jackson, Miss.: University Press of Mississippi, 1989.

———. "James Baldwin Back Home." Report of interview by Robert Coles. *New York Times Book Review,* 31 July 1977, 1.

———. "James Baldwin, an Interview." Inteview by Wolfgang Binder. In *Conversations with James Baldwin*, edited by Fred Standley and Louis H. Pratt, 190-209. Jackson, Miss.: University Press of Mississippi, 1989.

———. "James Baldwin Interviewed." Interview by John Hall. In *Conversations with James Baldwin*, edited by Fred Standley and Louis H. Pratt, 98–107. Jackson, Miss.: University Press of Mississippi, 1989.

———. "James Baldwin: Looking toward the Eighties." Interview by Kalamu ya Salaam. In *Critical Essays on James Baldwin*, edited by Fred L. Standley and Nancy V. Burt, 35–42. Boston: G. K. Hall, 1988.

———. "James Baldwin Writing and Talking." Interview with Mel Watkins. *New York Times Book Review,* 23 September 1979, 3.

———. *Just Above My Head.* New York: Dial, 1979; New York: Laurel-Dell, 1990.

———. "The Last Interview (1987)." Interview with Quincy Troupe. In *James Baldwin: The Legacy*, edited by Quincy Troupe, 186–212. New York: Touchstone-Simon and Schuster, 1989.

———. *Little Man, Little Man: A Story of Childhood.* Illustrated by Yoran Cazac. New York: Dial, 1976.

———. "The Male Prison." In *The Price of the Ticket: Collected Nonfiction, 1948–1985*, 101–5. New York: St. Martin's and Merk, 1985.

———. "Many Thousands Gone." In *The Price of the Ticket: Collected Nonfiction, 1948–1985*, 65–78. New York: St. Martin's and Merk, 1985.

———. "Me and My House." *Harper's* 211 (November 1955): 54–61. Reprinted as "Notes of a Native Son." In *Notes of a Native Son* and in *The Price of the Ticket: Collected Nonfiction, 1948–1985*, 127–45. New York: St. Martin's and Merk, 1985.

———. *Nobody Knows My Name.* New York: Dial, 1961; New York: Dell, 1963.

———. *No Name in the Street.* New York: Dial, 1972; New York: Delta-Dell, 1973.

———. *Notes of a Native Son.* Boston: Beacon Press, 1955; Boston: Beacon Press, 1984.

———. "Of the Sorrow Songs: The Cross of Redemption." *New Edinburgh Review* 47 (August 1979): 18–22.

———. *One Day When I Was Lost: A Scenario Based on Alex Haley's " The Autobiography of Malcolm X.* New York: Dial, 1972; New York: Laurel-Dell, 1992.

———. "An Open Letter to My Sister, Miss Angela Davis." *New York Review of Books,* 7 January 1971.

———. "The Preservation of Innocence." *Zero* 1, no. 2 (1949). Reprinted in *Out/Look: National Lesbian and Gay Quarterly* 6 (fall 1989): 40–45.

———. *The Price of the Ticket: Collected Nonfiction, 1948–1985.* New York: St. Martin's and Marek, 1985.

———. "Sonny's Blues." *Partisan Review* (summer 1957). Reprinted in *Going to Meet the Man,* 86–122. New York: Dial, 1965; New York: Laurel-Dell, 1976.

———. *Tell Me How Long the Train's Been Gone.* New York: Dial, 1968; New York: Dell, 1969.

Baldwin, James, and Nikki Giovanni. *A Dialogue.* Philadelphia: J. B. Lippincott, 1973.

Balfour, Lawrie. "Finding the Words: Baldwin, Race Consciousness, and Democratic Theory." In *James Baldwin Now,* edited by Dwight McBride, 75–99. New York: New York University Press, 1999.

Balliett, Whitney. "Father and Son." Review of *Just Above My Head,* by James Baldwin. *New Yorker,* 26 November 1979, 218.

Beam, Joseph. "Not a Bad Legacy Brother." *Gay Community News,* 20–26 December 1987, center, 12. Reprinted in *Brother to Brother: New Writings by Black Gay Men,* edited by Essex Hemphill, 184–88. Boston: Alyson Publications, 1991.

Bell, Pearl K. "Blacks and the Blues." Review of *If Beale Street Could Talk,* by James Baldwin. *New Leader,* 27 May 1974, 3–5.

———. "Roth and Baldwin: Coming Home." Review of *The Ghost Writer,* by Philip Roth, and *Just Above My Head,* by James Baldwin. *Commentary,* December 1979, 72–75.

Benjamin, Walter. "The Storyteller." In *Illuminations.* Translated by Harry Zohn, edited by Hannah Arendt. New York: Schocken, 1968.

Bergman, David. *Gaiety Transfigured: Gay Self-Representation in American Literature.* Madison: University of Wisconsin Press, 1991.

Billingsley, Andrew. *Climbing Jacob's Ladder: The Enduring Legacy of African-American Families.* New York: Touchstone-Simon and Schuster, 1992.

Bloom, Harold, ed. *James Baldwin.* New York: Chelsea House Publishers, 1986.

Bobia, Rosa. *The Critical Reception of James Baldwin in France.* New York: Peter Lang, 1997.

Boggs, Nicholas, "Of Mimicry and (Little Man Little) Man: Toward a Queer Sighted Theory of Black Childhood." In *James Baldwin Now,* edited by Dwight McBride, 122–60. New York: New York University Press, 1999.

Bozkurt, Saadet. "Harmony within and without: James Baldwin's Quest for Humanity." *American Studies International* 20, no. 1 (1981): 45–51.

Broyard, Anatole. "No Color Line in Cliches." Review of *If Beale Street Could Talk,* by James Baldwin. *New York Times,* 17 May 1974, 37.

Bruck, Peter. "Dungeon and Salvation: Biblical Rhetoric in James Baldwin's *Just Above My Head.*" In *History and Tradition in Afro-American Culture,* edited by Gunter H. Lenz, 130–47. Frankfurt: Campus Verlag, 1984.

———. *Von der "Storefront Church" zum "American Dream": James Baldwin und der amerikanische Rassenkonflikt.* Amsterdam: 1975.

Burks, Mary Fair. "James Baldwin's Protest Novel: *If Beale Street Could Talk.*" *Negro American Literature Forum* 10, no. 3 (1976): 83–95.

Campbell, James. "Sweet Memory." Review of *Just Above My Head,* by James Baldwin. *New Statesman,* 16 November 1979, 771.

———. *Talking at the Gates: A Life of James Baldwin.* New York: Penguin Books, 1991.

Carby, Hazel V. *Reconstructing Womanhood: The Emergence of the Afro-American Woman Novelist.* New York: Oxford University Press, 1987.

Carson, Warren J. "Manhood, Musicality, and Male Bonding in *Just Above My Head.*" In *Re-viewing James Baldwin: Things Not Seen,* edited by D. Quentin Miller, 215–231. Philadelphia: Temple University Press, 2000.

Chametzky, Jules, ed. *Black Writers Redefine the Struggle: A Tribute to James Baldwin.* Amherst, Mass.: University of Massachusetts Press, 1989.

Churchill, Ward, and Jim VanderWall. *Agents of Repression: The FBI's Secret Wars against the Black Panther Party and the American Indian Movement.* Boston: South End Press, 1988.

Clark, Keith. "Baldwin, Communitas, and the Black Masculinist Tradition." In *New Essays on "Go Tell It on the Mountain,"* edited by Trudier Harris, 127–58. New York: Cambridge University Press, 1996.

Cleaver, Eldridge. *Soul on Ice.* New York: Delta-Dell, 1968.

Crouch, Stanley. "Cliches of Degradation." Review of *Just Above My Head,* by James Baldwin. *Village Voice,* 29 October 1979, 39.

Dance, Daryl. "James Baldwin." In *Black American Writers Bibliographical Essays,* edited by Thomas Inge et al., 73–120. Vol. 2. New York: St. Martin's, 1978.

Davis, Charles T. "From Experience to Eloquence: Richard Wright's *Black Boy* as Art (1979)." In *Black Is the Color of the Cosmos: Essays on Afro-American Literature and Culture, 1942–1981,* edited by Henry Louis Gates Jr. , 281–97. New York: Garland Publishing, 1982.

Davis, Charles T., and Henry Louis Gates Jr. "Introduction: The Language of Slavery." In *The Slave's Narrative,* edited by Daryl Dance and Henry Louis Gates Jr., xi–xxxiv. New York: Oxford University Press, 1985.

DeGout, Yasmin Y. "'Masculinity' and (Im)maturity: 'The Man Child' and Other Stories in Baldwin's Gender Studies Enterprise." In *Re-viewing James Baldwin: Things Not Seen,* edited by D. Quentin Miller, 128–53. Philadelphia: Temple University Press, 2000.

Detweiler, Robert. "Blues Lament." Review of *If Beale Street Could Talk,* by James Baldwin. *Christian Century,* 31 July 1974, 752.

Dixon, Melvin. *Ride out the Wilderness: Geography and Identity in Afro-American Literature.* Urbana, Ill.: University of Illinois, 1987.

Douglass, Frederick. *Narrative of the Life of Frederick Douglass, an American Slave, Written by Himself.* Edited by Houston A. Baker Jr. 1845. Reprint, New York: Penguin American Library, 1982.

Du Bois, W. E. B. *The Souls of Black Folk.* 1903. Reprint, New York: Signet-New American Library, 1969.

Eckman, Fern Marja. *The Furious Passage of James Baldwin.* New York: M. Evans, 1966.

Edelman, Lee. *Homographesis: Essays in Gay Literary and Cultural Theory.* New York: Routledge, 1994.

Edwards, Thomas R. "Can You Go Home Again?" Review of *If Beale Street Could Talk,* by James Baldwin. *New York Review of Books,* 13 June 1974, 37–38.

Ellis, Cassandra M. "The Black Boy Looks at the Silver Screen: Baldwin as Moviegoer." In *Re-viewing James Baldwin: Things Not Seen,* edited by D. Quentin Miller, 190–213. Philadelphia: Temple University Press, 2000.

Ellison, Mary. *Lyrical Protest: Black Music's Struggle against Discrimination.* New York: Praeger, 1989.

Ellison, Ralph. *Invisible Man.* New York: Random House, 1952; New York: Vintage-Random House, 1972.

Fabre, Michel. "Fathers and Sons in James Baldwin's *Go Tell It on the Mountain.*" In *James Baldwin: A Collection of Critical Essays,* edited by Keneth Kinnamon, 120–38. Englewood Cliffs, N.J.: Prentice-Hall, 1974.

Farrison, William Edward. "If Baldwin's Train Has Not Gone." In *James Baldwin: A Critical Evaluation,* edited by Therman B. O'Daniel, 69–81. Washington, D.C.: Howard University Press, 1977.

Feldman, Susan. "Another Look at *Another Country*: Reconciling Baldwin's Racial and Sexual Politics." In *Re-viewing James Baldwin: Things Not Seen,* edited by D. Quentin Miller, 88–104. Philadelphia: Temple University Press, 2000.

Ferguson, Roderick. "The Parvenu Baldwin and the Other Side of Redemption: Modernity, Race, Sexuality and the Cold War." In *James Baldwin Now,* edited by Dwight McBride, 233–61. New York: New York University Press, 1999.

Fiedler, Leslie. *Love and Death in the American Novel.* Rev. ed. New York: Third Scarborough Books Edition, 1982.

Fleming, Robert. "Baldwin's Gospel: Treading Stagnant Waters." Review of *Just Above My Head,* by James Baldwin. *Encore American and Worldwide News,* 1 October 1979, 40–41.

Floyd, Samuel A. Jr. *The Power of Black Music: Interpreting Its History from Africa to the United States.* New York: Oxford University Press, 1995.

Fuller, Hoyt. "Books." Review of *Just Above My Head,* by James Baldwin. *Black Collegian,* February–March 1980, 26, 28.

Gates, Henry Louis Jr. "The Black Man's Burden." In *Fear of a Queer Planet: Queer Politics and Social Theory,* edited by Michael Warner. Minneapolis: University of Minnesota Press, 1993.

———. *The Signifying Monkey.* New York: Oxford University Press, 1988.

———. "What James Baldwin Can and Can't Teach America." *New Republic,* 1 June 1992, 37–43.

Gibson, Donald B. "James Baldwin: The Anatomy of Space." In *The Politics of Literary Expression: A Study of Major Black Writers*, edited by Donald B. Gibson, 99–123. Contributions in Afro-American and African Studies, no. 63. Westport, Conn.: Greenwood Press, 1981.

Gilman, Richard. Review of *Just Above My Head*, by James Baldwin. *New Republic*, 24 November 1979, 30–31.

Hacker, Andrew. *Two Nations: Black and White, Separate, Unequal.* New York: Scribners, 1992.

Hajek, Friederike. "James Baldwin: Beale Street Blues." *Weimarer Beitrage: Zeitschrift fur Literaturwissenschaft, Asthetik und Kulturtheorie* 23, no. 6 (1977): 137–50.

Hakutani, Yoshinobu. "If the Street Could Talk: James Baldwin's Search for Love and Understanding." In *The City in African-American Literature*, edited by Yoshinobu Hakutani and Robert Butler, 150–67. London: Associated University Presses, 1995.

Handy, W. C., and Edward Abbe Niles. *Blues: An Anthology.* Edited by Jerry Silverman. 1949. Reprint, New York: Macmillan, 1972.

Harris, Trudier. *Black Women in the Fiction of James Baldwin.* Knoxville, Tenn.: University of Tennessee Press, 1985.

———. "The Eye as Weapon in *If Beale Street Could Talk*." *MELUS* 5, no. 3 (1978): 54–66.

———. "The South as Woman: Chimeric Images of Emasculation in *Just Above My Head*." In *Studies in Black American Literature*, edited by Joe Weixlmann and Chester J. Fontenot, 89–109. Vol. 1. Greenwood, Fla.: Penkevill, 1984.

———, ed. *New Essays on "Go Tell It on the Mountain."* New York: Cambridge University Press, 1999.

Hernton, Calvin C. "A Fiery Baptism." In *James Baldwin: A Collection of Critical Essays*, edited by Keneth Kinnamon, 109–19. Englewood Cliffs, N.J.: Prentice-Hall, 1974.

Hicks, Granville. "From Harlem with Hatred." Review of *Tell Me How Long the Train's Been Gone*, by James Baldwin. *Saturday Review*, 1 June 1968, 23–24.

Hole, Jeffrey. "Select Bibliography of Works by and on James Baldwin." In *James Baldwin Now*, edited by Dwight McBride, 393–409. New York: New York University Press, 1999.

Holland, Patricia. "(Pro)Creating Imaginative Spaces and Other Queer Acts." In *James Baldwin Now*, edited by Dwight McBride, 265–88. New York: New York University Press, 1999.

Howe, Irving. "Black Boys and Native Sons." *Dissent* 10 (autumn 1963): 353–68. Reprinted in *A World More Attractive*, by Irving Howe, 98–122. New York: Horizon, 1963.

———. "James Baldwin: At Ease in Apocalypse." Review of *Tell Me How Long the Train's Been Gone*, by James Baldwin. *Harper's* 237 (September 1968): 94–100. Reprinted in *James Baldwin: A Collection of Critical Essays*, edited by Keneth Kinnamon, 96–108. Englewood Cliffs, N.J.: Prentice-Hall, 1974.

Hughes, Langston. *Selected Poems of Langston Hughes.* New York: Knopf, 1959. New York: Vintage-Random House, 1974.

Jackson, Joyce Marie. "The Changing Nature of Gospel Music: A Southern Case Study." *African American Review* 29, no. 2 (1995): 185–200.

Jackson, Katherine G. "Books in Brief." Review of *Tell Me How Long the Train's Been Gone,* by James Baldwin. *Harper's* 237 (July 1968): 104.

Jefferson, Margo. "There's a Heaven Somewhere." Review of *Just Above My Head,* by James Baldwin. *Nation,* 3 November 1979, 437–38.

Jones, LeRoi. *Blues People: Negro Music in White America.* New York: William Morrow, 1963.

———. "Brief Reflections on Two Hot Shots." In *Home: Social Essays.* New York: William Morrow, 1966.

Jordan, June. "If Beale Street Could Talk." Review of *If Beale Street Could Talk,* by James Baldwin. *Village Voice,* 20 June 1974, 33–35.

Joseph, Michael. "Blacks and Blues." Review of *If Beale Street Could Talk,* by James Baldwin. *Times Literary Supplement,* 21 June 1974, 656.

Julian, Faith. Review of *Just Above My Head,* by James Baldwin. *The Critic* 38, no. 11 (1980): 2, 8.

Julien, Isaac, and Kobena Mercer. "True Confessions: A Discourse on Images of Black Male Sexuality." In *Brother to Brother: New Writings by Black Gay Men,* edited by Essex Hemphill, 167–73. Boston: Alyson Publications, 1991.

Kaiser, Ernest. "Recent Books." Review of *Just Above My Head,* by James Baldwin. *Freedomways* 19, no. 3 (1979): 174–75.

Kaplan, Cora. "'A Cavern Opened in My Mind': The Poetics of Homosexuality and the Politics of Masculinity in James Baldwin." In *Representing Black Men,* edited by Marcellus Blount and George P. Cunningham, 27–54. New York: Routledge, 1996.

Katz, Ned. *The Invention of Heterosexuality.* New York: Plume-Penguin, 1996.

Kelsey, George D. "George D. Kelsey Preaches and Leads Congregation in Gospel Music in Washington, D.C." Recorded 22 August 1948. Sound recording. M579 bd.2, Voice Library. Michigan State University, East Lansing, Mich.

Kinnamon, Keneth, ed. *James Baldwin: A Collection of Critical Essays.* Englewood Cliffs, N.J.: Prentice-Hall, 1974.

Kollhofer, Jakob, ed. *James Baldwin: His Place in American Literary History and His Reception in Europe.* New York: Peter Lang, 1991.

Koponen, Wilfrid R. *Embracing a Gay Identity: Gay Novels as Guides.* London: Bergin and Garvey, 1993.

Kubitschek, Missy Dehn. "Subjugated Knowledge: Toward a Feminist Exploration of Rape in Afro-American Fiction." In *Studies in Black American Literature,* edited by Joe Weixlmann and Houston A. Baker Jr., 43–56. Vol. 3. Greenwood, Fla.: Penkevill, 1988.

Lee, Dorothy. "The Bridge of Suffering." *Callaloo* 6, no. 2 (1983): 92–99.

Leeming, David. *James Baldwin: A Biography.* New York: Alfred A. Knopf, 1994.

Levy, Paul. "American Giants." Review of *The Executioner's Song,* by Norman Mailer, *Just Above My Head,* by James Baldwin, *Sophie's Choice,* by William Styron, *Birdy,* by William Wharton, and *Chamber Music,* by Doris Grumbach. *Books and Bookmen,* December 1979, 13–15.

Lilly, Mark. *Gay Men's Literature in the Twentieth Century.* New York: New York University Press, 1993.

Llorens, David. Review of *Tell Me How Long the Train's Been Gone,* by James Baldwin. *Negro Digest* 17, no. 10 (1968): 51–52, 85–86.

Long, Robert E. "From Elegant to Hip." Review of *Tell Me How Long the Train's Been Gone,* by James Baldwin. *Nation,* 10 June 1968, 769–70.

Loewenstein, Andrea. "James Baldwin and His Critics." *Gay Community News,* 9 February 1980, 10, 11, 17.

Lynch, Michael. "The Everlasting Father: Mythic Quest and Rebellion in Baldwin's *Go Tell It on the Mountain.*" *CLA Journal* 37, no. 2 (1993): 156–75.

———. "Just Above My Head: James Baldwin's Quest for Belief." *Literature and Theology* 11, no. 2 (1997): 284–98.

———. "Staying out of the Temple." In *Reviewing James Baldwin: Things Not Seen,* edited by D. Quentin Miller, 33–71. Philadelphia: Temple University Press, 2000.

Macebuh, Stanley. *James Baldwin: A Critical Study.* New York: Third Press, 1973.

May, Vivian M. "Ambivalent Narratives, Fragmented Selves: Performative Identities and the Mutability of Roles in James Baldwin's *Go Tell It on the Mountain.*" In *New Essays on "Go Tell It on the Mountain,"* edited by Trudier Harris, 97–126. New York: Cambridge University Press, 1996.

McBride, Dwight A., ed. *James Baldwin Now.* New York: New York University Press, 1999.

McCluskey, John. "If Beale Street Could Talk." Review of *If Beale Street Could Talk,* by James Baldwin. *Black World,* December 1974, 51–52, 88–91.

McKee, Margaret, and Fred Chisenhall. *Beale Black and Blue: Life and Music on Black America's Main Street.* Baton Rouge, La.: Louisiana State University Press, 1981.

Mead, Margaret, and James Baldwin. *A Rap on Race.* Philadelphia: J. B. Lippincott, 1971.

"Milk Run." Review of *Tell Me How Long the Train's Been Gone,* by James Baldwin. *Time,* 7 June 1968 , 104.

Miller, Joshua. "The Discovery of What It Means to Be a Witness." In *James Baldwin Now,* edited by Dwight McBride, 331–59. New York: New York University Press, 1999.

Miller, D. Quentin "James Baldwin, Poet." In *Re-viewing James Baldwin: Things Not Seen,* edited by D. Quentin Miller. 233–54. Philadelphia: Temple University Press, 2000.

———, ed. *Re-viewing James Baldwin: Things Not Seen.* Philadelphia: Temple University Press, 2000.

Mitchell, Louis D. Review of *If Beale Street Could Talk,* by James Baldwin. *Best Sellers,* 15 May 1974, 106–7.

Möller, Karin. *The Theme of Identity in the Essays of James Baldwin: An Introduction.* Göteborg, Sweden: Acta Universitatis Gothoburgensis, 1975.

Morrison, Toni. *The Bluest Eye.* New York: Holt, Rinehart and Winston, 1970; New York: Pocket Books-Washington Square Press, 1972.

———. "Life in His Language." In *James Baldwin: The Legacy,* edited by Quincy Troupe, 75–78. New York: Touchstone-Simon and Schuster, 1989.

Nash, Julie. "'A Terrifying Sacrament': James Baldwin's Use of Music in *Just Above My Head.*" *MAWA Review,* December 1990, 107–11.

Nelson, Emmanuel S. "Continents of Desire: James Baldwin and the Pleasures of Homosexual Exile." *James White Review: A Gay Men's Literary Quarterly* 13, no. 4 (1996): 8, 16

———. "Critical Deviance: Homophobia and the Reception of James Baldwin's Fiction." *Journal of American Culture* 14, no. 3 (1991): 91–96.

———. "James Baldwin." In *The Gay and Lesbian Literary Heritage,* edited by Claude J. Summers, 71–73. New York: Henry Holt, 1995.

———. "James Baldwin (1924–1987)." In *Contemporary Gay American Novelists: A Bio-bibliographical Critical Sourcebook,* edited by Emmanuel S. Nelson. Westport, Conn.: Greenwood Press, 1996.

———. "Towards a Transgressive Aesthetic: Gay Readings of Black Writing." *James White Review: A Gay Men's Literary Quarterly* 11, no. 3 (1994): 17.

Nordell, Roderick. "Baldwin's World of Black Gospel Singers and Evangelists." Review of *Just Above My Head,* by James Baldwin. *Christian Science Monitor,* 26 September 1979, 16.

Oates, Joyce Carol. "A Quite Moving and Very Traditional Celebration of Love." Review of *If Beale Street Could Talk,* by James Baldwin. *New York Times Book Review,* 26 May 1974, 1–2. Reprinted in *Critical Essays on James Baldwin,* edited by Fred L. Standley and Nancy V. Burt, 158–61. Boston: G. K. Hall, 1988.

O'Daniel, Therman B., ed. *James Baldwin: A Critical Evaluation.* Washington, D.C.: Howard University Press, 1977.

Odets, Clifford. *Three Plays, by Clifford Odets: Awake and Sing, Waiting for Lefty, Till the Day I Die.* New York: Covici-Friede, 1935.

Olson, Barabara K. "'Come-to-Jesus Stuff' in James Baldwin's *Go Tell It on the Mountain* and *The Amen Corner.*" *African-American Review* 31, no. 2 (1997): 295–301.

Peters, Erskine, ed. *Lyrics of the Afro-American Spiritual: A Documentary Collection.* Westport, Conn.: Greenwood Press, 1993.

Pinckney, Darryl. "Blues for Mr. Baldwin." Review of *Just Above My Head,* by James Baldwin. *New York Review of Books,* 6 December 1979, 32–33. Reprinted in *Critical Essays on James Baldwin,* edited by Fred L. Standley and Nancy V. Burt, 161–66. Boston: G. K. Hall, 1988.

Porter, Horace. *Stealing the Fire: The Art and Protest of James Baldwin.* Middletown, Conn.: Wesleyan University Press, 1989.

Pratt, Louis H. *James Baldwin.* Boston: Twayne Publishers, 1978.

Puzo, Mario. "His Cardboard Lovers." Review of *Tell Me How Long the Train's Been Gone,* by James Baldwin. *New York Times Book Review,* 23 June 1968, 5, 34. Reprinted in *Critical Essays on James Baldwin,* edited by Fred L. Standley and Nancy V. Burt, 155–58. Boston: Hall, 1988.

Rainwater, Lee, and William L. Yancey. *The Moynihan Report and the Politics of Controversy.* Cambridge, Mass.: MIT Press, 1967.

Rawley, James. Review of *Just Above My Head,* by James Baldwin. *Saturday Review,* 5 January 1980, 49.

Reckley, Ralph, ed. *James Baldwin in Memoriam: Proceedings of the Annual Conference of the Middle Atlantic Writers' Association, 1989.* Baltimore: Middle Atlantic Writers' Association Press, 1992.

Review of *If Beale Street Could Talk,* by James Baldwin. *Black Books Bulletin,* fall 1974, 42–43.

Rich, Adrienne. "When We Dead Awaken: Writing as Revision (1971)." Reprinted in *The Norton Anthology of Literature by Women: The Tradition in English*, edited by Sandra M. Gilbert and Susan Gubar, 2045–56. New York: W. W. Norton and Co., 1985.

Robins, Natalie. *Alien Ink: The FBI's War on Freedom of Expression* (New York: William Morrow, 1992), 345–49.

Romano, John. Review of *Just Above My Head*, by James Baldwin. *New York Times Book Review*, 23 September 1979, 3, 33.

Sarotte, Georges Michel. *Like a Brother, Like a Lover: Male Homosexuality in the American Novel and Theater from Herman Melville to James Baldwin*, translated by Richard Miller. Garden City, New York: Anchor Press/Doubleday, 1978.

Savoy, Eric. "Other(ed) Americans in Paris: Henry James, James Baldwin, and the Subversion of Identity." *English Studies in Canada* 18, no. 3 (1992): 335–46.

Segal, Lynne. *Slow Motion: Changing Masculinities, Changing Men*. London: Virago Press, 1990.

Shin, Andrew, and Barbara Judson. "Beneath the Black Aesthetic: James Baldwin's Primer of Black American Masculinity." *African American Review* 32, no. 2 (1998): 247–61.

Smith, Barbara. "We Must Always Bury Our Dead Twice." *Gay Community News*, 20–26 December 1987, center, 10.

Spillers, Hortense. "The Politics of Intimacy: A Discussion." In *Sturdy Black Bridges: Visions of Black Women in Literature*, edited by Roseann P. Bell, Bettye J. Parker, and Beverly Guy Sheftall, 87–106. Garden City, N.Y.: Anchor Books, 1979.

*Spirituals and Gospels*. New York: Wise Publications, 1975.

Standley, Fred L., and Louis H. Pratt, eds. *Conversations with James Baldwin*. Jackson, Miss.: University Press of Mississippi, 1989.

Standley, Fred L., and Nancy V. Burt, eds. *Critical Essays on James Baldwin*. Boston: G. K. Hall, 1988.

Standley, Fred L., and Nancy V. Standley. *James Baldwin: A Reference Guide*. Boston: G. K. Hall, 1980.

Stepto, Robert B. *From Behind the Veil: A Study of Afro-American Narrative*. Urbana, Ill.: University of Illinois Press, 1979.

Straub, Peter. "Happy Ends." Review of *If Beale Street Could Talk*, by James Baldwin. *New Statesman*, 28 June 1974, 930.

Summers, Claude J. *Gay Fictions: Wilde to Stonewall*. New York: Continuum, 1990.

Sylvander, Carolyn Wedin. *James Baldwin*. New York: Frederick Ungar, 1980.

Taylor, Clyde. "Celebrating Jimmy." In *James Baldwin: The Legacy*, edited by Quincy Troupe, 29–37. New York: Touchstone-Simon and Schuster, 1989.

Thomas, David. "Too Black, Too White." Review of *If Beale Street Could Talk*, by James Baldwin. *Listener*, 25 July 1974, 125.

Thompson, John. "Baldwin: The Prophet as Artist." Review of *Tell Me How Long the Train's Been Gone*, by James Baldwin. *Commentary* 45, no. 6 (June 1968): 67–69.

Thwaite, Anthony. "Apocalyptic Gospel." Review of *Just Above My Head*, by James Baldwin. *Observer*, 28 October 1979, 38.

Tinney, James S. "Struggles of a Black Gay Pentecostal." In *Black Men/White Men: A Gay Anthology*, 167–71. San Francisco: Gay Sunshine Press, 1983.

———. "Why a Black Gay Church?" In *In the Life: A Black Gay Anthology*, 70–86. Boston: Alyson Publications, 1986.

Traylor, Eleanor. "I Hear Music in the Air: James Baldwin's *Just Above My Head*." *First World* 2, no. 3 (1979): 40–43. Reprinted in *James Baldwin: The Legacy*, edited by Quincy Troupe, 95–106. New York: Touchstone-Simon and Schuster, 1989.

Troupe, Quincy, ed. *James Baldwin: The Legacy*. New York: Touchstone-Simon and Schuster, 1989.

Wald, Alan. "The Writer as Witness." Review of *Just Above My Head*, by James Baldwin. *In These Times*, 5–11 December 1979, 20.

Wallace, Maurice. "'I'm Not Entirely What I Look Like': Richard Wright, James Baldwin, and the Hegemony of Vision; or, Jimmy's FBEye Blues." In *James Baldwin Now*, edited by Dwight McBride, 289–306. New York: New York University Press, 1999.

Warren, Nagueyalti. "The Substance of Things Hoped for: Faith in *Go Tell It on the Mountain* and *Just Above My Head*." *Obsidian II* 7, nos. 1 and 2 (1992): 19–32.

Washington, Bryan R. *The Politics of Exile: Ideology in Henry James, F. Scott Fitzgerald, and James Baldwin*. Boston: Northeastern University Press, 1995.

Watkins, Mel. "James Baldwin Writing and Talking." *New York Times Book Review*, 23 September 1979, 3, 33.

Weatherby, W. J. *James Baldwin: Artist on Fire*. New York: Dell Publishing, 1989.

Webster, Ivan. Review of *If Beale Street Could Talk*, by James Baldwin. *New Republic*, 15 June 1974, 25–26.

Weissman, Steve, ed. *Big Brother and the Holding Company: The World behind Watergate*. Palo Alto, Calif.: Ramparts Press, 1974.

Werner, Craig. "The Economic Evolution of James Baldwin." In *Critical Essays on James Baldwin*, edited by Fred L. Standley and Nancy V. Burt, 78–93. Boston: G. K. Hall, 1988.

———. "James Baldwin: Politics and the Gospel Impulse." *New Politics: A Journal of Socialist Thought* 2, no. 2 (1989): 106–24.

———. *Playing the Changes: From Afro-Modernism to the Jazz Impulse*. Urbana, Ill.: University of Illinois Press, 1994.

White, Edmund. "James Baldwin Overcomes." Review of *Just Above My Head*, by James Baldwin. *Washington Post Book World*, 23 September 1979, 5.

Williams, Sherley Anne. *Give Birth to Brightness: A Thematic Study in Neo-black Literature*. New York: Dial Press, 1972.

Winfield (Miller), Orilla. Interview by author. August, 1989. Manistee, Mich.

Wright, Richard. *Black Boy*. New York: Harper and Brothers, 1945; New York: Perennial Classic, 1966.

———. *Native Son*. New York: Harper and Brothers, 1940; New York: Perennial Classic, 1966.

# Index

Bergman, David, 14, 15, 164–65
Bible, xv, 50, 51, 64, 93–94
bibliographies, 179n. 12
Bildad, 95
biographies, xiv, 5, 6
Birmingham, 101, 155
bisexuality, xvii, xxv, 13, 17, 23, 32, 49,
    61, 116, 160, 165
Black Arts movement, 76
Black Belt, 40–41
"Black is beautiful," 74
Black Muslims, xx
black militants, 9, 12, 15, 22–23, 32, 51
black nationalism, 3, 17, 23, 50, 60, 147
Black Panthers, xxi, xxii, 22, 66, 73,
    183n. 7
Black Power movement, xiii, xx, xxi, 10,
    22, 23, 32, 78
*Black Scholar* interview, 71, 72, 75, 76, 105
black studies, 6, 178n. 5
Blaxploitation movies, 147
blood, 131–32
blues, xiv, xviii, xxv, 33, 36, 51, 62, 78–79,
    89–93, 101, 122, 130, 131, 133, 143,
    150–54, 158
blues culture, 65
*Blues for Mister Charlie,* xxiv, 9, 109–10,
    126, 146
blues heroes, 123, 131
blues stories, 88
Bobia, Rosa, 5
Boggs, Nicholas, 179–80n. 15
Bone, Robert, 13
bourgeois aesthetics, xxix, 8, 9
Boyer, Horace, 150
Bozkurt, Saadet, 208n. 70
Brando, Marlon, xxii
bridges, 140, 142, 167
brothers, xxv, 60, 128, 134, 148
Brown, Marie, 2
Bruck, Peter, 208n. 70
Burks, Mary Fair, 112, 194n. 57
Byerman, Keith, 7

■ C

California, 138
call and response, 141, 150, 156–57, 159
Callahan, John, 7
Campbell, James, 6, 122, 204–5n. 11
canonization, 7–8, 14
Capouya, Emile, xvi
Carmichael, Stokely, xxi-xxii
Carson, Warren J., 207n. 42
Carzac, Yoran, 67
categories of race and sex, xiii–xiv, 4, 5, 7,
    23, 81, 117–18
celebrity, x, 27
Central Park, xxvi, 52, 53–54
Cezzar, Engin, xxi
Charles, Ray, 140
The Chi-Lites, 147
child preachers, xv, 127, 131, 135
Chisenhall, Fred, 90
chronology, 27, 38, 137
Church, Robert Reed, 90
The church, ix, xxviii, 63, 93–94, 97–100,
    108, 124, 125–26, 141, 150, 156, 198n.
    113, 209n. 90; leaving the, 209n. 90
Civil Rights movement, xx, xxii, 10, 13,
    20–22, 47, 52, 67, 68, 74, 106–7, 126,
    139, 151, 152, 156, 166, 192n. 49
Civil War, xvii, 150
Clark, Keith, 177n. 52
Clark, Kenneth, xx, 107
Clark, Mark, 66
Cleaver, Eldridge, 9, 12–13, 14, 15, 16,
    72–73, 74, 202n. 4
coded language, 130, 138, 144, 145, 166
cold war, xxii
color line, 39, 40
Coltrane, John, 140
"Come out the Wilderness," 63, 84
*Commentary,* xxix
Communist party, viii, 73
*Communitas,* 40–43
*Conversations with James Baldwin,* xii
conversion, xv, xxv, xxx, 57, 87, 98, 105,

125, 198n. 113, 208n. 70

Cooke, Michael, 7

CORE, ix, xx, xxi

*The Corn Is Green,* 34–36, 41, 46, 53, 156

country houses, xxvi, xxvii

courage, 3

critical essays, 5

Crouch, Stanley, 13, 202n. 5, 203n. 6

Cruse, Harold, 7

crying, 142

Cullen, Countee, xvi

cultural studies, xiii

### ■ D

dancing, 42, 56, 133, 136–37

Davis, Angela, xxii, 76

Davis, Charles T., 29

Davis, Miles, 140

DeGout, Yasmin Y., 179n. 14

Delaney, Beauford, xviii, 189n. 120

*The Devil Finds Work,* vii, xvi

De Witt Clinton High School, xvi

*A Dialogue,* 67

Dickens, Charles, ix, 202–3n. 5

*Differance,* n. 157

difference, xiv, 7–8, 14, 149, 165

dignity, viii

"The Discovery of What It Means to Be an
   American," 176n. 21

disillusionment, 67–70, 73

Dixon, Melvin, 7, 16, 168–69, 175n. 13,
   203–4n. 7, 207n. 42, 208n. 70

domestic abuse, 81–82

Dorsey, Thomas A., 151

double-consciousness, 37, 38, 40, 41, 127,
   171

double resistance, 8

Douglass, Frederick, 26, 27–30, 33, 35, 40,
   93, 166, 186n. 56

dreams, 87, 91, 132, 141, 206n. 38

Du Bois, W. E. B., xxi, 26, 37–39, 154,
   171, 212n. 157

### ■ E

Eckman, Fern Marja, xxvi

Edelman, Lee, 16, 167–68, 181n. 35, 212n.
   157

Edwards, Thomas R., 193–94n. 57

Ellington, Duke, 154

Ellis, Cassandra M., 179n. 13

Ellison, Mary, 166

Ellison, Ralph, xxiii, 6, 10, 26, 43–47, 123,
   186n. 68

eloquence, x

"The Emperor Jones," 32

empty bottles, 96, 97, 167

Estes, David C., 120, 124

Eugene F. Saxton Foundation, xix

Europe, 139

Evers, Medgar, xxi, 22

"Every Good-Bye Ain't Gone," 177n. 44

"Everybody's Protest Novel," xix, xxviii, 8,
   111, 176n. 23

*Evidence of Things not Seen,* 9

### ■ F

FBI, 22, 183n. 6

Fabre, Michel, 176n. 36

family, xiv, xvi, xxiii–xxviii, xxx, 6, 52,
   63–64, 83, 98–110, 113–17, 119, 121,
   122, 140, 141, 143, 170, 206n. 22

Fanon, Franz, 212n. 157

Farrison, William Edward, 114, 183–84n.
   8, 201n. 169

fascism, 70

fathers, xiv, xviii, 55–57, 102–4, 108,
   116–17, 134, 152–53, 161–62, 210n.
   102

Feldman, Susan, 189n. 110

female characters, 5, 16–17, 80–81, 117,
   119, 194n. 57

feminine identity, 59, 84

feminist criticism, 16–17, 116, 178n. 5,
   190n. 5

Ferguson, Roderick, 176n. 23, 177n. 49

Fiedler, Leslie, 60

*The Fire Next Time,* vi–vii, xv, xx, xxix, 5, 9, 49, 70, 126
first-person narrators, 11, 25–26, 83–84, 88, 131
Fleming, Robert, 203n. 6
Floyd, Samuel, 136, 150, 157
"Follow the Drinking Gourd," 166
Fort, Charles, 209n. 90
Foucault, Michel, 130
The Four Tops, 147
France, xix, xx, xxii, xxiv–xxv, xxvii, 4
Franklin, Benjamin, 29–30
Frazier, E. Franklin, 107
"Freaks and the American Ideal of Manhood," 175n. 13
Frederick Douglass Junior High School, xvi
freedom songs, 166
Freudian psychology, 60, 189n. 118
Frost, David, 69
Fuller, Hoyt, 202n. 3
funeral of James Baldwin, 2–4
funerals, 135–36, 137

■ G

Garrow, David, 7
Garvey, Marcus, 23
Gates, Henry Louis, Jr., 7, 9–10, 73, 174n. 2
*Gay Community News,* 3
gay critics, 14–16, 178n. 5
gay identity, 17, 166
gay studies, 5, 14–16
Gaye, Marvin, 147
gender theory, xiii, 5
German Nazism, 67, 69
Germany, 66
Gibson, Donald B., 87, 111, 182n. 4, 193n. 57
Gide, Andre, 8, 13
"Gide as Husband and Homosexual," 175n. 13
Gilman, Richard, 202n. 4
Ginsberg, Allen, 60

Giovanni, Nikki, xii, 67, 69, 72, 74, 76, 81, 93, 94
*Giovanni's Room,* xix, xxiv–xxv, 6, 14, 15, 22–23, 25, 48, 75, 83–84, 116
*Go Tell It on the Mountain,* xv, xx, xxiii–xxv, xxx, 6, 8, 9, 11, 48, 50–58, 64, 66, 76, 79, 84, 87, 95, 97, 99, 102, 111, 116–17, 122, 123, 125–26, 145, 152
"Go Tell It on the Mountain," 50, 166, 187n. 83
"Go the Way Your Blood Beats," 209n. 90, 212n.155
"Going to Meet the Man," 110
Golden Gate Quartet, 150
gospel, xiv, 121, 122, 126, 133, 135, 139, 141, 142, 144–46, 148–52, 158, 169
Great Depression, viii, 150
Greenwich Village, xvii–xviii, xxiv, xxvii, 11, 48, 63, 66
Grimes, John, xv, xxvi, xxx, 48, 50–58, 84, 95, 102, 116, 125–27
group orientation, 41

■ H

Hajek, Friederike, 195n. 57
Hakutani, Yoshinobu, 87, 195n. 58
Haley, Alex, xx, 27, 67
Hampton, Fred, 66
Handy, W. C., 89–90, 92
Happersberger, Lucien, 20
Harlem, viii, xiv, xvi, xviii, xxiv, xxv, xxvi, 2, 11, 21, 38, 40–41, 44, 48, 54, 55, 56, 58, 62, 66, 67, 69, 89, 90, 92, 100, 101, 120, 125, 126
"The Harlem Ghetto," xix
Harris, Trudier, xxv, 5, 6, 16, 79–81, 87, 93, 176n. 38, 208n. 70, 210–11n. 114
Heart attack, 31, 43, 46–47, 132
Henry, John, 31
Herbert, John, 67
"Here Be Dragons," xix, 168, 175n. 13
Hernton, Calvin C., 187n. 77, 188n. 99

progress, 11, 12, 17, 22, 24–25, 43, 47

propaganda, 9, 12, 21

prophetic tone, 38

prophets, 12, 21, 64, 70

protest fiction, xxviii, xxix, 8, 9, 18, 21, 64, 75, 77, 92, 102, 111–16, 182n. 4

Proudhammer, Leo, xxv, xxvi, 11, 21, 22, 24, 26, 29–60, 65, 79, 102, 116, 126–28, 132, 154, 156, 160, 182n. 4

public speaking, ix, x, 28, 35

Puzo, Mario, 9, 21, 26

Pygmalion, 87

■ Q

quartets, 135, 143, 145, 150–55

queer baiting, xvii

queer theory, xiii

■ R

race representation, xxviii

racial categories, xiii–xiv

racism, xiv, xvi, xxiv, xxx, 23, 48, 51, 66–67, 109, 110, 113, 114, 116, 144, 158, 171

rap music, 150

A Rap on Race, 67, 70

rape, 59–60, 110, 138

Rawley, James, 202n. 5

Reagan, Ronald, 68

reconciliation, 142–43, 149, 165–66, 169, 208n. 70

Reed, Ishmael, 191n. 40

religion, 76, 93–94, 126

religion and homosexuality, 148–49

religion and sexuality, 98, 144–46, 169

religious vocation, xv

resistance, xiii, xiv, xxiv, xxviii, 11, 29, 50, 63, 77, 88, 102, 105, 108, 110, 115–16, 121, 170–71

responsibility, 67–68, 69, 75–76, 81–82

retrospective voice, 27–28, 30, 33

re-vision, 63, 190n. 5

revivals, 210n. 109

Rich, Adrienne, 63–64

"ring shout," 136

rites, 42

ritual ground, 40–41

rituals, 98, 136, 156

Rivers, Tish, 11, 62–64, 77–80, 82–88, 92, 94–97, 99, 101–5, 108–10, 113–18, 132

rivers, 92

Rivers family, 63, 71, 92, 98–02, 105, 108, 113–15, 200n. 158, 201n. 169

Robins, Natalie, 183n. 6

Romano, John, 204n. 8

running, 43–44, 47

■ S

SNCC, xxi

sacred language, 88–89, 93, 96–97

salvation, 7, 17, 50–52, 64, 96

San Francisco, 20, 42, 53–54, 120, 186n. 64

sanctified churches, 101, 150, 152

Sarotte, Georges-Michel, 14, 15

Savoy, Eric, 7–8

school, 63, 113

sculptors, 62, 65, 86–87, 103, 114

Seale, Bobby, xxii

segregation, viii, xvi, 39

self-made men, 29–30

self-representation, 126–27

sermons, 130, 135, 137

sexism, 77, 79

sexual categories, xiv, 81

sexual oppression, 171

Shabazz, Betty, xx, xxi

Shin, Andrew, 141, 211n. 114

siblings, xxiii, xxiv, xxv, 128

"signifying," 174n. 2, 177n. 49

sin, 101

singers, xxv, 101, 126, 128, 130

singing, slave, 186n. 56

slave narratives, 26–29, 59, 93, 113, 185n. 18

slavery, 28, 29, 82, 112, 114, 186n. 56

Smith, Barbara, 3